PrestaShop 1.3

Beginner's Guide

Build and customize your online store with this speedy, lightweight e-commerce solution

John Horton

BIRMINGHAM - MUMBAI

PrestaShop 1.3
Beginner's Guide

First published: June 2010

Production Reference: 1080610

Published by Packt Publishing Ltd.
32 Lincoln Road
Olton
Birmingham, B27 6PA, UK.

ISBN 978-1-849511-14-8

www.packtpub.com

Cover Image by Vinayak Chittar (vinayak.chittar@gmail.com)

Credits

Author

John Horton

Reviewers

Tomer Grassiany

Ardian Yuli Setyanto

Acquisition Editor

Dilip Venkatesh

Development Editor

Tarun Singh

Technical Editors

Shadab Khan

Hithesh Uchil

Copy Editor

Lakshmi Menon

Indexer

Hemangini Bari

Editorial Team Leader

Akshara Aware

Project Team Leader

Lata Basantani

Project Coordinator

Shubhanjan Chatterjee

Proofreader

Aaron Nash

Production Coordinator

Shantanu Zagade

Cover Work

Shantanu Zagade

About the Author

John Horton comes from a retail sales background where he learned the importance of selling, rather than the mere passive offering of a product or service. By 2005 he was disillusioned with the greedy, integrity-lacking, low-reward, corporate world, and was looking for a way to earn a living without the grind of the 9 to 5 and without having to sell his soul. He decided to investigate an e-commerce venture.

John started his first e-commerce website in 2005. Although only a modest success initially, it was the seed of a eureka moment, a blindingly obvious moment that comes only once in a lifetime. If you can start and run a business with virtually no costs (one that once up and running, has virtually no ongoing time commitment), why not make lots of businesses around the same idea?

John now has numerous e-commerce sites as well as other types of web businesses, earning revenue in different ways. John's latest venture is a product comparison website with a unique slant.

It is the low-time commitment model of John's businesses that has allowed him to write books aimed at helping others who want to achieve the same thing. He has published training manuals and books with other publishers on the same subject area and this is his first book for Packt. He is an avid fan of all things open source.

John has no formal, technical, or programming background, had no relevant previous business experience, no related educational qualifications, has never borrowed startup capital, is of average intelligence at best, does not have the gift of the gab or any other magical quality, is not especially "lucky" and would sincerely like to point out that it doesn't matter if you are in the same situation as him!

John works from home and spends his spare time with his family, Jo, Jack, and James, in Norwich, UK and pursues his hobbies of running, computer gaming, and reading.

Acknowledgement

To Jack for being such a wonderful son. I am so proud of you. James for being the loveliest little fellow anybody could wish to know. Jo, whom I love so much, for accepting me and my mad ideas and for your love. Ray for being someone I admire so highly and Rita as well. Olivia and Casey for being the prettiest girls, bar none, and Stan for being a great dad to them. And also to my newly found friend Mary Patel.

Sylvia for actually wanting a copy of my crazy ramblings and the first person in the whole world (and probably the last) to ask for my autograph.

A big thanks to all the people at Packt who made this a better book than I could ever have done on my own. A big thanks to the technical reviewers, Tomer Grassiany in New York and Ardian Yuli Setyanto, for pointing out improvements and blunders.

Also worth a mention: Higgsy, John (eboy) Barton, and Peter EggbuttNoBacon for being my friends. David Swinnerton for being a friend, doing my math homework and completing Bounty Bob Strikes Back. A long overdue thanks to the Ebbutt family for putting up with me and letting me in their house so often, especially when mine was empty. And to Chris, I sincerely apologize about the loft, bucket, shower thing—it was Pete's idea!

And mostly to those whose memory has inspired me all my life, especially this last year, who will sadly never read the next sentence. To Valerie and Ann, I dedicate this book.

About the Reviewers

Tomer Grassiany, born in Israel, has been interested in computer science since an early age. His serious work in computers and computer networks began during his high school years in Israel. Prior to coming to the U.S. at the age of 19, he administered networks at two Israeli computer animation schools.

As Chief Technology Officer and later Chief Software Architect of Meaningful Machines, a New York-based company, Tomer was in charge of research and development, including bringing the inventors' ideas to life. His focus was on the company's new and sometimes experimental applications. From 1999 to 2007, Tomer developed applications that brought the company's new technologies from concept to reality in the fields of Machine Translation, Data Mining, and Artificial Intelligence. During this time, he worked closely on machine translation with Professor Jaime Carbonell, the Allen Newell Professor of Computer Science at Carnegie Mellon University.

Tomer went on to found COMET Classifieds in 2007. The leading classifieds website in COMET's portfolio is TennisLessons.com, which has coaches listed in over 400 cities across 40 countries. Helping to connect over 30,000 students and coaches every month, it has become the most popular website for finding tennis lessons.

Tomer has been working since the start of 2009 doing custom PrestaShop projects for new and existing shops worldwide. He is also a PrestaShop Moderator on the English and Hebrew forums.

Tomer's newest venture is Presto-Changeo.com. Created in 2009, the website offers his PrestaShop modules and provides tips on how to troubleshoot and customize PrestaShop. His modules help shops to create a better experience for their customers, and increase productivity and sales.

I would like to acknowledge my parents, Dalia and Telo Grassiany, who supported and backed me throughout my life, and Eli Abir, who taught me a lot and always believed in me and my abilities.

Ardian Yuli Setyanto is a 22-year-old website developer from Indonesia and currently specializes in PrestaShop module and theme creation. He also moderates the PrestaShop local forum for Indonesian users.

Being a freelancer and a householder for a year has been a wonderful experience for him and he thanks his wife, Niela Pratamasari, for always supporting him.

You can get an update on PrestaShop tutorials and modifications on Ardian's blog (http://ardianys.com/) and follow him on Twitter (http://twitter.com/ardianys). His opinion about PrestaShop: "Although currently PrestaShop lacks in documentation, I have already found the great PrestaShop documentation in its source code."

Table of Contents

Preface

PrestaShop is a hidden gem. There are many, much more widely known online shopping cart solutions but none of them have anything like the number of features, the potential, and the ease-of-use that this OSL-licensed, completely free-to-use system has. PrestaShop is definitely a very big part of the future of e-commerce!

This book is called a 'beginner's guide' only because that is where it starts! Using both realistic and unusual case studies throughout, PrestaShop 1.3 Beginner's Guide will take you on a click-by-click, yet whirlwind journey to the realization of a fully featured, highly professional e-commerce business.

And then a bit further!

To make sure you are ready to sprint off the starting blocks let's talk about:

- Why PrestaShop?
- Open source and OSL licenses
- The order of events
- Which hosting environment?
- What if I get stuck?

So let's get on with it...

Why PrestaShop?

I have already enthusiastically introduced PrestaShop. But there is so much to PrestaShop that the only way to really grasp its innovation is to open a shop and make money with it, which we will do really soon! First, here are some of the ways that PrestaShop stands out from the crowd.

Simplicity and function

There are dozens of shopping cart solutions to choose from. But with my hand on my heart I can say that NONE are so damn easy to use! Every feature has a clearly labeled button or tab. And some of the previously most frustrating tasks like product attributes, customization, and statistics, are now, thanks to PrestaShop, a breeze. And PrestaShop achieves this simplicity without cutting back on options. To get anywhere near the advanced options available (as standard in PrestaShop when using other carts) you will need to install add-ons, upgrades, and even mess with the PHP code that makes the software. Yuck!

Stability and progress

PrestaShop is stable as a table! It is highly unlikely to crash on you or your customers. It doesn't lose their shopping cart or fail to find searched-for products.

And it is getting better all the time. The development team at PrestaShop is working on new features and bug fixes, probably even as you read these words. So often when a shopping cart reaches a certain stage of development, the team sits back and reaps the fruits, leaving a community of tens of thousands of users wondering, "What's next?" Not so with PrestaShop. During the writing of this book, PrestaShop went through many improvements, including the jump from version 1.2 to 1.3. So this guide is suitable for both.

It's cool!

I am serious. It's important! If your customer thinks it's cool, they are much more likely to shop with you. Check out the live shops. Go to www.prestashop.com. Click on **SHOWCASE** and then on **Live shops**.

Look how fresh, modern, and functional they are. The only differences between these shops and the default PrestaShop are some nice images, well-presented products, and a bit of customization. All of this and more is covered in this book.

Open source and OSL are the best!

PrestaShop is free because of the open development model chosen by its creators. This means you can download it, use it, modify it, and even distribute it! No charge.

Open source and OSL (the PrestaShop license) work by offering a reward model for developers/contributors outside of the traditional pay per item used for just about everything else on our planet. This means typical users like you and I get tons of great software for nothing. You don't even have to say thank you!

Availability

There's an instant download of just about anything you might need. This book uses only open source software to achieve everything.

Cost

It costs nothing! This is hard to elaborate on!

Updates

It is because distribution costs the developers nothing that open source (and OSL) teams can concentrate more on offering improvements, bug-fixes, and new versions at a much faster rate than the conventional software companies with their unwieldy software-in-a-box distribution methods.

As previously mentioned, PrestaShop improved from version 1.2 to 1.3 in the months it took to write this book. And it is probably a safe bet they will be working on 1.4 by the time you read this. This book deals with the fundamental and critical issues of starting and running a real business with PrestaShop. So no matter what the current version, this book should serve you well. Visit `www.prestashop-book.com` for regular updates and amendments.

Support

Now we know the software is free and the availability is high. This makes the really good stuff very popular. So there is often a whole community of enthusiastic users associated with an open source software title. The quality and responsiveness of any given community does vary. But you can usually solve almost any e-commerce problem within a few hours with a simple forum post or a well-directed e-mail.

If that doesn't sound impressive, try ringing Microsoft next time Windows crashes. Try even finding their phone number!

My golden rule of e-commerce

Keep your wallet shut! Don't buy any software until you have checked out `www.sourceforge.net`. This is the largest repository of high quality, free software. I will point out free software titles as and when they might be needed throughout this book.

What this book covers

Now I am really impatient. Whenever I get an idea for a business I always want to do it straight away. Waiting around for "professionals" to finish a website for me or a supplier to get back to me about a new product drives me mad. The good news is we are not going to hang around before getting your PrestaShop up and running.

I am going to try and be thorough and I will cover some of the less talked about topics that you might need, but I am NOT going to delay the day when you get that glorious e-mail saying that you have your first customer.

What follows is a really quick introduction to the topics covered in this book. They are approached in precisely the order that might be used when setting up a real business. So there is no study or theorizing, unless you choose to.

The only assumption I make is that you have already chosen a range of products to sell from your new e-commerce store. If you haven't—don't panic! Get on over to `www.prestashop-book.com` and download my PDF on choosing a business model and a product range. It's free.

John's 7-day challenge

When somebody first pointed out PrestaShop to me, I just had to have one yesterday. I stayed up half the night installing it, putting in great product descriptions, connecting the checkout, and customizing the look. In the morning, I started organically (free, not paid-for) promoting my new site. My first order came in seven days after the installation.

Can you beat seven days to your first sale? I really want you to and if you dive in and really go for it, you will. Please contact me and let me know if you do, or if you come close. Or even if you just want to share your joy at your first order, no matter how long it takes.

Here is how you can achieve my 7-day challenge.

Installing, configuring, and stocking-up

The first four chapters are a lightning (but thorough) guide to get your shop online—stocked up looking smart and unique, including some really cool and really simple product features to quickly show off your wares in style.

Customers, search engines, and customization

Chapters 5, 6, and 7 are quite diverse and cover some exciting stuff: newsletters, loyalty schemes, alternative revenue streams, statistics, analytics, and... breathe! Also, we cover security, disaster recovery, payment handling, currencies, taxes, shipping, and a bit more.

Now and the future

The last two chapters cover the final preparations before going live, handling orders in PrestaShop, and how to promote your store and get customers queuing up to spend their money with you. Once the money is starting to flow, we look at the future of e-commerce and your PrestaShop business. Then we discuss how to get on top of your niche and stay there. Not to forget "the big secret". Don't skip ahead!

Here are the chapter contents in more detail:

Chapter 1, *Building Your PrestaShop*, covers how to download and prepare the PrestaShop files, make a database, install PrestaShop, and implement post-install security. We will have a look at your shop from a customer's viewpoint and also have a look around your new admin control panel.

Chapter 2, *Shop Fitting and Layout*, sets the shape of your store including the logo. We will make your home page, make some more key pages such as "Contact us" and "Conditions of use", and also configure and enter manufacturer and supplier information, change and customize themes, and add a few more touches to your shop's configuration.

Chapter 3, *Merchandising for Success*, discusses and implements an efficient category structure. We will add high quality product descriptions that sell and take a look at all the different ways you can use PrestaShop to highlight products. We will also take a look at product features, attributes, accessories, and customization.

Chapter 4, *Giving Customers More and Getting More Customers*, provides information on how to choose the best keywords and provide food for the search engines. We will refine PrestaShop search. We will also cover Tag clouds, using the PrestaShop CMS, URLs in PrestaShop, robots and site maps, and using PrestaShop language features.

Chapter 5, *Tools, Newsletters, Extra Income, and Statistics*, looks at all of the most useful things on the Preferences tab. We will also explore the best stuff on the Tools tab. We will set up a newsletter and notifications system, talk about running an e-mail marketing campaign, set up PrestaShop statistics, and also set up Google Analytics.

Chapter 6, *Security and Disaster Recovery*, looks at the ways your shop can be damaged. We will add users, profiles, and permissions to increase security. We will talk about and optionally implement SSL to protect your customers' private information. We will learn how to back up and restore your shop in case everything else fails. We will also talk about upgrading PrestaShop and how this helps keep your business secure.

Chapter 7, *Checkouts and Shipping*, helps us choose and set up a payment provider. We will look at alternative payment methods, take a look at sales taxes, discuss and implement gift vouchers, and learn how to accept foreign currencies. We will look at the multitude ways to set up shipping options for your customers to choose from and make sure they get charged correctly.

Chapter 8, Get Set..., will show us how to create a customer account and place an order. We will look at the PrestaShop customer loyalty scheme and at how to get some feedback on your products using the PrestaShop comments module. We will tell the search engines about your cool new shop. We will also look at a multi-pronged marketing campaign including vouchers, forums, social media, and Google AdWords. The last thing we will do is cover some functionality on the Customers and Orders tabs that we haven't covered already.

In *Chapter 9, Go... To the Future*, we will cover analyzing, optimizing, and adding in PrestaShop. We will see "the big secret" and also the future of e-commerce and PrestaShop.

Appendix A, Control Panel Quick Reference, lists a reference to find everything in your PrestaShop control panel.

Appendix B, Web Resources, lists all the most useful websites for e-commerce entrepreneurs.

Who this book is for

This book is for anybody who wants a fully functional, real e-commerce store using PrestaShop. You do not have to have any previous knowledge of PrestaShop or any aspect of e-commerce or business in general. If you do, then you will probably find this guide really valuable as well. The book covers all you need to know but you must just bring the desire to have your own e-commerce business.

Which hosting environment?

Before you get down to building your PrestaShop, you need to choose how you are going to host your new business.

Option 1: Developing on your own PC

There is a generally accepted principle that you should develop a website privately, test it, and then transfer it to a "live" server.

If you want to go that route, then that's OK. But I am not recommending that here. PrestaShop is so smooth, so problem free that I don't see the point of the extra step. You really can buy a domain name, transfer the necessary files to your hosting account, and be up and running in not much more time than it takes to read this book.

Here is a suggestion. If you are planning on having thousands of products, why not get your shop up and running as described in this book and then add your range steadily to your store when it is already open and earning you money?

Obviously, if you are just checking out PrestaShop or you are working for a company who insists on a private environment to develop your shop, then fine, do it that way.

If you opt for developing PrestaShop on a private PC, have a look at WAMP (www.wampserver.com). This is a quick, easily configured environment that will allow you to develop PrestaShop on your PC.

Alternatively, go and download my guide on running a web server from home. It will talk you, click by click, through setting up the perfect environment for running a PrestaShop on your home PC. It's free and you can find it on www.prestashop-book.com.

It is my goal, however, to give you the chance to realize a trading, profitable, e-commerce business in a hurry. And the specific guides and tutorials will describe live development on a hosting account. It should be very easy to adapt these guides should you choose to do things on your own PC.

Option 2: Live hosting accounts

This is definitely my preferred way. Get it up, get it open, and get the money coming in.

If you go for this option, here are a couple of things to help you choose. A quick survey of web hosts showed that most would do the job nicely. One of the big names that's fine is www.godaddy.com. Their economy plan is more than sufficient. Don't book it on their website! Ring them up. Pretend you are not sure if Go Daddy is right for you and they will give you a discount. Nice, isn't it? This is true with most web hosts.

One big name you can't use is 1&1. They are still using a dodgy version of PHP that PrestaShop doesn't like. No talking or pleading with 1&1 seems to do any good.

If you already have a web host, here are the system requirements for PrestaShop. Give your host a call if you are unsure, change if they can't accommodate you. Most good hosts will be fine, as the requirements are very "normal":

- Linux, Unix, or Windows
- Apache web server
- PHP 5.0 or later
- MySQL 4.1.14 or later

PrestaShop is working from MySQL 4.1.14 to 5.0 too, but some features do not work (for example, product duplication) or have strange behaviors.

Some PHP 5 versions are bugged (like 1&1) and prevent PrestaShop from working correctly:

- PHP 5.2.1 (authentication is impossible)
- PHP 5.2.6 (authentication is impossible under 64-bit servers)
- PHP 5.2.9 (image management/upload broken)
- PHP < 5.2 (invalid date time zone)

PrestaShop turn-key hosting

If you want to save yourself a few hours setting up your PC or 10 minutes uploading the files, you can use PrestaShop-recommended turn-key hosting. That is, you can pay a monthly fee and use a ready-installed PrestaShop. The advantage is the hosting environment is specifically designed for PrestaShop and you will save a bit of time.

If money is no object, great, do it, but it really is not hard to get PrestaShop up and running without the turn-key option. And of course they charge much more than a regular web host as well as a commission on all your sales. Ugh! If you want to use the turn-key option, then visit www.prestabox.com.

Get your hosting ready to go

Considering all that we have just discussed, it is time to decide what is right for you and put your plan into action:

1. Choose your hosting environment.
2. Buy a domain name.
3. Set up home hosting or buy pro-hosting.

Your hosting environment is ready!

Now let's look at the help and support available to you.

What happens if I get stuck?

PrestaShop really is as intuitive and user-friendly as they come. But there are loads, and I mean loads, of options in the PrestaShop control panel. And it is likely that the large array of different hosting providers as well as the varying objectives of different readers will mean that different issues and problems arise for everybody.

That's OK. Help is at hand.

www.prestashop-book.com

This is the official website of PrestaShop 1.3 Beginner's Guide. There will be a regularly updated F.A.Q. and an errors and omissions section (hopefully, quite small) as well. You can visit as the need arises or register free for e-mailed updates.

www.prestashop.com

This is the official PrestaShop website. Here you can view the PrestaShop wiki and other official documents. You can log into their trial admin area and experiment with the features discussed in this book without fear of the effect.

Best of all though is the PrestaShop forum. You can ask anything about PrestaShop. And I can say from experience the community is responsive, knowledgeable, and most of all, very friendly. So many times in the forums of other shopping carts newcomers have been slated for minor breaches of somewhat draconian rules. This is not so in the PrestaShop forum.

www.businessdreams.net

Here you can ask anything you want about online business. Click on Forums and select the most appropriate category for your question. You can talk about marketing, affiliate programs, finance, open source software, and much more. There is even a PrestaShop category. And you can sign up for a hints and tips newsletter for great advice and up-to-the-minute e-commerce news.

Help others to help you

Now it's time to introduce yourself to e-commerce and PrestaShop entrepreneurs who are more than happy to help you. And maybe you can help them too.

1. Go and register on `www.prestashop-book.com` for free updates, extra tutorials, and (OK, I admit it) the occasional correction.

2. Register and introduce yourself in the official PrestaShop forums for all things PrestaShop.

3. Register and introduce yourself on the Business Dreams forums for all manner of support and advice.

You are now ready to set up your first PrestaShop.

Remember

My first rule of e-commerce: keep your wallet shut (assuming you have already bought this book—it's too big to put up your jumper). Hold onto your entrepreneurial hat. You will be in business before you know it.

Conventions

In this book, you will find several headings appearing frequently.

To give clear instructions of how to complete a procedure or task, we use:

Time for action – heading

1. Action 1

2. Action 2

3. Action 3

Instructions often need some extra explanation so that they make sense, so they are followed with:

What just happened?

This heading explains the working of tasks or instructions that you have just completed.

You will also find some other learning aids in the book, including:

Pop quiz – heading

These are short multiple choice questions intended to help you test your own understanding.

Have a go hero – heading

These set practical challenges and give you ideas for experimenting with what you have learned.

You will also find a number of styles of text that distinguish between different kinds of information. Here are some examples of these styles, and an explanation of their meaning.

New terms and **important words** are shown in bold. Words that you see on the screen, in menus or dialog boxes for example, appear in the text like this: "Click on the **Modules** tab and then click on **Configure** next to the **Product Comments** module."

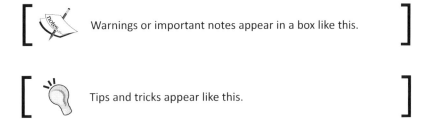

Warnings or important notes appear in a box like this.

Tips and tricks appear like this.

Reader feedback

Feedback from our readers is always welcome. Let us know what you think about this book—what you liked or may have disliked. Reader feedback is important for us to develop titles that you really get the most out of.

To send us general feedback, simply send an e-mail to feedback@packtpub.com, and mention the book title via the subject of your message.

If there is a book that you need and would like to see us publish, please send us a note in the **SUGGEST A TITLE** form on www.packtpub.com or e-mail suggest@packtpub.com.

If there is a topic that you have expertise in and you are interested in either writing or contributing to a book on, see our author guide on www.packtpub.com/authors.

Customer support

Now that you are the proud owner of a Packt book, we have a number of things to help you to get the most from your purchase.

Errata

Although we have taken every care to ensure the accuracy of our content, mistakes do happen. If you find a mistake in one of our books—maybe a mistake in the text or the code—we would be grateful if you would report this to us. By doing so, you can save other readers from frustration and help us improve subsequent versions of this book. If you find any errata, please report them by visiting http://www.packtpub.com/support, selecting your book, clicking on the **let us know** link, and entering the details of your errata. Once your errata are verified, your submission will be accepted and the errata will be uploaded on our website, or added to any list of existing errata, under the Errata section of that title. Any existing errata can be viewed by selecting your title from http://www.packtpub.com/support.

Piracy

Piracy of copyright material on the Internet is an ongoing problem across all media. At Packt, we take the protection of our copyright and licenses very seriously. If you come across any illegal copies of our works, in any form, on the Internet, please provide us with the location address or website name immediately so that we can pursue a remedy.

Please contact us at `copyright@packtpub.com` with a link to the suspected pirated material.

We appreciate your help in protecting our authors and our ability to bring you valuable content.

Questions

You can contact us at `questions@packtpub.com` if you are having a problem with any aspect of the book, and we will do our best to address it.

1
Building Your PrestaShop

I don't believe in hanging around! So let's get right on with setting up PrestaShop. Take a look at what we will do next.

In this chapter we will:

- Download and prepare the PrestaShop files
- Make a database
- Install PrestaShop
- Implement post-install security
- Have a look at your shop from a customer's viewpoint
- Have a look around your new admin control panel

Here we go...

Case studies

To make this book realistic, I will refer to two fictitious stores—fluffyteddies.com and guns4u.com. The diverse and extreme nature of the case studies will help to clearly demonstrate the "real" application of some PrestaShop features. I will refer to the case studies from time to time to discuss how the topic in question might fit in with one or perhaps both of them. Here is a bit more about the case studies.

◆ Fluffyteddies.com

Fluffy Teddies is a brand new small scale business. It is the fulfillment of a dream for a teddy bear, doll, and accessories hobbyist. It is his plan to offer a wide and diverse range of the most delightful and collectable products of their type, available in one place.

He is passionate about his range and aims to project this to his customers through an interesting and useful website content as well as good quality merchandise.

◆ Guns4u.com

Guns4u is the web outlet for a major arms reseller. Guns4u has a very wide range of weapons from small arms to intercontinental ordinance with various warheads as well as state-of-the-art missile defense systems.

Guns4u plans to make their product range available to a wide and diverse range of customers. Operating from the independent island of Tropicano in the South Pacific, it is not governed by restrictive laws on arms sales.

Just as long as Guns4u complies with the stringent tax laws of the ruling dictator of Tropicano, it will have a free reign to sell its wares to whoever it chooses. Guns4u intends to offer a retail range to anybody and a bulk discounted range for its bigger customers.

Downloading PrestaShop

Visit `www.prestashop.com` to get your free copy of PrestaShop. Click on the **Download PrestaShop** option. Fill in the very brief registration information and click on the big blue button. Finally click on the **Download** button and you should have a zipped file called `prestashop_1.x.x.x.zip`, where `x.x.x` is the version of PrestaShop you have downloaded. The version number you have doesn't matter. As long as you follow the download link from the PrestaShop home page, you will have the latest stable version.

In the next tutorial, we will upload all the loose unzipped files to your web server. It is worth pointing out that you might save some time by uploading the zipped file and then using your web host's file manager to do the unzipping. As most web hosts use a slightly different system, I will guide you through by unzipping first. But if you know how to use your web hosts file manager to do this, then you could save a short wait while uploading. You decide. Unzip it now to prepare for the next guide and you will be left with a folder called `prestashop`.

Now that you have downloaded and unzipped the PrestaShop files, it's time to put them onto your website ready to install. If you are hosting at home, this is a simple matter of putting them in the Apache home folder (see my downloadable guide if you're unsure where this is).

If you are developing on a live server, then you need to transfer the files via FTP. Let's do that step by step.

Time for action – transferring files to your web host

To make this as quick and easy as it can be, I will use a few Windows shortcuts in this short click-by-click guide. Just before you dive in, you will need your FTP username and password. If you don't know it already, you can usually find this quite easily by looking in your account details in your web host's control panel. Any doubts, give them a ring. That's what you pay them for.

1. Hold down the *Windows* key and tap the *E* key twice. You will have two Explorer windows pop up. Arrange them neatly one above the other. Alternatively, you can grab a copy of a dedicated FTP program such as FileZilla from `www.sourceforge.net`. There is a small learning curve doing this, but once you're used to it, you will have more options when using FTP. This guide assumes you do not have FileZilla, but if you do, it won't be a problem to interpret the guide.

2. Browse to the unzipped `prestashop` folder at the bottom of the window. Actually click into it. We do not need the folder itself, just the contents.

3. At the top window, you need to log into your website via FTP. In the address bar at the top of the screen, type `ftp://yourdomain.xxx` and press *Enter*. When a pop-up window appears, enter your FTP username and password that you obtained earlier.

4. Now at the bottom of the window, left-click on the very first file. Hold down the *Shift* key and then using the *down arrow* key, while still holding down *Shift*, scroll to the very bottom of the screen so that all the files and folders are highlighted. Every single one.

5. Now let go of all the keys on the keyboard. Left-click and hold the left mouse button. You can now drag all the files from the `prestashop` folder on your PC up to your website in the top window.

6. Wait for the files to upload. The time will vary according to the speed of your Internet connection.

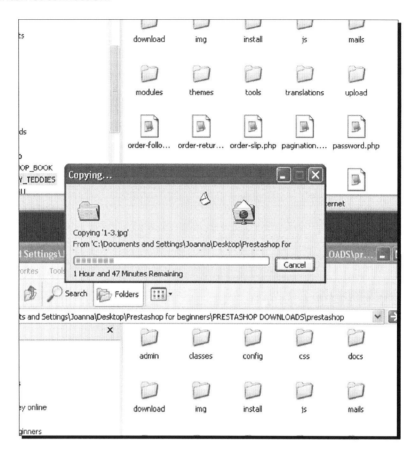

What just happened?

What you have done is put all of the files and folders containing the entire computer code, data, images, and other resources into your web host's server ready for the next phase of installation.

So let's move on.

Making a database

PrestaShop needs a MySQL database to function. The files we have just uploaded are the web pages that will become your store and the PHP programming code that performs the actions required by your store.

For example, when a customer creates an account in your new shop, the programming code contained in the files that we uploaded will fill out and store the information in a completely separate computer program. This program is called a database server and the type of database server that PrestaShop uses is called MySQL. Usually, when you are pro-hosting, this server will be an entirely different physical computer to the one holding your files (the web server).

As with many servers/computer programs, you need a username and password to access its functions. You also need a unique name for a database for your shop on that server, and you need to know the address locating the server. As an example, this could be `aserver.myhost.com`. Or it could be something completely different.

Now many web hosts will have already allocated database server details to your hosting account. If this is the case, then you only need to find them and make a note of them for the next phase of the installation.

Most likely your web hosts have a simple two- or three-click process for creating a database. You can then access the details of this newly created database in order to proceed.

Precise details will vary from host to host and also the order in which the options are presented (if at all). The database creation process goes like this.

If you already have a created database, that is okay. PrestaShop can function on a database used by other applications. However, to make sure that they do not conflict, or worse, damage each other, pay close attention to the *How to install PrestaShop* section to be sure you create a table prefix!

Time for action – creating a database

First of all, you need to log in to your hosting control panel. You are looking for an option called "MySQL", "MySQL databases", or perhaps just "databases".

1. Click on **MySQL databases** or something similar.

2. Now we need to make another database. Look for the option **Create new**, **Make a database**, or perhaps just **add**. Click on it to see the options presented. Below is a screenshot of the database creation page on the Godaddy.com control panel. It serves as a good example because it has more options than most. If your screen has fewer options, that is okay. Just follow the guide for the bits you need to.

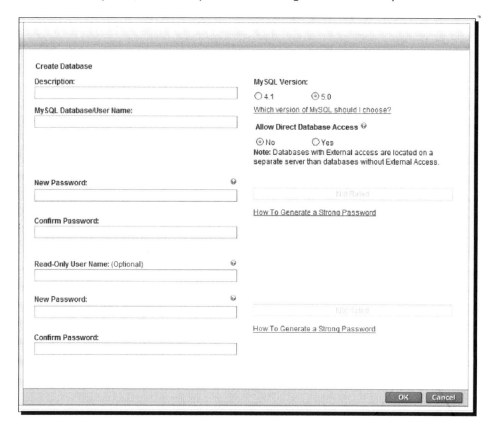

3. **Description**: This is an arbitrary field. Suppose over the years you open a couple of dozen stores, all requiring a database; eventually just a database name might not be enough to identify its purpose. Put something quite descriptive here, like **1st PrestaShop on www.mydomain.com**. Abbreviate it if there is not enough space.

4. **Database username**: This is an important detail that needs to be remembered. It is case sensitive, so upper and lower case must be accurately recorded. Choose a username; again, it is arbitrary, but use something appropriate and not easily guessable, like **mydomainsomesecretnumber**. There will be a maximum number of characters, so you might need to use a shortened version. Write it down or copy and paste it into Windows Notepad or on a similar application. It is possible that you do not have a field for a name or it has already been filled out automatically. That's fine. Just write it down.

5. Enter a memorable but un-guessable password. Again this might be decided for you and it might not have this option at all. Re-enter the password if required. Write it down or copy and paste it in Notepad or something similar.

6. **Read-Only User Name** and **Password**: This is not required for PrestaShop, so leave it blank.

7. If you get the choice to select versions for MySQL, tick/check the option for 5 or later.

8. And, if as shown in the screenshot you get the option to **Allow Direct Database Access**, this is a definite **No**. We don't want people to fiddle with our database from far away.

9. When you're done, click to create the database— **OK**, **Finish**, **Create**, or whatever your web host decides to label their button with.

10. Now you should be able to see a summary of the database you created. Complete with the values you chose and the values chosen for you. The following screenshot will give you an idea. As usual, write it all down or copy and paste it into Notepad or some similar application.

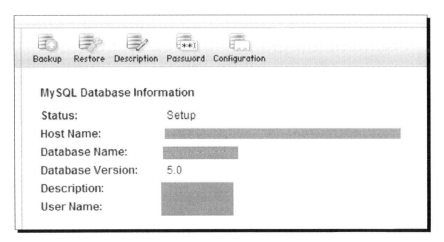

What just happened?

Now we have a fresh database just itching to be filled up and manipulated. We also have the database information we need to do so. Next we can go to the most interesting part of the process and get our very first glimpse of PrestaShop in action. We'll set up the program right away.

How to install PrestaShop

Now for the fun part when you get to see some results. What we are going to do is run the PrestaShop auto-installer. This will be a series of web pages where you will enter information to allow the auto-installer to configure your store.

The sort of information that we will be entering is business information such as your shop name, personal details, and of course the database information gathered previously.

Time for action – the PrestaShop auto-installer

To get started, type your shop domain name into your web browser. It will automatically redirect to the default start of the PrestaShop installation program. You should see the following window:

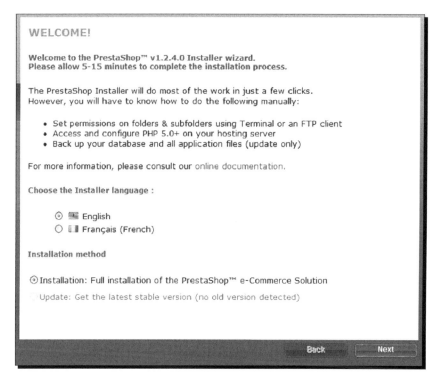

1. First up, just choose your language and click on **Next** to move to the **SYSTEM AND PERMISSIONS** screen:

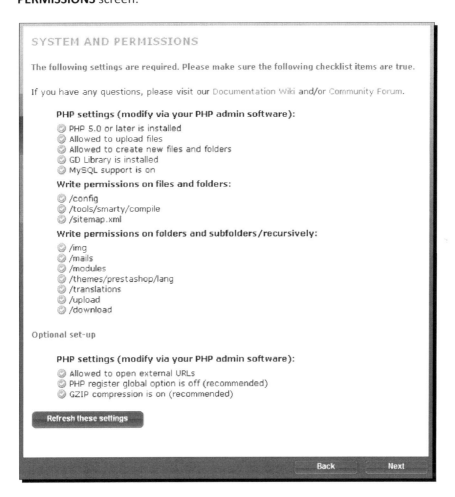

2. Check that you have all green ticks, as in the preceding screenshot. If you do, then click on **Next** to proceed and jump to the next number. If you see some scary red crosses, don't panic because there are some simple solutions. And here they are. If you have all green ticks move on to step number 6.

3. If you have any red crosses under the PHP settings, then you need to contact your web host and ask them to make some changes for you. If your hosting package has the system requirements discussed earlier, it is most unlikely you have any crosses here. Also, if you have installed hosting on your own PC as described in my free guide, they will all be ticks. If you have crosses and need to contact your web host read the next point first.

4. Next is **Write permissions on files and folders**. This is the most likely area to have some crosses and also the easiest to remedy. In order for PrestaShop to install itself, it needs to be able to modify (write to) various files and folders. A red cross indicates that the folder cannot be written to. Changing this is nice and easy. Log in to your website with FTP just as we did when we transferred the PrestaShop folders there. Locate any folders with a red cross, right-click on them, and select **Properties**. Then put a tick in the top two checkboxes under the **Write** column. Done! It is possible that you might need to use your web host's file manager to do this step. Also, if you extracted the files on your web server, then the file permissions will probably not need amending at all. The last optional settings are just that, entirely optional. And again if you are pro-hosting, your web host will need to resolve this for you. But PrestaShop will still be functional without them.

5. Click on the **Refresh these settings** button to check if you have solved the problem(s) and then press **Next** and read on.

6. Next is the **DATABASE CONFIGURATION** screen:

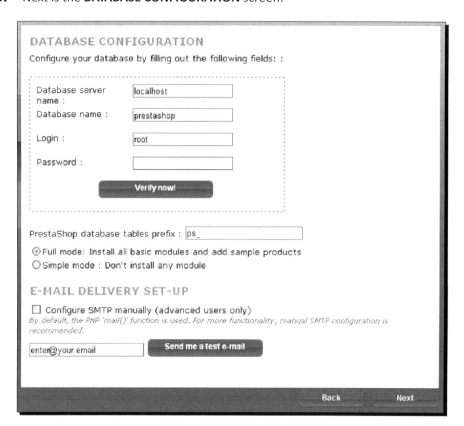

7. You have probably guessed that this is where you will fill in all the database information that we collected earlier. I will go through each setting one at a time because some of the fields are described differently from host to host and by PrestaShop. I feel the need for a small table of explanations. Here it is:

PrestaShop field	Explanation/alternative name
Database server name:	The address of the computer (server) with your database on it: Sometimes called 'address', 'host name', or just 'the database server'. Type this in here exactly as it appears in your web hosting control panel.
Database name:	Simply a name given to the database on the database server: On shared hosting environments, this is often the same thing as the username (or login as PrestaShop calls it). Enter exactly as it appears in your hosting control panel.
Login:	Your MySQL username: On shared hosting environments, this is often the same as database name. Enter exactly as it appears in your hosting control panel.
Password:	Your top secret sequence of letters and numbers (Shhh...).
PrestaShop database tables prefix:	This is a short series of letters placed before all the tables (sections) of your soon-to-be-created database. When an e-commerce shop of any type is created, there are dozens of "tables" created to store all the necessary information. If you think about it, all stores are likely to have similar table names (perhaps 'customers' or 'products'). When this occurs, adding a unique prefix prevents the new table destroying the old. A prefix is a good idea at any time, a very good idea if you have any other uses for your database and *essential* if you have more than one PrestaShop on your database. If this is your first PrestaShop, I suggest leaving the prefix as it is, that is ps_. But if this is your second or third, I suggest changing it to ps2_ or ps3_.

8. Select the **Simple mode** checkbox. This gives us a nice clean slate to work with. The other option sets up your store with sample products and lots more features all ready to go. That's cool. But do we know what we want yet? At the end of the day it is up to you. If you want to do it the **Full mode** way, that's fine. This book assumes that you have gone for the **Simple mode** installation, but the coming chapters would be quite easy to interpret if you want to do it the other way. I suggest **Simple mode**, but you decide.

9. Leave the **Configure SMTP manually** box unchecked. This is unnecessary for a pro-hosted environment.

10. Now enter your preferred e-mail address on your shop's domain that you would like PrestaShop to use. PrestaShop will send e-mails to customers to thank them for orders, notify them of dispatch, and more. PrestaShop will also contact you to let you know about important events such as when people spend money!

11. Click on **Next** and your shop database will be made. You will see this screen:

12. This page is really simple but with a little twist. Just fill in your first and last names along with the password you want to use to log in to your admin control panel. Do not select the **Receive notifications by e-mail** checkbox, as we will enable this later. There is a small bug in PrestaShop and this step avoids it. The one field that I haven't covered is the **Shop logo** box. I will cover this later, but if you just happen to have a 230x75 pixel graphic logo on your PC, feel free to browse to it and include it right away. Click on **Next** and rejoice.

What just happened?

You have just made your first PrestaShop. Cool! A few more bits and pieces to fiddle with and you're done. Was that difficult? In my opinion, if there is a technical side to running a PrestaShop e-commerce business, then that was probably about as geeky and technical as it gets! If you are reading this, you are heading for success.

Post-install security

Just a few, very quick modifications to your PrestaShop files and it's done.

Deleting the install folder

What we need to do is delete the entire folder called `install` from your web server. The reason for this is that it contains the PHP code that configured your store. So it might be very easy for anybody who knows it is there to rerun the install process with erroneous information and mess up your store.

Time for action – how to delete the install folder

This is probably the quickest and easiest way to do it:

1. Hold down the *Windows* key and hit *E* once. This will bring up a new Explorer window.

2. In the address bar, type `ftp://yourdomain.com` and hit *Enter/Return*.

3. Enter your FTP username and password.

4. Find the `install` folder. It is nice and prominent, near the top, under the `img` folder.

5. Right-click on it and select **Delete**. That's it. Don't close the FTP window, and read on.

What just happened?

Without the PrestaShop install files nobody can run the install process again. So we just prevented anyone with a little bit of knowledge from reinstalling over our PrestaShop and causing us to have a bad day. Next we will take another precaution to protect our new shop.

Renaming the admin folder

The admin folder holds all the web pages and PHP code that allows you to manage your shop. Almost any customization or configuration that you will make using your control panel, including the ability to log in, relies on this folder and the knowledge of its location. So you obviously don't want any Tom, Dick, and Harry sitting on their PC at www.yourdomain. com/admin trying to guess your password. And anybody who knows anything about e-commerce software knows that the default folder name for such functions is often admin. So we will now name it something more secret and personal.

Time for action – renaming the admin folder

You should already have an FTP window to perform these steps. If not repeat Steps 1 to 3 in the previous *Time for action* section and then come back here.

1. Find the admin folder.

2. Right-click on it and select **Rename**.

3. Rename it something that is easy to remember but difficult to guess. I suggest treating your admin folder name like a password. Perhaps, admintrickypassword. Make sure to leave the admin bit at the start. Then it should be safe from prying eyes and tampering fingers, but you and the PrestaShop system will know where it is.

4. Close your FTP window.

What just happened?

You just made your store's **Control Panel** practically inaccessible to anybody except you.

Your shop-front explained

Now, at last, it is time to see your shop! Visit www.yourdomain.com. It should look like the following screenshot:

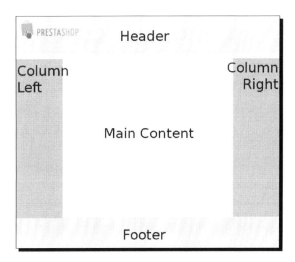

I have made a couple of notes to indicate a few areas that we will discuss next. It helps to name areas so that we can refer to them precisely and easily, instead of talking vaguely about the different parts of your site. PrestaShop refers to even more positions than this, but they are all related to these main ones.

If you haven't already, go and have a look at a PrestaShop that has some content. This will help you visualize approximately how your own store will take shape. You can do this at http://www.prestashop.com/en/showcase_demo/.

Header

This includes the little PrestaShop graphic in the top left. We will soon replace it with yours. As we progress, we will optionally add features and functions to this part of the store.

Column (left & right)

These areas are for navigation and just about anything outside of the main content area. Exactly how and where you position things will be up to your business objectives and your personal preferences. We will discuss all the options along the way.

Main content

The big bit in the middle! This is where your customer can find the most significant information. The home page, the product description, the product category, an article you have written, among others.

Footer

This is the full width of the website, right across the bottom.

Your admin control panel

Now log in to your store control panel. This is where 90 percent of this book will take place. This is what you will see:

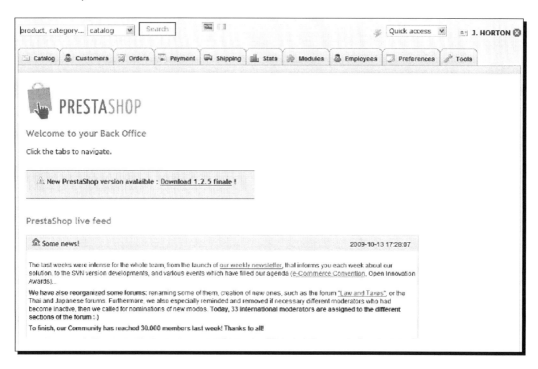

Time for action – logging in to your PrestaShop control panel

Here is how to get there.

1. In your web browser type `www.yourdomain.com/youradminfoldername`, where `youradminfoldername` is the same name that you chose for your admin folder previously.

2. Enter the e-mail address you registered with and the password you gave on the last configuration page when you installed PrestaShop.

3. Hit enter and you're in.

4. Why don't you have a look at the PrestaShop live feed? This contains topical news and information about PrestaShop direct from the creators. If there is an update available for PrestaShop, you will hear about it here.

What just happened?

You took your first look inside your store control panel. Now let's click some buttons.

Control panel guided tour

Here I will quickly run through some of the general functions contained within each tab and drop-down box and mention when, approximately, we will cover them in more detail. Why not explore as we run through them? A full control panel reference is contained in Appendix 1. From left to right, we have:

- **Catalog**: On this tab we have everything we need to manage our product range and all related aspects. For example, as well as creating the products (*Chapter 3*) themselves, we can give our customers manufacturer and supplier information to aid their buying decision (*Chapter 2*). We can assign advanced features to our catalog such as attributes, features, customizations, and attachments (*Chapter 3*). We can also assign product tags to help customers and search engines easily find what they want (*Chapter 4*).

- **Customers**: The **Customers** tab allows us to view and edit our list of customers as well as creating groups of different types of customers. This as we see can be very useful (*Chapter 8*).

- **Orders**: Here we can manage every aspect of post-purchase communication. Things like notifying customers of dispatch or a problem and making invoices available and printing packing slips. All of this will be covered (*Chapter 8*).

◆ **Payment**: This tab lets us connect to payment providers like Google and PayPal as well as offering options such as cash on delivery and bank transfer (*Chapter 7*). We can also add and configure the currencies we allow for payment, and create and manage gift vouchers that can be purchased (*Chapter 7*) or given away as a promotion (*Chapter 8*).

◆ **Shipping**: Unfortunately, this tab can't actually deliver stuff for you. It does just about everything else that is related to delivering your customers' orders. You can configure shipping types, costs, and durations in just about any combination to suit your business (*Chapter 7*).

◆ **Stats**: This topic is crucial. And it is a very significant area where PrestaShop stands head and shoulders above its competitors. Capturing and using statistics (*Chapter 5*) will allow you to measure success and decide how to change and improve your shop (*Chapter 9*).

◆ **Modules**: Just about everything in PrestaShop is a module. If you put a shopping basket here, it's a module; if you put a menu there, it's a module. We will be in and out of the module tab all the time. We will also go into greater depth about modules (*Chapters 2* and *5*).

◆ **Employees**: If you have someone else helping to run your business, the employees tab will help you manage your staff and how they interact with PrestaShop (*Chapter 6*).

◆ **Preferences**: The second-most varied tab in the whole of PrestaShop. There are many things you can do here. We will be popping in here from time to time and then covering everything we missed (*Chapter 5*).

◆ **Tools**: The most varied tab in the whole of PrestaShop. There are several things you can do here. We will be popping in here from time to time and then covering everything we missed as well (*Chapter 5*).

◆ **Search box** and **drop-down**: Select a PrestaShop aspect, type a related word, and hit **Search**. When you can't quite remember which tab is hiding the function you need, the **Search box** and **drop-down** menu in the top left is a life saver.

◆ **Quick access** drop-down: Know exactly where you want to go but don't want to click multiple buttons to get there? Select your destination from the quick access drop-down. This handy feature is in your control panel at the top-right corner.

Have a go hero – hunt the PrestaShop thimble

Here is a little challenge for you. Nothing very technical but a sort of PrestaShop 'hunt the thimble'. What if you wanted to temporarily disable your shop? Maybe you wanted to close it for maintenance. Perhaps you want to close it down during development when you're not actually viewing it. Can you find where to do it?

I promise you the solution is simple but can you work out where it is hiding?

Solution: Click on the **Preferences** tab. Scroll down to **Enable Shop** and select **No**. The Maintenance IP box even enables you to enter your unique Internet (IP) address so that only you can see the shop. This is a perfect, secure manner to develop your store. To get your IP address visit `http://www.whatsmyip.org/`. Enter it in the box on your preferences tab and press **Save**.

Before we continue

It is not important to know where everything is and how it works at this stage. As I mentioned before, we will approach each topic in the likely order of setting up a new business and not in a left-to-right manner. I just thought it might be nice to have a look under the hood before we get stuck in! This will hopefully help you to master PrestaShop more logically and to achieve my 7-day challenge.

Pop quiz – a few questions about Chapter 1

1. Many web hosts charge per database or have a limit before forcing you to upgrade your package. How would you create almost unlimited PrestaShop installs on the same domain name and same database without overwriting the original?

2. Once configured, which tab is the most likely you would use to see how many visitors your website has had?

3. Could you think of what would be the fastest way (least clicks) to begin the process of creating a new product?

Summary

We learned a lot in this chapter about PrestaShop.

Specifically, we covered the following:

- Obtaining PrestaShop: Where to download it from and how to prepare the files, including how to transfer them via FTP to your website.
- MySQL databases: How PrestaShop uses the database, how to create a MySQL database, and how the different terms are used to refer to the database location.
- PrestaShop installer: How to complete each step of the installer and filling out the slightly trickier pages like the database configuration page, and how to get round an intermittent bug in the installer.
- The shop front: How to refer to different parts of the shop front.
- The admin control panel: A brief look at where the different functions and tasks can be performed.

We're now ready to fit out your shop with a visually pleasing, unique, and sales-efficient design. This is the topic of the next chapter. So let's get stuck in then!

2
Shop Fitting and Layout

Your shop front as it stands is quite bland. But in around 20 pages time in will be bristling with modules, search boxes, navigation boxes, a smart header, and much more.

In this chapter, we will:

- ◆ Set the shape of your store including the logo
- ◆ Make your home page
- ◆ Make some more key pages, such as contact us and conditions of use
- ◆ Configure and enter manufacturer and supplier information
- ◆ Change and customize themes
- ◆ Add a few more touches to your shop's configuration

So let's get on with it...

Arranging key modules

What is a module? Well just about everything is a module or perhaps more accurately uses a module to be displayed. The best way of demonstrating is to get on and do something.

First, here is a list of key PrestaShop modules and their uses. I will then go through step by step, enabling, configuring (where necessary), and positioning them. I will also suggest positions and give reasons for my suggestions.

It is important to remember that everyone's shop will have varying objectives and it is perfectly reasonable, maybe even likely, that you will want to vary some of my suggestions. This is good, and if you feel you know best having read my suggestions and reasons, then you probably do know best. It's your shop (obviously) and the whole point of all the flexibility of PrestaShop is that there is no one best place. And every shop should be unique.

Below is a look at the **Modules** tab in your control panel:

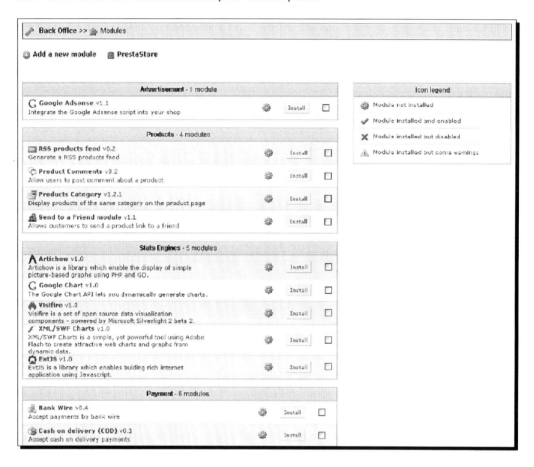

Take a look at the screenshot or click on the **Modules** tab in your PrestaShop control panel. On the left, you have a list of modules divided into categories. In a column to the right of the module description, there is a small gear wheel icon. This indicates the status of each module.

Just to the right in a narrow second block, there is a legend for the meaning of the module status icons. We can see that the gear wheel means that the module is not activated. If you choose the same install method as I suggested, then this is how all your modules will look. Note that an installed module has a nice green tick. An installed but temporarily disabled module has a cross and a module with personal issues has a warning triangle.

Now there are dozens of modules. We are just going to look at the most common or key examples. Now, having said what I have, there are some key modules, like payment modules (quite important for a shop), that we will skip over and deal with in a specific section that deals with payment.

I will go into click-by-click detail with a *Time for action* section for the first module. I will go into the same level of detail whenever there is anything new or different, perhaps when configuration options are required. But if the setup of a module is identical or even closely identical to a previous one, I will just point this out. You can then refer back to a previous click-by-click *Time for action* tutorial or set it up from memory. Maybe this will save a tree or two.

So let's get on with it.

Cart block

Every self-respecting shop has a shopping cart. It is a part of the web page that summarizes the customer's current situation with regard to product choices. It will show an abbreviated list of all the items selected for possible purchase so far as well as running money total. I said I would make suggestions about likely use of the different modules and I cannot think of any good reason why a shop would not display this particular module.

I would also suggest it should be highly prominent. Its very presence alerts visitors to the fact that you are a shop and not just an information website. It has a similar physiological effect to a "real" shopping cart. If you haven't got one, you can't put anything in it!

Why not check a few of the major online retailers and see what they do with their shopping cart? Many if not most have it in the top or right-hand column near the top. This is how I will show you how to position yours.

Time for action – installing the shopping cart module

We are now going to create a shopping cart module:

1. Log in to your PrestaShop control panel and click on the **Modules** tab. You should see the same window as shown in the previous screenshot.

2. Scroll down the list of modules and under the heading **Blocks** you will see the **Cart block** module. Just to the right of the description, click on the **Install** button.

3. Now scroll back to the **Cart block** module. Notice the green activated tick icon. Click on **Configure**.

4. Here you have the option to select an **Ajax cart** or not. AJAX is a suite of technologies that enables some really cool and smooth web effects. Sound like a good idea? Thought so. The reason you have the option to switch AJAX off is that some older templates that we will look at later in this chapter do not get along with AJAX and you would need to switch it off. For now at least, I suggest leaving it on. Click **Save** when you're ready.

5. Go and have a look at your shop front. You should see the same as the picture below. Why not click on the **Cart** and **Check out** buttons to see the effect? Understanding the experience your customers will have is a good idea.

What just happened?

Congratulations! Your first of many modules is enabled. Now let's move on to the categories block.

Categories block

This module is simply a list of product categories. That is, when you create categories for your products, they will appear in this module. And if you change, delete, or add to your categories, then the categories module will dynamically change. This means you never have to worry about changing your site when you change your product range.

This module is activated in exactly the same way as the previous one and is located just below it. Activate it now, then click into the configuration options and I will explain them next.

There are two options. Here they are from the top. The **Maximum depth** option is first. We will discuss good category design in the next chapter, but for now just to understand this option, here's a quick explanation. If you have a complicated or large selection of products, it makes good design sense not to try and ram the whole range on your customer's screen at the same time. **3** is a good default setting. I suggest leaving it as it is until we have looked at category structure in the next chapter.

If you want your category titles to slide around in a cool animated fashion, then leave this setting as it is. Have a look at your store front and see what you think. Obviously, there are no actual categories in it yet, but there will be soon.

User info block

Nice and simple, no configuration required. Install this module as normal. Then visit your store. You will see three links at the top right-hand corner. Next is **Your account** option; this will take your customer to an account creation page. **Log in** takes the customer to a sign in page and in case they do not have an account then this link also gives them the option to create an account. And finally, a minimalist version of a shopping cart. You can use this instead of the shopping cart module but most customers will probably appreciate a permanent and clear visual reference to their shopping status. You decide.

My account block

This is probably the most optional of all the modules so far. Enable it and then we will discuss what is in it and you can decide if it suits your shop. Of course, whatever your decision is with any module, you can always change your mind with a click of the button. Install **My account block** and read on about creating a test account.

Time for action – making a customer account

Now it is time to create an account for yourself in your own shop. This will be useful now and later as well. It is especially useful because the **My Account** module is only visible to customers who have logged in.

1. Click on **Your Account** at the top-right of your store front. In the **Create your account** box, enter your e-mail and click on the **Create your account** button.

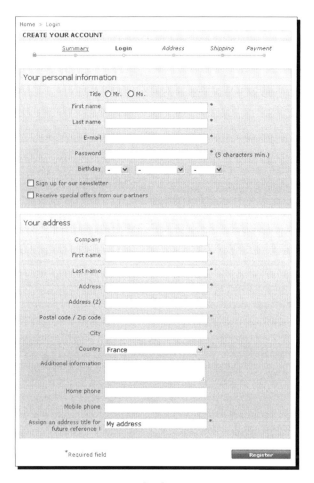

2. The form is very self-explanatory. Fill it out and click the green **Register** button at the bottom of the screen. You are now at the **MY ACCOUNT** page, as shown in the following screenshot:

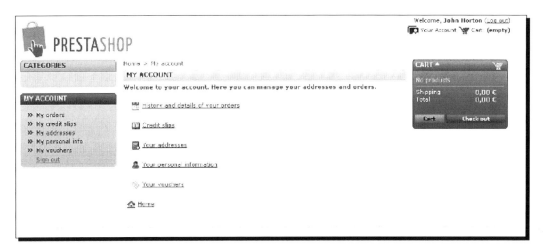

3. Take a close look at the now visible **My Account** module and compare it to the links on the main content area of the page. They are just about identical. So we can simply devise from this that the purpose of the **My Account** module is a permanently visible version of the main **MY ACCOUNT** page.

4. Click on **My account** at the top-left just to confirm this.

What just happened?

Now you have a customer account, which as we saw is useful for testing. You have also checked out the **My Account** block, which should help you decide if you want one in your PrestaShop.

Just in case you are not sure if you want this module, consider your customers and your future store. Will your store be a place that is regularly visited by repeat purchase customers? For example, my Guns4u.com sells occasional purchase weapons and accessories to governments and other organizations. I don't think the average Guns4u customer needs a permanent link to their orders, credit slips, delivery addresses, and so on. The screen real estate saved could be used to highlight special offers or new products like missile defense shields or something similar.

However, FluffyTeddies.com also sells a huge range of build-it-yourself dolls, houses, and furniture. I expect enthusiasts to be constantly adding to their collections, checking on the progress of orders and buying vouchers for friends and family. They are also probably interested in ordering gift items to be sent to alternate shipping addresses. A **My Account** module will definitely be useful in the teddy shop.

Permanent links block

Found in roughly the same place as all the modules so far. Install it and visit your shop front. Notice that you now have three key links added to the top of your store. They are these: **contact**, **sitemap**, and **bookmark**. Why not try them all now? See what they do.

Your **Sitemap** page is very cleverly created for you. So as you add products and other pages, PrestaShop updates your site map. **Contact** is a contact form for your customers or soon-to-be customers to quickly and easily contact you. Notice the **Subject** drop-down box? We will talk more about that later in the chapter. And the **bookmark** button enables visitors to bookmark your site just a little bit quicker than doing so through the button in their web browser.

Suppliers and manufacturers blocks

Install both of these; they are located in the same section as the others have been. Visit your store front and you will notice they are both just empty blocks. They will, if you choose to do so, contain drop-down boxes so that your visitors can find out more about your suppliers and manufacturers as well as sort products based on them as well. We will add suppliers and manufacturers to your store later in the chapter.

Quick search block

This is almost certainly a must have. If your visitors can't find things quickly they will probably give up. The search function in PrestaShop is very efficient and works well. Install it and check out the effect on your store front.

Footer links block

Install it and then scroll back down and click on the **Configure** link. I would suggest that unless you have a really unique reason not to, you should check all the boxes and PrestaShop will create links and pages for all those topics. Notice on your shop front the links to what I call must-have pages. Click on these links and you will see that the content of these pages is just some sample text. We will put this later in the chapter.

Notice also some links to product pages such as specials, new products, and top sellers. These will automatically become relevant when we add products to your store in *Chapter 3*.

Have a go hero – moving the blocks around

Maybe you don't like where PrestaShop has put your blocks. So can you work out how to move them about? A clue to get you started is that the answer is on the **Modules** tab. You probably guessed that.

Click on the **Positions** sub tab. You can then click on the **show** drop-down to control which modules are visible for editing. This is useful because there are loads of modules and hiding the unnecessary ones makes things clearer. Now click on a transplant module, select the module and then the position you want it to appear in. The most commonly used would be left to right or vice versa.

Visit your store to see the effect. Notice that the block is actually duplicated! Go back to the admin control panel, find the block in the original position and click the red cross to delete the original. Do you notice the black up and down arrows? Move the block up and down in priority to change its location within the same position. This is useful if you want to customize the order/layout of the left and right columns, header, or footer. Moving modules around is covered step by step with screenshots later in the chapter.

Creating your home page

This is the page that visitors will see if they type your shop's URL without any extra bits. There is much debate about the best way to present your home page and what type of information should be on it. I think the right answer lies in what is "appropriate" for your business. I will talk you through creating some key elements for your home page, along with why they are probably a good idea. As with positioning the modules, if my argument for any given element doesn't hold up for your business, then do it your way.

What goes on your home page?

First let's discuss what goes on the home page and then it's *Time for action* to actually add your new content to the home page.

Unique Selling Proposition

Every business should have a USP. It stands for Unique Selling Proposition, that is, a reason in the form of a statement that compels customers to stick around and spend money at your shop. It is this USP that is a viable option for going right at the top of your home page. So how do you make one?

You need to think about your business and your products. What makes you different and unique? What is your "thing" that people can buy, which is so brilliant that they will want to find out more? By "thing" I don't mean a product, I mean a benefit that a key product or key range from your shop gives your customer (selling) and how can you present it to them (the proposition).

Let's look at an example. How many shops sell teddies? There is probably a multitude. So a half-hearted "Welcome to my shop; we sell teddy bears; and we really look after our customers", although sincere, won't sell much fluff!

But if I think about what is unique and will benefit my customers, I will start to make some progress. I sell teddies, they are fluffy. So how fluffy are they? I happen to know they are really fluffy. In fact, I can't remember ever hugging a teddy that was fluffier. But is fluffiness really a benefit to my customer? Who shops with me? It is not three-year-olds with Visa and American Express. No. They are mums and dads. So what benefit do mums and dads want to get from my products? They want a happy, secure, and safe little toddler who has a teddy bear they really love that didn't break the bank.

How about this -"At Fluffyteddies.com, all our bears are made from the perfect mix of natural and man-made fibers to guarantee that your special little one feels snuggled and loved by their new bear. And because we specialize only in bears and the like, we are never beaten on price."

A good USP is often made from a mixture of key facts, emotive reassurances, and a guarantee. Your USP could be much shorter: "The crumbliest, flakiest milk chocolate in the world" or "The softest, most huggable teddy bear at the picnic!" Or it could be much longer. What's important is that it is not just a greeting or a statement of facts and it specifically reveals a benefit to the purchaser.

Most important facts or navigation

Next up should be some key facts about your shop. By key I mean things that are important or useful to your customers. Perhaps you have free world-wide delivery. You could even have a really generous price promise. Maybe your store is divided into two or more very disparate areas. By this last point I don't just mean different categories such as golden teddies or brown teddies, I mean perhaps you have a wholesale area and a separate retail area or something else significant.

Products

By far the most significant use of space on your home page should be for products. In the next chapter, we will add some products to your store and learn how, with a couple of clicks, we can add the most important selection to your home page.

Time for action – how to add your content to your home page

PrestaShop has a really easy-to-use CMS. CMS is an acronym for Content Management System. It will allow you to create and label content and then make links to it. We will see more of this when we create your "must-have" pages in a minute and when we look at the CMS in more depth in *Chapter 4*. PrestaShop deals with home page content in a slightly different way. It uses another module called the **Home text editor**. Here goes:

1. Click on the **Modules** tab and scroll down to the section titled **Tools** (not the **Tools** tab!), find the **Home text editor**, and click on **Install**.

2. Now come back to it again and click on **Configure**. I have divided the page you will see into two screenshots.

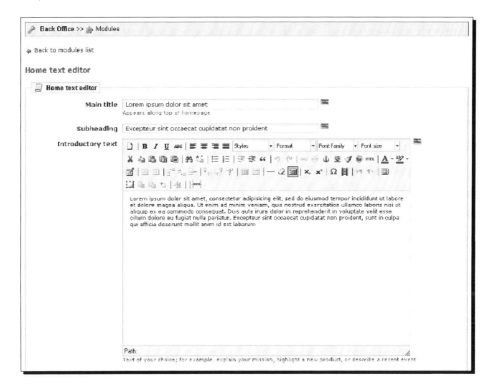

3. Now visit your store's home page. This will show you what the default content in the **Home text editor** is. It will make it much easy to follow when we change it all next.

4. Click into the **Main title** box and change the text to suit your shop. Your shop title could go here.

5. Now click into the **Subheading** box. This is the perfect place for your USP.

6. Now click into the **Introductory text** box. This is the ideal place for your most important facts or navigation, as described earlier. You could also put other information such as a news article, the most significant product, or a mission statement as suggested by PrestaShop.

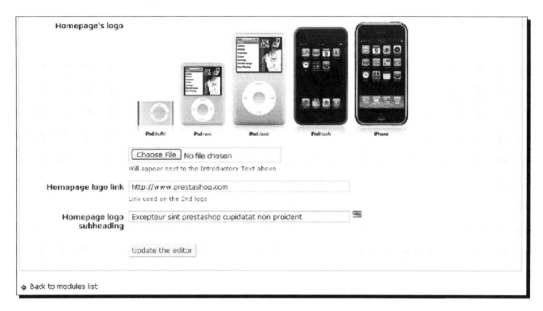

7. Next up is what PrestaShop describes as **Homepage's logo**. It probably shouldn't be the same as your shop/company logo that will soon replace the PrestaShop logo. It is more suited to a themed/generic picture or perhaps a product showcase/montage. Visit www.prestashop-book.com and you can download my free guide to creating logos and editing pictures and graphics in general. The guide uses completely free, open source, fully-featured editing software called GIMP. Keep your wallet shut! The ideal width for your new home page image creation is 530 pixels and the height can be whatever looks right on your site. But remember, optimize your image for faster download (as described in my guide). When you have created your masterpiece, click on the **Choose File** button, browse to it on your hard drive, and upload it.

8. Enter a subheading for your image.

9. Click on **Update the editor**, check if your home page looks as you want it to. Make any corrections then repeat this step until you are satisfied.

What just happened?

You now have the most prominent page on your website. Take a look at your home page. Coming together nicely, I think. Remember you can and should update this page as and when it is relevant to do so.

Now we will use the PrestaShop CMS to create your 'must-have' pages.

Creating the 'must-have' pages

What follows is a discussion of the pages you would probably expect to find on any e-commerce website. I will go through each in turn, discuss its purpose, and make some suggestions about creating your version of the page.

Delivery

This should contain everything a customer, future or current, needs to know about delivery time's return and refund policies. Depending upon the complexity of your offering, this whole page might amount to a couple of paragraphs or more.

Just make sure it is clear and complete, and if it needs to be long, make sure it is easy to use. This page is probably more important than the other information pages, as it is statistically the most likely to be referred to before a purchase is made. There is a sample template to extend or cut is on `www.prestashop-book.com`.

Legal notice

This page attempts to disclaim any unreasonable liability you might encounter. Even if your content and products are not controversial, you might want to get proper legal advice for this one.

Obviously, however, if you sell something that could leave you open to legal action, then you should definitely get proper legal advice and probably insurance as well.

This is one of the few areas where it might be worth getting your wallet out!

There is a text template available as a free download. You can get the file on `www.prestashop-book.com`. Download the file, amend it, or get legal advice as you see fit.

Terms and conditions

They are any rules and regulations you might have for your customers and visitors. Often this can be incorporated into the legal notice. The template mentioned above has sample terms and conditions for you to amend, leave, or get legal advice on as you see fit.

About us

This is the place to put the non-sales, non-product-specific stuff that so many new e-commerce sites make the mistake of putting on their home page. You can write this much better than me.

What are your values? How long have you been in the business? Have you got an interesting startup story? How big is your business?

Your aim is not to sell anything except YOU. Build trust and familiarity so that when your visitors find a product they want, they would feel all warm and friendly towards you. Then they will get their wallets out.

Secure payment

I have provided a template for you. You can get the file on `www.prestashop-book.com`. Download the file and read on. Be sure to change the parts (bold in brackets) to whatever is appropriate for your store.

Of course, my template is just a suggestion. It is short, reassuring, and non-technical. If you want to do it another way, that's great. But people will visit this page (even if they don't read it all) to make sure you take their security seriously.

Time for action – using the content management system

Having decided upon the text for all your pages, it is time to actually create them.

1. Click on the **Tools** tab. Next click on **CMS**.

2. From the list of pages, click on the first one that you want to edit. The **Edit** button is the little pencil and paper picture in the middle of the three icons on the right.

3. Type or copy and paste your content as discussed previously. Click on the **Save** button when done.

4. Repeat for each page. Notice that there is a little red cross icon next to the edit icon. You can delete a page if you feel you do not need it. For example, many stores combine their terms and conditions with their legal notice.

5. Visit all your new pages to make sure they are formatted as you want them.

What just happened?

The 'must-have' pages are hardly the most exciting pages of your shop to create. However, they are really important. And once they are done, you can usually leave them alone and get on to more exciting things! For example, next we will define suppliers and manufacturers. Read on.

Suppliers and manufacturers

Do you use lots of different suppliers and manufacturers? Are they relevant to your product offering? What do I mean by this? As an example, if you sell technology gadgets, then the manufacturer is very important: Apple iPod, Nintendo Wii, Sony Vaio, and so on. The manufacturer and the name is a part of the product. Another example of where the manufacturer is important relates to the many sorts of components. For example, PC components, bicycle, or motor-spares are often relevant. Also, think about brand names. Sometimes brand names are synonymous with manufacturers but often they are not, albeit still important. Think about clothing and other fashion accessories.

What I am getting at is this: Is it important to distinguish, in some way, between the different brands/manufacturers of the products you sell, other than just a simple mention in the product description? Would it be beneficial for you or your customers to be able to sort by brand or manufacturer? In your product range, does the manufacturer or brand name make a real difference to price or quality (perceived or actual)?

If you answered yes to one or more of the three questions in the last paragraph, then it is almost certainly beneficial for you to complete this short section to define your manufacturers and give you and your customers more usability, search ability, and product clarity.

If you conclusively answered no to the previous three questions, it might not be worth defining your manufacturers and you could save 20 minutes. And remember, either way, if you make the wrong decision, you can always come back and add or delete them.

By defining manufacturers now and adding a manufacturer's module to your store front, when you come to create your products, you will be able to assign them to manufacturers and facilitate the extra PrestaShop search and sort options. I would suggest you use the term manufacturer and brand interchangeably except where there is an obvious reason not to.

For example, I would use manufacturer for a fashion brand with no obvious actual manufacturer, but perhaps for something like Sony Vaio, I would use Sony as the manufacturer and Vaio in the product description.

What about suppliers?

Suppliers are the actual place/company you get a product from. It is usually of less relevance to your customer apart from in a few examples. But if you have a large range of products and suppliers, it could be worth defining them because it can help with stock control. Imagine getting PrestaShop to print you off a low stock report for any given supplier. This could be really useful.

Decide if you want to define manufacturers and suppliers, just one or the other or none. If you do, it's *Time for action*. If you don't think you need to, feel free to skip this next practical.

Time for action – defining manufacturers and suppliers

Defining manufacturers and suppliers is, like most things in PrestaShop, a fairly simple affair. If you are only defining manufacturers and not suppliers or vice versa then just follow the steps relevant to you.

1. First, click on the **Catalog** tab and then on **Manufacturers**. Click on **Add new**. Near the top you will see the following screen:

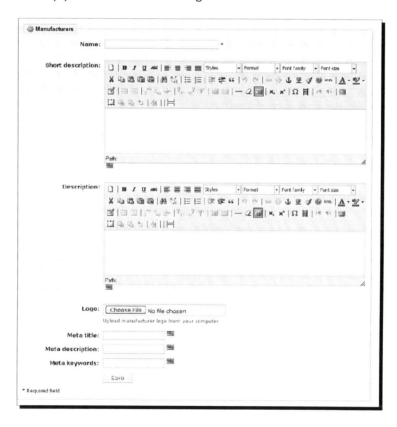

2. Fill out all the details and if possible upload an image. This is especially relevant where the manufacturer/brand name is trusted or admired in your field of business. By writing a short but concise description and adding a smart image, you associate your business with that of the brand. This can only be good for sales. The last three options are **Meta title**, **Meta description**, and **Meta keywords**. If you know what you want to put here, great, do it! I recommend leaving them empty until later when we discuss search engine optimization. We will look at the different types of metadata and ways to use keywords and consider a site-wide strategy. Then we can implement these three options and many more all at once. Click on **Save** near the bottom.

3. Click on **Add new** underneath **Manufacturer addresses** to add a new address. Select the manufacturer that you just defined in the drop-down box at the top, enter the address, and click on **Save**.

4. Moving onto the suppliers.

5. Click on **Suppliers**, then click on **Add new.** You will see the following screenshot:

6. Enter the supplier's details and press **Save**. Notice that the fields for suppliers are quite minimal. This reflects the probable lower importance to your customer.

7. Click on **Modules**, scroll down to **Manufacturers block** and/or **Suppliers block,** and enable them. If you click on **Configure** next to either of these modules after enabling them, you can determine the type and length of list displayed on your store front.

8. Go and have a look at your store front and see the added functionality. As you start to add products in the next chapter, you will see additional ways that your customers can interact with and use this information.

What just happened?

We just discussed whether suppliers and manufacturer modules are right for you. You then added the manufacturer and supplier modules where appropriate.

Now we can go on to explore or discuss key aspects of the topic.

Contacting your store

What if someone needs to contact you? Perhaps they need to ask a question, complain, or just want to say hello.

Contacts

You need to have relevant contacts for the different types of messages that people will send. Don't panic, you don't need to employ staff. All you need is to tell PrestaShop that certain types of message go to different e-mail addresses. This makes you look more professional and makes your customers feel that their message is not going into an empty black hole to be ignored.

Time for action – creating departments to contact

We are going to divide your shop into departments to give it a more professional feel and to create confidence in customers sending you messages. Remember that when we create these contacts and assign e-mail addresses, you will need to have previously created them through your hosting account.

1. Click on the **Employees** tab and then **Contacts.**

2. Click on **Add new** and enter the details of the new department/contact. Be sure to write something informative in the **Description** box because this is displayed to the customer. Then **Save** the information.

3. Repeat for each department/e-mail address combination you require.

4. Visit your **Contact** page and send test messages to each department to make sure everything is working as expected.

What just happened?

You just made your shop seem much more professional.

PrestaShop themes

Themes are what distinguish one PrestaShop from another. They are sometimes called as templates. They define the color, graphics, and even the actual ambience of your store. For example, if you are running a shop selling guns, you will want a very different theme to one selling teddy bears.

Themes are readily available for PrestaShop—many are free and many are not. What follows is a low down on where and how to find a theme for your shop. In my view, getting the right theme is only the start of creating the perfect look for your e-commerce establishment.

I strongly recommend hunting high and low for the theme that most closely suits your purposes and then installing it. All this is covered here and now. I also suggest, probably once you are up and running, that you embark on a process of further customization. This will truly separate your store from everybody else's and, along with all the other elements discussed in this book, leave you with an absolutely unique store.

The process of template customization is a bit more advanced than simply choosing and installing a readymade template, but we will explore the basics in a bit. It has to be said, however, that you might be completely happy without customizing. I have a real shop with the regular PrestaShop theme and it does just fine.

Let's get on with finding and installing a great template.

Finding themes

First of all, you need to have plenty of great themes to choose from. Visit www.prestashop-book.com and you will find a list of great resources free and otherwise for PrestaShop themes.

Choosing a great theme

Now here is how to pick a great one. If you visit one of the theme (template) resources listed on www.prestashop-book.com, you can find some really sleek-looking templates. Very often these will require an additional configuration change (as well as uploading files), which will all be covered in a bit.

Here is a quick word of warning when you're choosing a new template, especially when you're paying for it. Look at the substance of the layout and not just the images used to display the template. Remember that (probably) every single image that you see on the demo site will need replacing! Think how cool it will look with your images in it instead. Is the template you are thinking to buy truly beautiful or is it just the images that look good?

Installing a template takes only minutes, so try as many free ones as you like, but consider the above advice carefully before getting your wallet out.

When you have found a truly beautiful theme and you are ready to try it out read on.

Installing the themes

As I mentioned, this is nice and easy. Choosing is the hard part.

Time for action – installing a PrestaShop theme

Here is how to do it.

1. Download the template to your PC.

2. Hold the *Windows* key and tap *E* twice. In one window, browse to your downloaded theme. In the other window, log into your website via FTP.

3. On your website, browse to the **themes** folder.

4. Drag the new **themes** folder onto your website.

5. Now log into your PrestaShop admin panel.

6. Click on the **Preferences** tab and then on **Appearance**. Scroll to the bottom of the page, select your new template, and click on **Save**. How quick was that?

7. Okay. Just one more step, might be required. View your template. Is it muddled or not appearing at all? If so, it is probably designed for an older version of PrestaShop. No problem. There is a button to fix this. Click on the **Preferences** tab again and scroll to the very bottom of the page. Click on **Yes** for **v1.1 version theme compatibility**. All should be well. Remember to change this setting back if you download a newer theme or switch back to the standard theme.

What just happened?

You can now switch themes at will. After this quick pop quiz, we will look at making your theme completely unique.

Pop quiz – themes and things

So how do you customize the theme? Maybe you like the general layout but want to change some elements?

◆ How do you think you change elements of the actual template itself? Here is a clue: It's not in your control panel.

◆ How about changing the background color?

◆ And, of course, you need to change the default images of your new template (unless you are really lucky).

Customizing your template

Here, as the heading suggests, we will look at customizing our chosen template. Creating a template from scratch is too in-depth for the space we have here and involves a skill I am not qualified to teach. The skill I am referring to is design. "Click here", "Click there" type of instructions don't help when trying to design something. If you really want to start from scratch, I would recommend you to get two books: the first on CSS and another on design and layout principles.

The beauty of customizing an existing template is that all the tricky code is done for us; all we need to do is identify key elements of somebody else's work and amend it. We can then choose a template we like the overall shape and style of as a starting point, and change it in subtle or not so subtle ways to better suit our business and to make sure that our website is unique.

Now we will look at some 'quick wins' for simple customization, look at the PrestaShop template and discuss changing the CSS code, which defines a template.

To do all this, I will be working with the default PrestaShop template, but everything I talk about should be just as relevant regardless of your chosen template. So let's get on with it...

Important preliminary point

Throughout this part of the chapter, I will be suggesting you change this and that, delete this, add that. It is entirely possible that it could all go horribly wrong. Therefore, you could be left with a template and a shop that doesn't work. Make sure you have a current backup of every file you alter and only make one change at a time, check the effect, and then move on. You have been warned.

Moving modules around

No technical jiggery-pokery required here. PrestaShop allows you to move modules around at will and decides if there are any pages on which a module should not appear. Here is a lightning guide to doing just that.

Time for action – moving modules

Make sure you are logged into your PrestaShop control panel and read on.

1. Click on the **Modules** tab and then the **Positions** sub-tab.

2. Click on the **Transplant a module** link.

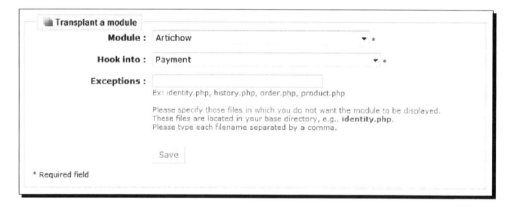

3. Select the module that you want to move in the top drop-down box and then where you want to move it to in the second.

4. Now specify a list of any pages that you don't want the module to appear on (if any).

5. Click on **Save**.

6. Notice that the module appears twice: in the original position and the new one. If this is not the desired effect, simply go back to your module positions page and click the red cross next to the one you don't want anymore.

7. Now you are back at the main **Positions** page, you can scroll down to the position you just moved a module to and using the up down arrows raise or lower the position it appears in. You can also drag and drop the modules.

What just happened?

Any module can now go anywhere. As usual do one change at a time because not everything works or looks good.

Customizing the default image sizes

The sizes of default images such as categories, products, scenes, and more can be defined by you. This is a really easy way to add more uniqueness to your PrestaShop. Also, you can create some great layouts and enhance your chosen template with just a few well-chosen dimensions.

Time for action – changing the default image size

This is really easy to do. The trick to achieving something unique here is to experiment. Try some really big sizes and perhaps consider decreasing the number of products per page at the same time, especially if you have a small niche range or sell products with interesting or detailed images. Here is how:

1. Click on the **Preferences** tab and then the **Image** sub-tab. Notice you can change the size of just about any image. This is really flexible and useful. Try experimenting with different image types.

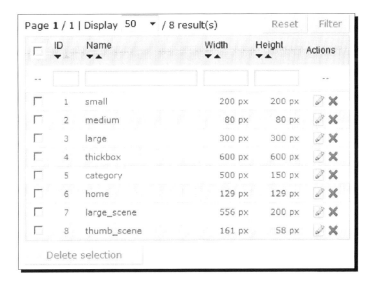

2. Click on the **Edit** button next to whichever image you are going to mess with and enter your new size. Be daring, you can always change it back. Click on **Save**.

3. Now scroll to the bottom of the page and click **Regenerate thumbnails**. Go and have a look at your products. Some of the images also need to be edited in your CSS file (more soon), but for some you will see the change right away.

4. Now, if necessary, we can reduce the number of products per page. Click on the **Preferences** tab and then the **Products** sub-tab. Scroll down to the **Products per page** and enter the number you want.

5. Go and have a look at the result. Repeat and tweak until you feel it is unique.

What just happened?

You can now vary the image sizes in your store. If doing so improves the look of your shop, make sure you use images that look good at their new size.

Now we can go on to explore or discuss key aspects of the topic

PrestaShop templates

PrestaShop makes it really easy to get started. All we need to do is have a selection of files and images that collectively make the template, put them into the folder structure on our web host in the right place, and we are ready to get modifying.

The easiest way to do this is to make a copy of the folder containing the template we want to modify, rename it (effectively making a new template), and put it into the folder structure. We will then be able to swap between our templates at will. I mentioned at the beginning of this section that it was important to back up files regularly while altering them. Of course, by making a copy of your chosen template, you are effectively safeguarding the original from harm. But I still suggest you make a regular backup of the files you work on as well. CSS files are necessarily complex and it is very easy to make a great change you really like, mess it up, and then not be able to get it back to the original. So make regular copies of the files you are working on, perhaps at different stages.

In the next guide, we will copy the default template, rename it, and enable it in our control panel. Then we can start to modify it.

Time for action – creating a new template

It's really easy to create a new template. The trick to achieving something unique here is to experiment. Try some really big sizes and perhaps consider decreasing the number of products per page at the same time, especially if you have a small niche range or sell products with interesting or detailed images. Here is how:

1. Open an FTP window on your web host.

2. Click into the `themes` directory in the main `prestashop` folder. Drag a copy of the folder you want to copy to your desktop. If working with the default theme, the folder is called `prestashop`.

3. Now right-click the folder on your desktop and select **Rename**. Rename the folder to whatever you want your new theme to be called (no spaces and all lower case is the best).

4. Drag the new folder onto your web server. You now have a new theme.

5. In your PrestaShop control panel, click on the **Preferences** tab and then the **Appearance** tab.

6. Scroll to the bottom and change to your new theme. Visit your shop and it will look no different. But now we can start to play with things.

What just happened?

We now have a canvas, so to speak, which we can start to do wonderful things with. So let's do it.

Editing your CSS file

The file that we are going to play with is called `global.css`. It is in the CSS folder inside our main template folder. A good way of working with it is to open it using a program like Notepad++ or something similar. Notepad++ is good because it does not add any extra formatting to a document and this is important. You can get a free copy of Notepad++ from `www.prestashop-book.com`.

We can make one change at a time, upload it to the live folder on the web server, and then go view the changes. Like it? Great! Don't like it? Change it back and have a rethink.

First I will point out a few parts of the CSS file that you can make interesting changes to, then a quick tutorial to show you how to implement the changes. I will discuss several potential changes all at once and then the tutorial, but remember to do it one at a time and to make a backup at regular intervals. Why not open up `global.css` now and have a look.

```
1   /*
2       PrestaShop CSS
3       18 used colors :
4       10 grays: #374853 #595a5e #5d717e #76839b #888 #bdc2c9 #d0
5       4 fushias: #f6dce8 #dd2a81 #971d58 #5d0630
6       2 yellows: #f8e1a0 #f9e400
7       1 green: #488c40
8       1 red: #da0f00
9   */
10
11  * {
12      padding:0;
13      margin:0;
14  }
15
16  body {
17      background-color: white;
18      font-size: 11px;
19      font-family: Verdana, Arial, Helvetica, Sans-Serif;
20      color: #5d717e;
21      text-align:center;
22  }
23
```

If you don't understand CSS, it will look very confusing. A complete explanation, as you might guess, is way beyond the scope of this book. The good news is that, generally speaking, it is quite easy to interpret and the code uses English words to help identify the purpose of each part of the code. So we can scan through and pick parts to change. Here are a couple of examples to get you started.

Background-color

On line 17 in the previous screenshot, you can change the entire background color in a stroke. Just change the word `white` to any CSS-recognized color. A few examples are aqua, black, blue, fuchsia, gray, green, lime, maroon, and navy. A full list can be found at `www.w3schools.com/css/css_colors.asp`.

Font-size

You can probably guess that this element determines the size of the font. Scroll through your `global.css` file. You can see dozens of references to font-size and they will all change the size of the font at different places.

```
567  ☐.price, .price-shipping, .pr
568      color: #da0f00;
569      font-size: 1.1em;
570      font-weight: bold;
571      white-space:nowrap;
572  └ }
```

Scroll down to line 569 (shown above) and change the value of **1.1** to **1.7**. From the context, can you guess where the font size will be changed? Try it out and then check your shopping cart totals. Press *F5* to refresh your browser.

Want more?

Why not visit `http://www.w3schools.com/css/` and get some great CSS tutorials as well as a complete list of CSS elements and their use. Now for a guide to actually making the modifications to your website.

Time for action – editing and updating your CSS file

This is really easy. Just consider that if your store is actually getting customers they will see the changes. So if you are up and running already, do another PrestaShop installation and use it to experiment before transferring the new CSS file to your live site.

1. Open the CSS file in Notepad++ or something similar.

2. Make one amendment to your file.

3. Be sure to retain any subtle parts of the code like commas or semicolons.

4. Save the modified file.

5. Via FTP, transfer the new `global.css` file to your web server and put it in exactly the same folder as it was on your desktop.

6. You will be prompted if you want to overwrite the existing file. As you have made a backup (right?) that is fine, because if there are any problems with the new file you can quickly replace it with the original.

7. Visit your store, refresh the page (*F5*), and view the changes.

8. Replace the file if necessary. Move on to your next tweak if happy.

What just happened?

We can now modify our chosen template a stage at a time.

Changing graphics

You already know how to change your logo and you might find that after modifying other parts of your site you want to change it. But what about all the subtle graphics? Here is how they work.

The CSS file refers to them in another folder. So we can view and change the graphics at will and as long as we keep the filenames the same, PrestaShop will use our new graphics instead of the originals. Here are all the default graphics that are in the `img` folder:

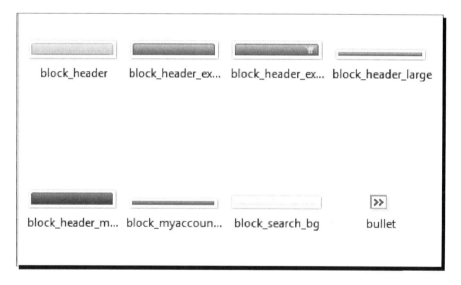

Buttons and icons

Perhaps the most fun change is to get a new set of icons/buttons. They are located in the `img/icons` folder. Here is what some of them look like:

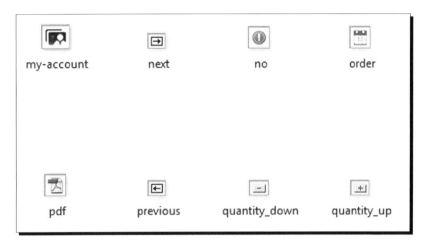

You can make your own in GIMP, amend the existing ones, or nip over to an image site like `www.dreamstime.com` and pick up a brand new set for around a dollar. Just rename the icons in the new set so that they replace the originals and PrestaShop will do the rest.

Themes summary

You have probably guessed that one of the keys to making your chosen template unique and stylish at the same time is a combination of all the things we have discussed along with a bit of extra research into the CSS elements. As usual don't put off further development or expansion of your business until you have achieved the perfect template because that day might never come.

As I mentioned in the beginning of this section, CSS and template design is a huge topic. If it is a topic that you want to find out about in detail, then further reading is essential. If you just want a smart, unique template in a hurry and then move on with the next phase of building your shop. Hopefully I have provided enough information here.

The other key to a great template has got to be planning. I didn't mention this until the end because it definitely helps to experiment a bit. Until you know what is possible it is hard to imagine what you might like to achieve. When you look at templates try and envision how you could change it to make it *yours*.

For more information about templates visit the PrestaShop forum. There is a whole section devoted to the very subject: `www.prestashop.com/forums`.

The cherry on top

Now let's fix up your company/shop logo. If you don't have one already and you don't know where to start to create one, grab hold of my free graphics and logos guide from `www.prestashop-book.com`. Create a new logo or modify your existing one to be approximately 230 pixels wide.

Time for action – uploading your company/store logo

So you now have your logo graphic. Here is how to add it to your shop:

1. Click on the **Preferences** tab.

2. Click on **Appearance**. This is what you will see:

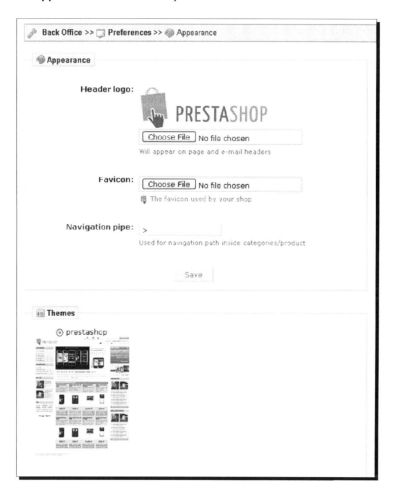

3. Click on the **Choose File** button underneath the PrestaShop logo and browse to your new logo.

4. While on this screen, you can also upload a new Favicon. That is a tiny graphic that displays in your visitors web browser. Just make a 16 x 16 pixels image in GIMP and save it with the `.ico` extension.

5. When you're done, save the changes by clicking on **Save**.

What just happened?

You now have a neat, well-optimized logo. It is starting to look like your very own PrestaShop.

Summary

We achieved quite a lot in this chapter. Specifically, we covered:

- Setting up the key PrestaShop modules: With a few clicks, we can add or remove quite significant features to our store.

- Creating content for our home page: The homepage is vital and should be updated occasionally. It is controlled by a module.

- Creating our 'must-have pages': PrestaShop has an easy-to-use **CMS** (**Content Management System**). This makes creating and managing unique pages really quick. There's more on the CMS in *Chapter 4*.

- Switching themes: It is not difficult to use a ready-made theme to customize our PrestaShop.

- We learned how to make basic but significant customizations to our chosen theme.

Now that you have got a shop with essential pages, features and content, it is time to give our customers some products to buy. That is the subject of the next chapter.

3
Merchandising for Success

The way we merchandise or set up an online shop is just as important as it is in a shopping mall. Would you buy from a shop that didn't have clear pricing, quality products, and an appealing offer?

In this chapter, we shall cover everything to do with presenting your products, and we will:

- Discuss and implement an efficient category structure
- Add high quality product descriptions that sell
- Take a look at all the different ways you can use PrestaShop to highlight products
- Look at product features, attributes, accessories, and customization

So let's get on with it...

Shop categories

Creating product categories, like most things in PrestaShop, is easy and we will cover that soon. First we need to plan the ideal category structure. And this demands a little thought.

Planning your category structure

You should think really hard about the following questions: What categories and subcategories will work best? What will make navigation simple and intuitive for your customers? What structure will support any plan you might have for expanding the range in the future? What do your competitors use? What could you do to make your structure better for your customers than anybody else's? When you have worked it out, we will create the category structure and then we will create the content (images and descriptions) for your category pages.

First you need to consider what categories you want for your product range. Here are some examples:

- Teddy Bears
- Dolls
- Houses
- Accessories

Next, to make your categories more organized, you might want to add subcategories. As an example, have a look at this:

Teddy Bears:

- Traditional
- Martial Arts
- Disney

Dolls:

- Cindy
- Traditional
- Other Dolls

Houses:

- Doll Houses
- Furniture
- DIY Kits

Accessories:

- Clothes
- Other Accessories

Perhaps you might even require categories within subcategories, but this is less common in a small store. Here are some examples:

Teddy Bears:

- Traditional
- Martial Arts
- Disney

Dolls:

- ◆ Cindy
- ◆ Traditional
- ◆ Other Dolls

Houses:

- ◆ Doll Houses
    - ❏ Terraced
    - ❏ Semi-Detached
    - ❏ Mansion
- ◆ Furniture:
    - ❏ Kitchen
    - ❏ Bedroom
    - ❏ Bathroom
    - ❏ Reception

You get the idea.

Obviously, my example was starting to get a bit silly, but it was deliberate to demonstrate a point. Don't have categories, subcategories, or anything deeper just for the sake of it. There are no prizes for compartmentalizing. If you think a fairly flat structure is what your customer wants, then that is what you should do.

If you are thinking, "Hang on, I don't have any subcategories let alone any sub-subcategories," don't panic. If your research and common sense says you should only have a few categories without any subcategories, then stick to it. Simplicity is the most important thing. Pleasing your customer and making your shop intuitive for your customer will make you more money than obscure compartmentalizing of your products.

Creating your categories

Have your plan close at hand. Ideally, have it written down or if it is very simple have it clearly in your head. Enough of the theory, it is *Time for action*.

Time for action – how to create product categories

Make sure you are logged into your control panel. We will do this in two steps. First we will create your structure as per your plan, then in the next *Time for action*, we will implement the category descriptions. Let's get on with the structure of your categories:

1. Click on **Catalog** and you will see the category creation screen. Notice at the top you have the option to add a category. We will be clicking that in just a moment and notice that further down the screen, you have the option to add a product to the **Home** category. This is where you put the products you want on your home page.

2. Now click on the green + symbol to add a new subcategory. PrestaShop calls even your top-level categories as subcategories because it considers the top-level to be home.

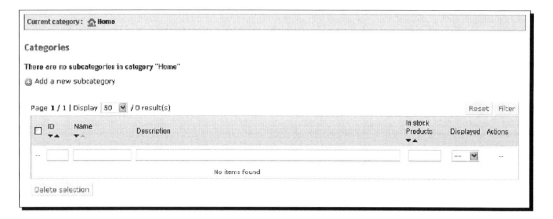

3. Just type in the title of your first main category. Don't worry about the other options. Descriptions are covered in a minute and all the rest is to do with the search engines and is covered in *Chapter 4*. Click on **Save** when you're done.

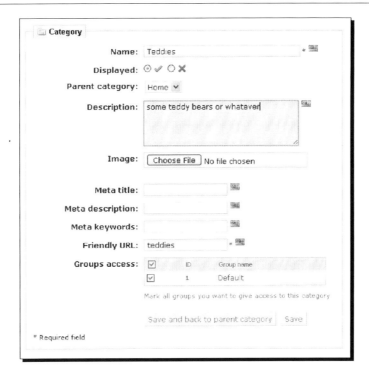

4. Now, as you might expect, you have created your first category. But as you might NOT expect PrestaShop has returned you to the product page of the category you first created. This means if you click to create another category now, it will be created as a subcategory of the category you just created. When you saved the category, you could have clicked **Save and back to parent category** as a one-click alternative. I suggest you create all your top-level categories first. So we want to get back to the **Home** category and then create the next one. Click on the **Home** link as indicated below.

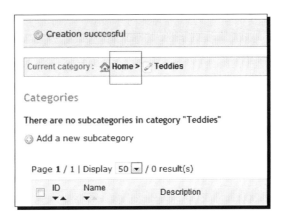

5. Now that you are back in the **Home** category, you can click on the green button again and create your next main category. Do so, save as before and remember to click the **Home** link, ready to create your next main category.

6. Repeat until all top-level categories are created. Have a quick look at your shop front to make sure you like what you see. Here is a screenshot from the PrestaShop demo store:

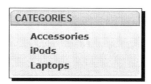

7. Now for the subcategories. We will create one level at a time as earlier. So we will create all the subcategories before creating any categories within subcategories. In your home category, you will have a list of your main categories. Click on the first one in the list that requires a subcategory.

8. Now click on the create subcategory **+** icon. Type the name of your subcategory leaving the other options and click on **Save**.

9. Now notice you are in the subcategory that you just created. Click on the link to take you back to the main category if you want to create another subcategory. Click the **Home** category where you can navigate to the right place to create your next subcategory.

10. Play around with clicking in and out of categories and subcategories until you get used to how PrestaShop works. It isn't complicated, but it is easy to get lost and start creating stuff in the wrong place. If this happened to you, just click the red cross icon to delete your mistake. Then pay close attention to the category or subcategory you are in and carry on. You can edit the **category order** from the main catalog page by selecting the box of the category you want to move and then clicking an up or down arrow.

11. Finish creating your full category structure. Play with the category and subcategory links on your shop front to see how they work and then move on.

What just happened?

Superb! Your category structure is done and you should be fairly familiar with navigating around your categories in your control panel.

Now we can add the category and subcategory descriptions. I left it empty until now because you might have noticed that the category creation palaver can be a bit fiddly and it makes sense to keep it as straightforward as possible. Here are some tips for writing good category descriptions followed by a quick *Time for action* for entering them into the category itself.

Creating content for your categories and subcategories

I see so many shops online with really dull category descriptions. Category descriptions should obviously describe but they should also sell! Here are a few tips for writing some enticing descriptions:

◆ Keep them short-two paragraphs at the most.

◆ The detail should be in the products themselves. Similar to a USP, category descriptions should be a combination of fact and emotive description that focuses on the benefit to the customer.

◆ Try and be as specific as you can about each category and subcategory so that each description is accurate and relevant in its own right. For example, don't let the category steal all the glory from a subcategory.

Time for action – adding category descriptions

Be ready with the text for all your categories or you can of course type them as you go:

1. Click on **Catalog** and then on the first categories' **Edit** button.

2. Enter your category description and click on **Save**.

3. Click into the subcategories of your first category, enter and save a description for each (if any).

4. Navigate to the second main category and enter a description, then do the same for each of the subcategories in turn.

5. Repeat for each category.

What just happened?

You now have a fully functioning category structure.

Now we can go on to look at adding some of your products.

Adding products

Adding products is a matter of navigating to the appropriate category or subcategory and clicking on the **+** link. There are a multitude of boxes and options to choose from and they deserve a little bit of consideration each.

In the *Time for action*, I will cover what to enter in each box as a separate item. However, I will skip over a few items like meta tags because they are best dealt with on a site-wide basis separately.

The other important option is the product description. This deserves special treatment because it needs to be effective at selling your product.

With the categories, I specifically showed you how to create the structure before filling in the descriptions because I and others I know have got into a muddle in the past. It is less likely but still possible to get into a bit of a muddle with the products as well. This is especially true if you have lots of them.

However, perhaps you should be the judge of whether to fill out your catalog before adding descriptions or add descriptions as you go. So here is a handy guide to create great product descriptions, and I will leave you to decide if you fill them in at the same time as the rest of the details, or if you just enter the product title, revisit them to fill in the rest of the details.

Product descriptions that sell

Don't fall into the trap of simply describing your products. It might be true that a potential customer does need to know the dry facts like sizes and other uninspiring information, but don't put this information in the brief description or description boxes. PrestaShop provides a place for bare facts—the **Features** tab (there will be more on this soon).

The brief description and description boxes that will be described in more detail soon are there to sell to your customers—to increase their interest to a level that makes them "want" the product and then actually suggests they pop it in their cart and buy it.

The way you do this is with a very simple and age-old formula that actually works. And, of course, having whetted your appetite, it would be rude not to tell you about it. So here it goes.

Actually selling the product

Don't just tell your customers about your product, sell them the product. Explain to them why they should buy it! Use the **FAB** technique—feature, advantage, benefit:

- Tell the customer about a feature:
    - ❏ This teddy bear is made from a new fiber and wool mix
    - ❏ This laptop has the brand new i7 processor made by Intel
    - ❏ This guide was written by somebody who has survived cancer

- And the advantage that feature gives them:
    - ❏ So it is really, really soft and fluffy!
    - ❏ i7 is the very first processor series with a DDR3 integrated memory controller!
    - ❏ So all the information and advice is real and has been actually tested!

- Then emphasize the real emotive benefit this gives them:
    - ❏ Which means your little boy or girl is going to feel safe, loved, and secure with this wonderful bear
    - ❏ Meaning that this laptop gives your applications, up to a 30 percent performance boost over every other processor series ever made
    - ❏ Giving you or your loved one the very best chance of beating cancer and having more precious time with the people they love

Don't just stop at one feature. Highlight the most important features. By most important features, of course I mean the features that lead to the best most emotive and personal benefits. Not too many though. If your product has loads of benefits, then try and pick just the best ones.

Three is perfect. Three really is a magic number. All the best things come in threes and scientific research actually proves that thoughts or ideas presented in threes influence human emotion the most. If you must have more than three features, summarize them in a quick bulleted list. Three is good.

- Soft, strong, and very long
- Peace, love, and understanding
- Relieves pain, and clears your nose without drowsiness

Ask for the sale

When you have used the FAB technique, ask the customer to part with their money! Say something like, "Select the most suitable option for you and click on **Add to cart**" or "Remember that abc is the only xyz with benefit 1, benefit 2, and benefit 3. Order yours now!"

Create some images with GIMP

If you have a favorite photo editor then great. If you haven't then I suggest you use GIMP. It's cool, easy, and *free*. Grab a copy of my PDF about creating graphics and logos to create some great images and how to get hold of GIMP for free. It's in the usual place: `www.prestashop-book.com`. Have your product images ready and read on.

Time for action – how to add a product to your PrestaShop

Let's add some products.

1. Navigate to the first category or subcategory that will have products.

2. Click on the **Add a new product** link. You will see the next screenshots. Okay, I admit it. It does look a little bit daunting. But actually it is not that difficult. Much of it is optional, and still more we will revisit after further discussion. So don't despair. There is a table of explanations for you after the screenshots.

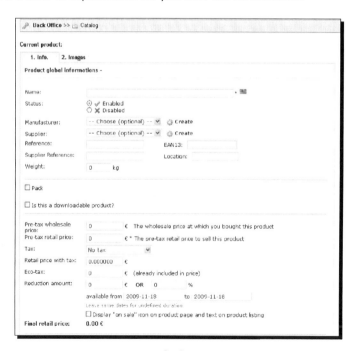

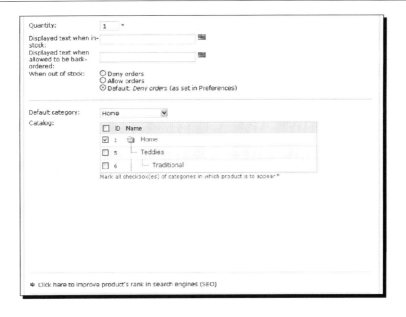

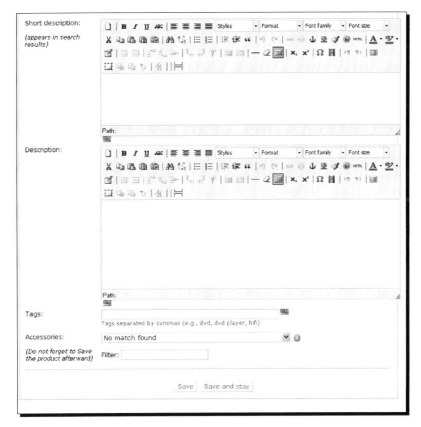

Field	Explanation
Name	The short name/description of your product. There is a brief description and a full description box later, but perhaps a bit more than a short name should go here.
	For example, 50 cm golden teddy bear—extra fluffy version.
Status	Choose **Enabled** or **Disabled**. If your product is for sale as soon as you're open, click **Enabled**. If your product is discontinued or needs to be removed from sale for any reason, click **Disabled**.
Manufacturer	If you decide to define your manufacturers in *Chapter 2*, then select one from the drop-down list.
Supplier	If you decided to define your suppliers in *Chapter 2*, then select one from the drop-down list.
Reference	An optional unique reference for your product.
	For example, 50cmFT-xfluff
Supplier Reference	An optional unique supplier reference. Useful when reordering low stock from the supplier.
EAN13	The European Article Number or barcode. If your product has one (and almost everything does), use it because some people use this for searching or identifying a product.
Location	Got a huge warehouse, stored it in another depot, or drop-shipping from elsewhere? You can specify the location here.
Weight	Optional. If the weight might be important to your customer, then specify it here. If you intend to charge shipping by weight, then this is essential (more in *Chapter 7*). If not, just leave it blank.
Pack	If this item is packed with other products or multiples of the same product included in the price, tick the box, and specify the product and the quantity.
Is this a downloadable product?	Just what it says. If you are selling a digital product like the ones described in my choosing a product guide, then tick the box and specify the file location, number of allowed downloads, and the time limit in days to complete the download.
Pre-tax wholesale price	What is the price you pay your supplier before tax? Optional but useful for profit calculations.
Pre-tax retail price	The price you sell to the customer before tax, if any.

Field	Explanation
Tax	The amount of tax specified as a percentage.
Retail price with tax	The resulting price to sell the product.
Eco-tax	Any eco-tax if applicable.
Reduction amount	If this item is on special offer, enter an actual or percentage amount (more detail later in this chapter).
available from - to	The dates of availability on the special offer. If it is for an indefinite period, then leave this blank.
Display "on sale" icon	Do you want PrestaShop to put a cool "for sale" label on your product?
Quantity	The number of items available for sale.
Displayed text when in stock	Add an extra description next to the quantity available. Perhaps "In stock—ships in 24 hours."
Displayed text when allowed to be back ordered	Want to encourage orders when you are out of stock? Perhaps, "Out of stock. More soon. Pre order now."
When out of stock	Decide if the product can be purchased even when you have none in stock.
Default category	Which category should this product be in? By default, you should be in the right category. If you accidentally start in the wrong category and don't want to quit and start typing all over again, change the default category here.
Catalog	Tick any extra categories you want your product to appear in.
Click here to improve product's rank in search engines (SEO)	Don't worry about this. We will look in detail at meta-tags and other search engine-related topics in *Chapter 4*.
Short description	A description long enough to capture an interest or entice a click. This short description will appear in searches and on the category pages with other products.
Description	Super sales copy as discussed earlier.
Tags	More in *Chapter 4*. Leave blank for now.
Accessories	Discussed later in the chapter. You need to enter the rest of your product range before we talk about accessories.
Filter	Filter the product drop-down for the above box. Useful if you have hundreds of products. Not important right now.

3. Fill in your product page as described above.

4. Click on the **Images** tab at the top of the product page.

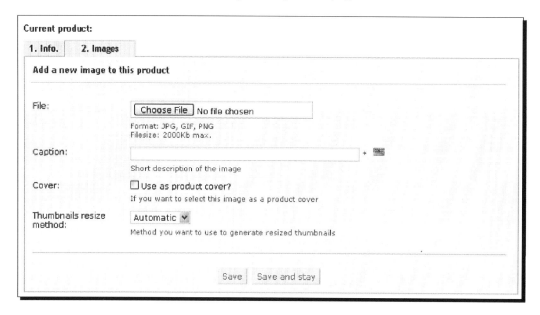

5. Browse to the image you created earlier and upload it. Note that PrestaShop will compress your image for you. It is worth having a look at the final image and maybe varying the amount (if any) that you apply when creating your product images.

6. Type a brief caption for your image.

7. Check the box for automatic thumbnail resizing. This means that the image you uploaded will be cleverly resized to be used at a smaller size where appropriate.

8. Click on **Save** and then go and admire your product in your store front.

9. Repeat until all your products are done, but don't forget to check how things are looking from the customer's point of view. Visit the category and product pages to check whether things are looking the way you expect them to. If you have a huge range that is going to take you a long time, then consider just entering your key products. Proceed with this book to get the money coming in and add the rest of your range a bit at a time over the course of time.

What just happened?

Now you have something to actually sell.

Let's go and showcase some of your products. Here is how to make some of your products stand out from the crowd.

Highlighting products

Next is a list of the different ways to promote elements of your range. There is also an explanation of each option and how to do it as well.

New products

So you have just found some great new products. How do you let your visitors know about it? You could put an announcement on your front page. But what if a potential customer doesn't visit your front page or perhaps misses the announcement?

Welcome to the new products module.

Time for action – how to highlight your newest products

1. Just follow the quick instructions below to enable and configure the highlighting of any new products you add. Once set up, this will happen automatically, now and in the future.

2. Click on the **Modules** tab and scroll down to the **New products block** module under the **Blocks** subheading.

3. Click on **Install**.

4. Scroll back down to the module you just installed and click on **Configure**.

5. Choose a number of products to be showcased and click on **Save**.

6. Don't forget to have a look at your shop front to see how it works. Click around a few different pages and see how the highlighted product alternates.

What just happened?

Now you are done with new products and they will never go unnoticed.

Specials

Special refers to the price. This is the traditional **special offer** that customers know and love.

Time for action – creating a special offer

Just follow the quick instructions below to create special offers and make sure they get seen.

1. Click on the **Catalog** tab and navigate to the category or subcategory that contains the product you want to make available as a special offer.

2. Click on the product to go to its details page.

3. Scroll back down to the section that says **Reduction amount**.

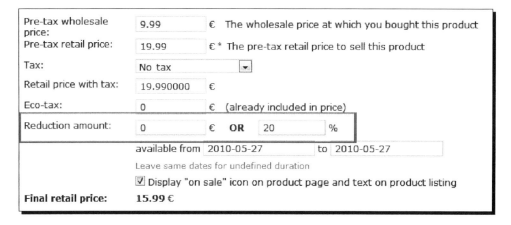

4. You can enter an actual monetary amount in the first box or a percentage in the second box. Monetary amounts work well for individual discounts and percentages work well as part of a wider sale. But this is not a hard rule. Choose what you think your customers might prefer. Save the product.

5. Now go and have a look at the category that product is in and click on the product as well. You'll notice the smart enticing manner that PrestaShop uses to highlight the offer. You can have as many or as few specials as you like.

6. But what if you wanted to really push a product offer or a wider sale? Yes, you guessed it, there's a module.

7. Click on the **Modules** tab and scroll down to **Specials block** and click on **Install**. Getting the hang of this? Thought so.

8. Go and have a look at the effect on your store.

What just happened?

Your first sale is underway.

Recently viewed

What's this then? When customers browse products, they forget what they have seen or how to find it again. By prominently displaying a module with their most recent viewings, they can comfortably click back and forth comparing until they have made a buying decision. Now you don't need me to tell you how to set this up. Go to the module, switch it on, and you're done.

Best sellers

This is just what it says. Not necessarily an offer or anything else is special about it. But if it sells, well there must be something worth shouting about. Install the best sellers module in the usual place to highlight these items.

Accessories

I love accessories. It's all about add-on sales. Ever been to a shop to buy a single item and come out with several? Electrical retailers are brilliant at this. Go in for a PC and come out with a printer, scanner, camera, ink, paper, and the list goes on. Is it because their customers are stupid? Of course they are not! It is because they offer compelling or essential accessories that are relevant to the sale. By creating accessories, you will get a new tab at the bottom of each relevant product page along with PrestaShop making suggestions at key points of the sale.

All we have to do is tell PrestaShop what is an accessory to our various products and PrestaShop will do the rest.

Time for action – creating an accessory

Accessories are products. So any product can be an accessory of any other product. All you have to do is decide what is relevant to what, follow the quick guide below, and you're done. Have a think about appropriate accessories for your products and read on:

1. Click on the **Catalog** tab then find the product you think should have some accessories.

2. Click on it to edit it and scroll to the bottom of the page and find the **Accessories** section as shown in the following screenshot:

3. Find the product that you wish to be an accessory by clicking the drop-down box and selecting it. Now click on the little green **+** button to add it as an accessory.

4. Save your amended product. You can add as many accessories to each product as you like.

5. Go and have a look at your product on your shop front and notice the **Accessories** tab.

What just happened?

You just learned how to accessorize. It's silly not to because it costs you nothing but a few clicks and it could significantly increase your turnover.

Now we can go on to explore more product ideas.

Features

This is very useful. Suppose you have a range of products and they all have features in common. Take for instance teddy bears. They are all made of something. But what about if within your range, what they were made of varied, and you wanted a simple way of making the information available without polluting the product description? An example would be useful.

I have a range of teddy bears and they are made from super-soft cotton, micro-fiber, or wool knit. I can create a feature and call it 'Material'. I can then create a range of 'Values' for 'Material'. Super-soft cotton, micro-fiber, and wool knit. And I can assign values to any products that I choose.

You can create as many features and associated values as you need. You might want a country of origin feature, with assigned values of 'Europe', 'China', and 'India'. You might have products with a manufacturer's rating. Take Intel processors for example. They all have a star rating from 1 to 5. You could create a feature of colors. The important point here is that features are usually used when it is not a fundamental part of the buying decision.

I will explain. When you create features and values, you then assign them, where appropriate, to products. PrestaShop very kindly creates an extra tab on the appropriate page with all the appropriate features and values. The customer might not bother checking these values so clearly; PrestaShop's **Features** is for additional information that the customer *might* want to read.

You probably wouldn't create a color feature for a T-shirt. That would be a critical or fundamental part of the buying decision and would almost certainly be in the product description, title, and image or attribute (more in a bit). Perhaps, however, the color of a computer cable would be a secondary or optional requirement and might make a good candidate for a feature.

One thing features are definitely not used for is when that feature makes a difference to the price. Variations like this would be handled by another aspect of PrestaShop we will cover very soon. Also, features will not show as part of the description when added to the customer's cart. If this is important to you, **Features** is not for you.

Think carefully about how PrestaShop features can be used for your product range and have a look at the really quick manner you can implement them.

Time for action – using PrestaShop's 'Features'

Here we will implement a range of features and values. I am using the country of origin example; you can choose what is appropriate to your product range.

1. Click on the **Catalog** tab and then on **Features**.

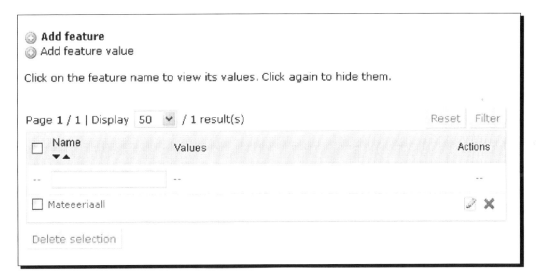

2. Now click on **Add feature** and type the name of your first feature and then click on **Save**.

3. Next click on the **Add feature value** and type the name of the first value of this feature and click on **Save**.

4. Repeat Step 3 for all values of that feature.

5. Repeat Steps 2 and 3 for all of the features you want to create.

6. Now click on the **Catalog** tab again and browse to the category of the first product you want to add a feature to. Click on the product to edit it.

7. Note at the top you now have an additional tab headed **Features**. Click on it:

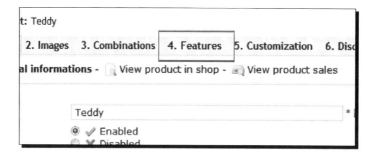

8. Select the feature and then the value from the drop-down list and click on **Save**.

9. Go and look at the cool **Data sheet** tab that has appeared with that product on the shop front.

10. Assign as many products and values as you need.

What just happened?

You have now implemented the features option on your product range and have learned that features are for optional or additional product information that does not affect the price.

Now we can go on to explore and discuss product attributes. **Attributes** sounds fairly dull but in fact is a very powerful feature and in my opinion is probably better implemented in PrestaShop than any other shopping cart software. This is because PrestaShop makes a potentially complicated process nice and simple.

Attributes

These are a lot more interesting than the name suggests. PrestaShop allows you to create attribute groups and then actual attributes within those groups, and then assigns them to products. A very quick and simplistic way of describing an attribute would be as a product variation.

For example, attributes are a perfect way to have a single product: teddy T-shirt. Then create a **Color** attribute group and lots of actual attributes—**Red**, **Blue**, **Pink**, and so on. The customer could then, from one single product page, select any of the available colors for that teddy T-shirt. Have a look at attributes in action below:

As you can see, the customer is able to click a drop-down box and choose from the different attributes (product variations). The first thing to note here is that this is a simplistic example and we will get a bit deeper into this before we try attributes out. The other thing to point out is that just because you might sell a product with multiple variations does not mean you must have attributes.

As an example, I might introduce a range of teddy T-shirts with karate, heart, or skateboarder pictures. I certainly could create an attribute group called **style** and attribute values of **karate**, **heart**, and **skateboarder**. However, I might decide that displaying all of the styles and their pictures in a list in the teddy T-shirts' category was very important, perhaps to make sure that all the options were clearly visible. In this instance, using attributes wouldn't be a good idea.

So as with other product options in PrestaShop, attributes and their usage needs to be considered and planned carefully. Always keeping in mind what is best for helping the customer make a purchase!

I said that my example was simplistic. You can actually do so much with attributes that it is really not possible to cover it all in this book. Here are some of the most likely scenarios where attributes are indispensable.

What if my teddy T-shirts came in white, green, blue, and pink? Consider if the white version was £5 and all the colored versions were £7. This is no problem at all. I can create attributes and groups and specify the different increases in price that the different attributes should have. Then when the customer uses the drop-down menu to browse the different options, they would be presented with the correct price. Not only this but the product image can also be varied to show the different options as and when they are selected.

PrestaShop even allows you to specify a new weight for each combination (for shipping purposes), an eco-tax, and different references/barcodes for each variation. PrestaShop even has a 'product combinations generator' to enable automatic assigning of specified attributes to any given product.

Time for action – an attributes example

Here we will see how to create several versions of a product. The customer can then select the one they want from a drop-down list. The product price and image will update.

1. Click on **Catalog** and then **Attributes and groups**.

2. Let's start by adding an attributes group. Click on **Add attributes group** and type in the name of your attributes group. In my case T-shirt styles.

3. Notice you have the option to enter a different public name. So you could call your attribute group something different in the admin and shop fronts. If this is important, perhaps to avoid using overly technical terms, then do so. If possible, I would keep them the same to avoid confusion. Our confusion.

4. The color checkbox gives you the facility to provide actual colors, not just descriptions. If you choose these, you will simply enter a color code as well as an attribute value for each option. If you are providing an image for each attribute option, this feature is unnecessary. I suggest leaving it unchecked unless your situation specifically requires it.

5. Click on **Save** when you're ready.

6. Next click on **Add attribute value**. I will be adding my first T-shirt style—Karate. Then **Save** it. Keep adding attribute values from different groups until you have added all that you need.

7. Now we will go to the first product that we need to add these newly created attributes to. So click on **Catalog**, find the appropriate product, and click it to edit it.

8. Notice the **Combinations** tab among the other product tabs. Click on it and we will create our product combinations from our attributes.

9. At the top, select a group and then a specific attribute from the two drop-down boxes.

10. Below this click on **Add** and it will be added to the box. You can add multiple attributes to this product this way, but keep it simple for now and leave it at just one.

11. You can now optionally add references, locations, and EAN codes.

12. Here is the really good bit. Suppose one option is a bit more expensive, a bit heavier, or has a different eco-tax to the original product to be applied, simply enter that next in the area indicated below:

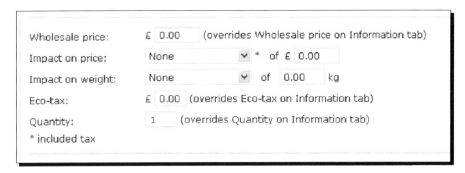

13. Enter an **Eco-tax**, **Quantity**, or **Wholesale price** if it is different from the original product. When it comes to impact on price, select none, increase or decrease, then in the quantity box put the amount of the increase or decrease. You can do the same with weight, but as explained when creating products, this is only necessary if you intend to calculate postage using weight.

14. If you want to create a different image for this combination, it needs to have been previously uploaded on the image tab. You can then simply check the box next to the appropriate image.

15. When you're done, click on **Add this combination**.

16. You can now click on the product again, select **Combinations** again, and add another combination based on different attributes.

17. Go and have a look at your product in the shop front to see it in action.

What just happened?

You now know how to create product combinations using attributes.

The last possibility I would like you just to consider is this. Remember accessories? Your customers are shown a range of pre-selected add-on sales to choose from. What about creating attribute groups to match product categories and values to match actual products? Your customers could click on a drop-down menu and instantly add the T-shirt of their choice to their teddy. Nice!

Have a go hero – the combinations generator

If like my teddy T-shirt example you only have a few combinations, that is not a problem. But what about if we had multiple combinations from multiple attribute groups each containing multiple values? The above process could be rather long and frustrating! Fortunately, there is a solution. The clue is in the *Have a go hero* title.

Here's the answer:

Simply click on the combinations generator at the top of the **Combinations** tab. Select all the attributes from the right-hand box that you want to use with this product, click on **Add**, click on **Generate**, and a table of all the combinations possible are generated. Delete with a single click those that are unnecessary and fill in the weights and prices of those you want to keep. Then click on **Generate**. Finished. There is an imperfection with generating attributes when you have lots of them. If you generate more than 10,000, you might run into problems. I am reliably informed that a fix/new module is in progress. Thanks TG.

Customizing

This is a bit more niche than the other product features we have seen and there is a good chance you might not need this. But just knowing that you have the customizing option might open your mind to new ideas. And if you do need to offer your customer's custom options then this quick explanation and guide will be invaluable.

So what is customizing in a PrestaShop context? Click on the **Customization** tab of one of your products.

Notice you have the option to specify the number of **File fields** and/or **Text fields**. If you do, then these would appear on the product page. Try it if you're curious. So let's say I am selling a teddy bear T-shirt. And I would like the customer to be able to specify a name to put on the T-shirt. All I need to do is put **1** in the number of text fields. PrestaShop would then pass on the details of the customization when the customer places the order. Of course, I could specify multiple text fields for a message. I could also specify a file field enabling the customer to upload a file to me. This could be a photograph for the teddy T-shirt or perhaps a picture to go on a custom gift tag.

All this assumes of course that I can produce the teddy T-shirts. PrestaShop obviously cannot do that for me. But the scope of the customization feature is only limited by your imagination. Here is a quick guide to add a customization to your product.

Time for action – allowing your customers to customize

Follow this simple guide to add customizations to your products.

1. Find and click on the product you want to add a customization option to.

2. Click on the **Customization** tab and enter the number of file and text fields you require to enable your customers to configure their customization.

3. Save the product.

4. Go and visit the product page to see the effect. How simple was that?

What just happened?

Although not needed by every store owner, this is a powerful product feature that is well worth being aware of.

Product mania!

Everything we have looked at in this chapter is fairly non-technical. But the huge range of options and features you have at your disposal can sometimes cause apparent complexity. It is well worth playing with the PrestaShop catalog options and, perhaps, rereading this chapter so that you can fully grasp how PrestaShop manages your catalog and how incredibly flexible and diverse it is.

Having said that, don't hold back on further development until everything is perfect. Any e-commerce store should be an ongoing cyclical thing that you constantly add to, improve, and refine. Also, don't forget my suggestion about opening your shop with just a core range of products and then adding more on an ongoing basis. If you can be making money while working on your catalog, then I think it makes sense.

Pop quiz – a few product marketing questions

1. Using what you have just learned, how could you sell a product for less than the cost price and still make a profit on the purchase?

2. Arrange the following into feature, advantage, and benefit:

   ❑ The women will love you

   ❑ Your abs will be rock solid

   ❑ The new body toner uses the latest fitness technology

Summary

We learned a lot in this chapter about e-merchandising. You now have well-presented products with descriptions that actually sell.

Specifically, we covered:

◆ Categories: We learned about planning, structure, creation, and describing them in an enticing manner.

◆ Products: We saw how to create and implement them as well as creating short, concise sales copy that sells.

◆ Product options: We looked at a whole range of ways to enhance, highlight, and offer options on your products, including special offers, linking accessories, attributes, recently viewed, and offering customization.

Now that your products are ready, it is time to look at the rest of the content of your site and how to give more to your customers and how to get more customers.

4
Giving Customers More and Getting More Customers

In this chapter, we will be looking at a number of topics related to getting more visitors on your website. There are two main ways we can achieve this. The first is by pandering to the whims of the search engines. We will look at the keywords: everything from choosing them to using them, and taking advantage of a whole range of PrestaShop SEO (Search Engine Optimization) utilities.

Then we will look at giving your customers a bit more. Your potential customer's visit to your site needs to be worthwhile and useful for them. We will achieve this by talking about writing articles related to your business and then we will use the PrestaShop content management features to highlight them.

Finally, we will look at a few really quick and simple methods to attract customers who speak a different language from us:

- How to choose the best keywords
- Making food for the search engines
- Refining PrestaShop search
- Tag clouds
- Using the PrestaShop CMS
- URLs in PrestaShop
- Robots and site maps
- Using PrestaShop language features

So let's get on with it.

SEO: Search Engine Optimization

It is my opinion that people are more important than search engines when creating your content. It is true though that there are lots of things you can do and not do, to try and improve your success with search engines, as regards how many visitors they send you.

You can read enormous technical books written by greatly esteemed gurus on the subject, but consider this. Search engine companies invest vast fortunes in their systems. They do this so that they can present to their users interesting, useful, and (here is the big one) **appropriate** content, based on the search their user performed.

Therefore, by understanding your customer, your business, and your product niche, you will achieve far more than any trick or secret that can be shared in a book. The important questions for us now are how well do we understand our customers and which keywords and search terms will our customers use?

Which keywords should we use?

Are you using the same keywords and phrases your customers will be using? Pretend you are selling big televisions and throughout your website you refer to them as "flat panel TVs". Is that the most popular phrase the type of person you are trying to attract will use to search for your product?

If people don't search for "flat panel TVs" but instead use "plasma screen", "LCD TV", "OLED television" or one of dozens of other phrases with a similar meaning, then you will miss out on loads of free visitors. What about this conundrum—laptop, notebook, or portable PC? That is the question; how would you decide?

There are a number of premium software programs and web services you can buy, but I am guessing you didn't buy this book just to be referred to someone else for more expense. There are various sites where you can have a limited time trial of products that help you find popular keywords in your industry. Later, in *Chapter 9*, we will look at Google Analytics, which has precise tools for choosing keywords.

But as this optimization process is ongoing, I don't recommend even the free ones, as you will have to pay eventually. And Google Analytics, although free, does not give you the hands-on experience and feedback that you will get by following this guide. Now if you are building a PrestaShop mega-store with thousands of products, then fine, get your wallet out. Otherwise try this.

Discovering the value of keywords

Visit Google, Bing, and the other search engines, and search for different terms. Keep it simple. Perhaps just two or three word phrases to start with. If there are a couple of paid-for adverts down the right-hand side or at the top, then you have probably chosen a phrase that is worth considering. I say this, because the fact that there is an advert means somebody else believes it is worth paying money for.

It is not necessarily the best phrase. If there are lots of adverts. Then you might have discovered a phrase that lots of people in your industry are prepared to pay for.

Different niches will have different volumes of competition, so you have to compare the phrases from your niche relatively to each other. Next, search again for the same terms and have a look at the number of results returned for that search. Be sure to have a pen and paper handy to make notes on your findings.

A keyword success story

Here is a real example—I know a guy who has a niche e-commerce business selling cloths and cleaners for a very specific type of item. Very niche, but the narrow range enables him to focus intently on his customers and SEO that the big stores who also sell this type of product cannot possibly match.

Initially, however, he was not particularly successful. He spent months finding the most popular search terms, he spent a lot of money on pay-per-click advertising (more in *Chapter 8*), getting visitors for the most popular terms, but this only brought him modest success.

Don't fall off your chair

In the end he spoke to people. I am not kidding. He actually went out of his front door and had conversations with human beings. He asked people how they would try and find his product. And almost overwhelmingly they said something completely different to what he expected. And it was completely different to what he and his competitors had been paying Google a small fortune for, in order to receive visitors.

Keyword clarification

So am I saying we should compete for the most sought-after keywords or the niche, untapped keywords? The answer is whichever your research leads you to feel is right. The point I am making is that you must research online and offline to fully understand your niche and your customers. When you do this, you will gain an advantage over the big companies. They cannot possibly focus as much as you can.

So, to get started on choosing your keywords, do some research. Do this online and face to face. Decide the best phrases to use for each product or product group and stick to them, just for the duration of this book until you have read *The big secret* section in *Chapter 9*. It is much better to focus on a single set of keywords, even if they turn out not to be the very best, than it is to use a smattering of everything. But don't choose the keywords without spending some significant time thinking, researching, and rubbing shoulders with fellow earthlings.

When we look at ongoing optimization again in *Chapter 9*, we will look at strategies for improving and optimizing your keywords as well as every other aspect of your business.

Notebook, laptop, portable PC, or whatever phrases are best for your shop; you decide, then stick to them and read on.

Meta tags

Meta tags are words and descriptions about the information on your PrestaShop that are not seen by your customer. They are in the code for your page that some search engines read to help determine the words they will index your site for. Implementing meta tags well can help the search engines accurately determine your site's content. Meta tags are not as important as they used to be—some search engines do not use them at all—but they are so simple to implement in PrestaShop that it is well worth doing so.

They should be a part of your overall keyword strategy and you have already come across where to enter them.

Meta tags can be defined for PrestaShop category, product, and article pages. Here I will show you how to easily add them into your category and product pages and you will see how to add them into your articles later in the chapter.

Types of meta tag

There are meta titles, meta descriptions, and meta keywords. We will start with a brief explanation of each type of meta tag, then a *Time for action* section where you can begin to implement them.

◆ Meta titles are a short title relevant to the specific page concerned. If this is an article, then the meta title could be the same as the title. If the page is a category or product, then a bit more imagination might be worthwhile. Perhaps a 50 cm fluffy teddy—extra fluff could become "Buy this 50 cm fluffy teddy with extra fluff finish".

◆ Meta description is easy for the products and categories. Often the brief description from the product page is suitable here. For articles, a brief summary of the title and key points would be good.

◆ Meta keywords are a list of keywords you deemed the most appropriate to use for any given page—just one, two, and three word phrases separated by a comma in a list. For example, fluffy teddy, teddies, extra fluff, 50 cm teddy bear, and so on.

Time for action – PrestaShop meta tags

This is where and how to enter your meta information in products and categories. Articles are covered later in the chapter.

1. Click on the **Catalog** tab and then click on the **Edit** icon of the first category to add meta tags. Scroll down to the meta information text boxes and enter your meta tags. **Save** the category.

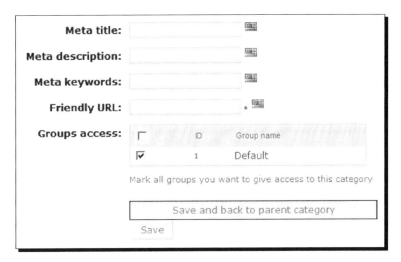

2. Repeat until all your categories have meta tags.

3. Click on the **Catalog** tab and then click into the category containing the first product that you want to add meta tags to. Scroll down to the meta information text boxes and enter your meta tags. **Save** the product.

4. Repeat until all your products have meta tags.

What just happened?

Your products and categories now have meta information so that search engines (that want to) can quickly assess the likely content of your website.

Search aliases

We have just spent a while discussing how to choose the best keywords and then how to use them. In a later section about writing articles, we will discuss density and formatting as well. In this brief but potentially profitable section, we will look at choosing and defining, through the PrestaShop system, some search aliases.

So if you remember the "laptop, notebook, or portable PC" conundrum, you can actually tell PrestaShop that they are the same thing. They are aliases. So when visitors use your PrestaShop search box, it wouldn't matter if they searched for laptops, notebooks, or anything else that meant the same thing. As long as you defined it, PrestaShop will return the right search results.

Choosing aliases

The previous laptop example is fairly obvious. If you sell a laptop and somebody on your site searches for "notebook", you want them to see your laptop. But when choosing your aliases, you should think as deeply as possible. Look at the category and product descriptions. If a relevant keyword is not contained in the product/category description, it is worth defining it as an alias.

Consider using less obvious aliases like plurals. If I write a wonderful description for a teddy but do not mention teddies in it, then anybody searching for teddies would get no results in search. Another worthwhile consideration is misspellings. If you have a product that is a challenge to spell, then creating an alias for the possibly incorrect searched-for words is well worth it.

Here is a suggestion. Make a list of all your major keywords and some of the lesser but still relevant ones as well. Then next to each keyword, make a list of any relevant aliases. When you're ready, follow this quick tutorial to prepare your PrestaShop.

Time for action – creating the article

Here we are going to enter all your keyword aliases to help your visitors find and buy the correct products.

1.   Click on the **Tools** tab and then on **Aliases**.

2. Click on **Add new** and you will see the following screen:

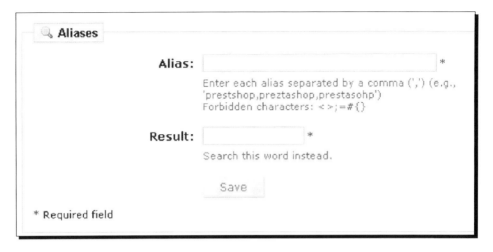

3. In the top box, type a list separated by commas between each word. And in the box below, type the actual keyword that is already contained in your descriptions that PrestaShop should search for instead.

4. Click on **Save**.

5. Then click on **Add new** and repeat the process until you have defined all the aliases that you want to.

6. Visit your store front, search for an alias, and see how you are magically returned results with the appropriate keywords.

What just happened?

You now have a comprehensive catalog of aliases that will enable a thoroughly professional search system for your customers. All this translates to more sales.

Tag clouds

Tag clouds are cool. They look good, the search engines like them and customers like them. But what are they? A tag cloud is a list of keywords and phrases arranged in a way as to tempt visitors to click them. But why would we do this? What is the point?

It doesn't matter how well you define your meta tags or how carefully you write your product descriptions and your articles. Some visitors will still turn up on your website and not be on the exact page they need to be in order to solve whatever it was they visited your site for in the first place.

A tag cloud is a bit like an unordered, highly relevant index. It contains the words and phrases you choose. So a visitor scans the words (because that is what brains do) and they see a word or phrase that means something to them, so they click it. And hey presto, they are on the relevant product page that has all the information they need. That's the theory anyway.

Actually, a tag cloud can seriously enhance your site's usability and profitability. Here is one from `www.amazon.com`.

If you want your own tag cloud read on.

Time for action – creating a tag cloud

Let's see how to create a tag cloud.

1. Click on the **Modules** tab and scroll down to **Tags block** and enable it.

2. Scroll back down to the **Tags block** and click on **Configure**.

3. Here you choose the number of tags you want to appear in your cloud. There is no best number present, just choose what is right for your shop. In a small PrestaShop that I made with 10 products, a cloud of 10 tags looked good and some really relevant tags were displayed.

4. Play with the number of tags and see what is displayed and what your tag cloud looks like on your shop front. Click on **Save** each time you try a different number.

What just happened?

You just made your shop front a lot friendlier. A tag cloud is a great for your visitors who do a one-click search. And lots of visitors who won't use a search box will use a tag cloud.

Search-friendly and canonical URLs

As promised, here is the low down on search-friendly URLs, and while we are on the subject of URLs, we will look at canonical ones as well.

Search-friendly

Friendly is much better than unfriendly, but what exactly is a friendly URL? Visit your shop front and click on one of your products. Then look at the address in the address bar of your web browser. It is probably something like this:

`http://www.fluffyteddies.com/category.php?id_category=6`

How friendly is that? Well, if you look at the beginning, it is not too bad, but after www.fluffyteddies.com it gets a bit grim. Search-friendly URLs enable PrestaShop to get rid of the `category.php?idxxxxxxx` and replace it with real category names, product names, and article titles. This has two major benefits. Firstly, your visitors are more likely to remember a URL such as `www.fluffyteddies.com/3-teddy` than one like the example above and also the search engines can reward you for having URLs relevant to the keywords on your site.

Time for action – how to get search-friendly URLs

So there are big benefits for completing this *Time for action*. We need to make a minor modification to the files on our website and then tell PrestaShop to enable friendly URLs. Here goes:

1. Click on the **Preferences** tab then scroll down to **Friendly URL** and click on **Enable**. Remember to scroll to the bottom of the page and click on **Save**.

2. Click on the **Tools** tab and then **Generators**. You will see the following option:

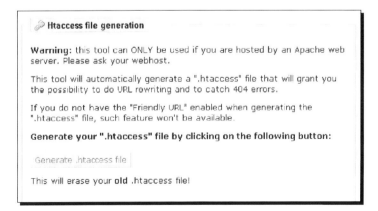

3. Despite the message saying the tool will generate a **.htaccess file**, it will only actually do so if there is a blank one already there waiting to be **generated**. This is easy. Open Windows Notepad or something equivalent and save a blank document as `.htaccess`. Now use FTP to transfer it to the main `prestashop` folder.

4. Now click on the **Generate .htaccess file** button.

5. That's it. Check out your friendly URLs. Now it is possible that this didn't work! It is even possible that you now get an error when you try to view your store. Don't panic. This means that your web host does not support "URL rewriting". Simply go back to Step 3 and disable friendly URLs and all will be well. A web host not supporting URL rewriting seems to be a fairly rare event these days, so it is probably unlikely this will be a problem.

What just happened?

First of all, when you clicked on the **Generate .htaccess file** button, PrestaShop created a file on your website that gives instructions to the Apache web server. This then enables PrestaShop to make use of a web server feature called URL rewriting. PrestaShop uses this to make up friendly URLs. We also mentioned that if your web host does not allow its server to do this, then you will need to disable the friendly URLs' feature.

Canonical

Canonical URLs refer to when similar or duplicate content appears on your website but on different URLS. The simplest explanation is `www.yoursite.com` and `yoursite.com`. Type either into a web browser and you will probably end up on your home page. This apparently harmless situation can cause problems with how highly search engines rate your page.

By specifying your preferred canonical URL as either `www.yoursite.com` or `yoursite.com`, PrestaShop will make minor but important modifications to the code in your web pages that tells the search engines what the situation on your website is. This helps avoid any of the pitfalls mentioned previously.

Time for action – choosing your canonical URL

Here is how to specify your canonical URL and tell PrestaShop to use it.

1. Click on the **Modules** tab, and under the **Tools** category, enable the **Canonical URL** module.

2. Now scroll back down to it and click on **Configure**.

3. Here you can enter the canonical URL for your shop. I suggest `www.yoursite.com` because it is most widely recognized, but you could also put `yoursite.com`. Obviously, you type your actual domain name and extension instead of `yoursite.com`.

4. Click on **Save** and you're done.

What just happened?

PrestaShop will now make sure that your chosen canonical URL is used exclusively. This, as we discussed, has great potential benefits for the search engine ranking of your site. Now let's take a look at adding some great articles to your PrestaShop.

Writing and displaying articles

Articles are what you give to people as an incentive to visit your website, especially when they are not considering a purchase. By creating high quality, useful articles, you attract visitors from search engines, create loyalty, and can use the article to subtly promote products.

Good ideas when writing articles

Most of your visitors are probably not planning on reading all your articles or even a single page. More likely they are looking for a fact, figure, or piece of information.

The goal is to make it very easy for them to find and even more compelling to continue reading.

Make your articles easy reading

Reading from a screen is more difficult than reading from this book. That is why you need to consider making readability as easy as possible when writing your articles. If you have a subject people are interested in, you know about it, and you focus your efforts in making your pages easy to get information from, then people will like your articles. And if we work on the assumption that search engines know what people want, they will also rank you higher and more sites will want to link to you. The result is more visitors. So by focusing on what your visitor wants, you will get what YOU want.

Consider carefully who your website and the specific page you are working on are aimed at. Under what circumstances would somebody want to read your page? Is the page worded and structured in such a way as to accommodate their circumstances? Do the most important pieces of information jump out of the page or are they hidden away in a huge section in the middle?

Think about your audience

Think about the level of expertise your customers have. What language or level of industry jargon will they like and what will bore them? Don't use technical jargon or clever words unless you are certain that is what your reader likes.

Don't use long words where short ones will do. Forget about preamble! Your first heading and paragraph should be 100 percent specific and lay out clearly what the rest of the article is about. By all means use colorful, interesting language but not at the expense of immediate clarity. The first heading should sum up the article: for example, you would put "How to write articles" and not "Hints and tips when getting started with writing".

Sell, but sell subtly

Don't go over the top. Don't flog a product. It is perfectly acceptable to turn a word or phrase in your article into a link to a product, as long as it doesn't trick the reader into viewing the product. But don't use too many product links. Links to information the reader is looking for are most important, or readers might find your web page too hard to navigate and leave. Don't forget the article is surrounded by your PrestaShop modules—new products, specials, and so on. They will find your products when they are ready.

Don't promote your products unless it is appropriate. In every industry, there are products that are right for different people in different situations. If you are 100 percent honest when a product might not be suitable, your reader will subconsciously recognize your honesty.

If you recommend a cheap, reliable laptop that is appropriate for a student, when someone who knows him is then after a top-of-the-range, all-powerful machine, you might get a recommendation. Also, when you explain how wonderful and appropriate another product is, they are more likely to believe you and get their wallet out.

I before e except after c

Grammar and spelling are very important. Spelling mistakes lose you credibility. Grammar is something I have always struggled with. I have never been taught how to write well-structured content for any medium. But that is no excuse not to make it as good as you possibly can. I read and reread all my work to make it the best it can be. I then pester my partner for her input (when I don't have the assistance of a Packt editor).

Now what?

All good articles tell the reader what to do next. Perhaps to click a link to more information, sign up for a newsletter (more in *Chapter 5*), or look at a product. If your content has been written well, proved useful, and not been too pushy, you will have built trust. It is called pre-selling. I don't know where the saying comes from, but I like it a lot and it is appropriate here.

People don't care how much you know until they know how much you care.

Page formatting and keyword density

Headers, underline, italics, image filenames, article titles, and so on—that's what formatting is. It's all the different ways you can present information or add relevancy and appropriateness to the article.

Name your pictures and pages with relevant keywords and phrases. For example:

```
15cm_fluffy_teddy.jpg
```

not

```
img012.jpg
```

Focus your effort on what is good for humans. Create an H2 heading containing the keywords/phrase at the start of the article. Use same keywords/phrases in the first paragraph. Consider making this bold or italic. Use H3 and H4 headings generously and appropriately again with similar or identical keywords/phrases later in the article. Lots of well–ordered, clear, nested headings make your articles easily scan-able and more likely to be read in full.

Use links (with keywords/phrases) to relevant parts of the same page or other pages in your shop. All the above techniques not only make your article easier to scan, but they also highlight the key bits of information, making your article genuinely useful. When you make useful articles, visitors will like you, and people buy from people they like.

How many times should the keywords/phrases be used?

This is probably one of the most widely sought after pieces of information to do with SEO. What percentage keyword density is perfect? That is, if your page has a hundred words how many of them should be the words you think people searching for you will use?

In a nutshell—sorry, I don't know. If you take Google for example, their formula for calculating page rank is a very closely guarded secret. If somebody tells you the percentage is "x", then they are lying, misinformed, or at best, estimating based on experience.

The truth is that there probably is no specific percentage anyway. It is in fact based on a publicly unknown and extremely complicated list of variables likely to include links to your site, their content, the rank of the site, and the page they appear on, the density, spacing, format, and the location on the page as well as the location of the page on your site and many more factors.

So how on earth do you optimize for such complexity? The most important thing you can do is make sure you choose the words your customers are likely to use. Use them in different formats and locations: headings, links, underlines, bold, and so on. Some should be near the end of the page, some in the links outside the main body of the page, and some in the pages linking to the page.

However, do not put more keywords or phrases than is natural to a human reader. If it sounds natural, looks natural, and uses the words and phrases your customers are using, that's good.

Quick tips

- If you have a complicated subject where you need to go into detail, this is not a problem. Try to keep the start of the article simple and build the complexity later in the article and pay extra attention to all the rest of the tips.

- Think and plan the structure of your article before you start writing. This includes deciding upon highly relevant, to-the-point titles and subtitles. Good and frequent subtitles divide up your article and help readers target what they want, and this makes the whole article easier to read.

- Use shorter paragraphs and sentences. They make your article easier to read.

- Use bulleted lists of key information. A bit like this one.

- Don't make the pages too long. Consider breaking the article into multiple articles if it seems heavy going to read it all.

- Most readers will scan the first line of a few titles and paragraphs to discover if your article has what they want. Make the first sentence of each paragraph highly relevant and precise.

Writing Summary

The above might all seem a bit daunting, but try to write with all that guidance in mind. Always go through and edit your articles with the guidance in mind, but don't wait until it is perfect. You wouldn't be reading this now if I had aimed for perfection. Is it useful? Is it clear and simple to scan and read? Is it professional-ish? Is so, publish it. You can always revisit it another time or react to feedback.

Using the CMS

Now that we have gone through the ins and outs of writing good articles for your website, it is time to actually put those articles on your website. If you have the articles to hand, ready to copy, and paste, that's great! If you like, you can write them as we go. Remember the tip about not waiting until its perfect?

Time for action – creating the article

Let's use the CMS to create your first article on PrestaShop.

1. Click on the **Tools** tab and then **CMS** and **Add new**.

2. You now know exactly what to do with the three 'meta' options.

3. Friendly URLs are cool. I suggest you enter the title of your article with a dash between each word. So "Why teddies are so fluffy" would be entered as "why-teddies-are-so-fluffy". Just leave of the speech marks and put all the characters in lower case.

4. Copy and paste or type your article as previously discussed.

5. Click on **Save**.

6. Create other articles in the same way.

What just happened?

You have written an article and put it into the PrestaShop system. There is just one thing that is not done. How can people read your article?

Time for action – displaying the article

Follow the next few clicks to publish your article and make it prominent.

1. Click on the **Modules** tab, again.

2. Scroll down to the **Blocks** category of modules and install the **Link block**.

3. Scroll back down to the installed **Link block** and click on **Configure**.

4. In the **Add a new link** section, you can add the text for the link. That is the words that are displayed to the visitor and are actually clickable. This could simply be the same as the article title, but if the title is too long or you have another reason to change the clickable words, do so here.

5. In the URL box, type `www.yourdomain.com/content/id-search-friendly-url`, where id is the ID number of the article you are linking to and search-friendly-url is the search-friendly URL you entered when creating your article. If you can't remember, just open another browser tab, log into your control panel, click on **Tools** then **CMS**, and you can read off the information from the summary presented.

What just happened?

Your article(s) can now be easily found by the search engines and by people who turn up on any page of your website. If your article is really vital to your products or particularly topical, why not introduce and link to it from a home page or product page?

Have a go hero – article prominence

You have written an article that must be seen, but you think the article list module is insufficient. So, how could you make it more prominent?

The answer is that there are lots of ways, and here are a couple of them: feature part of the article on your home page with a "read more" link to the full article or introduce the article on relevant category and product pages with a link to read the full article.

I am a robots.txt

Search engines are our guests. They should be looked after and treated respectfully because when they get grumpy with you they can cause all sorts of problems. For example, stop sending you visitors. Never forget: the search engines are businesses themselves. They are not obliged to feature you in their search results.

Creating a file and placing it conveniently on your website server will let the search engines know they are welcome, but also point out that there are some places that a guest should not go. That's fine they won't be offended. In fact, they will be quite pleased you saved them the bother of searching areas that are not needed. Want to see what robots.txt looks like? Have a look at the following screenshot or download yours from the main top-level folder of your website:

You can see that the robots.txt file is not brain surgery, but there are many things you can do with one. For a full exploration of robots.txt files, have a look at www.robotstxt.org, or to quickly generate the recommended PrestaShop default, complete the *Time for action* section below.

Time for action – creating robots.txt

Here we will create a robots.txt file and place it on your web server. It will keep the search engines from indexing unnecessary pages like account pages. This is good as it prevents search results about your site from becoming polluted.

1. Create a file with Windows Notepad and save it without any content as robots.txt.

2. Log in to your web server via FTP and transfer the file to the main/root directory of your store. This is where you uploaded all the PrestaShop files to.

3. In your PrestaShop control panel, click on the **Tools** tab, then on **Generators**. The second option down to generate a `robots.txt` file is the one you want. Click it now.

4. PrestaShop will generate a useful default `robots.txt` file suitable for a typical PrestaShop installation.

What just happened?

You have just respectfully marked a few areas of your store as off-limits to the search engines. However, please note this is not a security feature. It does not block access, but merely asks search engines (99 percent) of them to avoid certain areas. We will cover actual security measures in *Chapter 6*.

Helping Google with site maps

A site map is just that—a map. It outlines the structure of your website and includes pertinent information such as last updated and update frequencies. Just suppose you add an important product to the bottom of a big subcategory. In all likelihood, Google must crawl through your entire site to find it and add it to the search results.

With site maps, Google can be aware of this page, any others, and any modifications. Google can then specifically crawl the new or updated pages. This is better for you and easier for Google.

Time for action – Google site maps tutorial

So how do we get one of these `sitemap.xml` files? You probably guessed. PrestaShop has a module that makes one. And as always it's a breeze to implement.

1. Click on the **Modules** tab and under the **Tools** category enable the **Google sitemap** module.

2. Scroll back down to it and click on **Configure**.

3. Now to generate the `sitemaps.xml` file and click on **Update sitemap file**.

4. You should do this every time you add to your site, such as adding products, categories, or articles. Also, do this if you make a significant change to the content as well.

5. Want to have a look what this `sitemap.xml` file looks like? Connect to your web server with FTP and download the `sitemap.xml` (NOT `sitemap.php`) file. Have a look at all the information PrestaShop has generated. It might look a bit like this:

```xml
<?xml version="1.0" ?>
- <urlset xmlns="http://www.sitemaps.org/schemas/sitemap/0.9" xmlns:xsi="http://www.w3.org/2001/XMLSchema-instance"
    xsi:schemaLocation="http://www.sitemaps.org/schemas/sitemap/0.9 http://www.sitemaps.org/schemas/sitemap/0.9/sitemap.xsd">
  - <url>
      <loc>http://tv-wipes.com/</loc>
      <priority>1.00</priority>
      <lastmod>2009-11-23</lastmod>
      <changefreq>daily</changefreq>
    </url>
  - <url>
      <loc>http://tv-wipes.com/content/1-delivery</loc>
      <priority>0.8</priority>
      <changefreq>monthly</changefreq>
    </url>
  - <url>
      <loc>http://tv-wipes.com/lang-fr//tv-wipes.com/content/1-livraison</loc>
      <priority>0.8</priority>
      <changefreq>monthly</changefreq>
    </url>
  - <url>
      <loc>http://tv-wipes.com/lang-de//tv-wipes.com/content/1-delivery</loc>
      <priority>0.8</priority>
      <changefreq>monthly</changefreq>
    </url>
  - <url>
      <loc>http://tv-wipes.com/lang-es//tv-wipes.com/content/1-delivery</loc>
      <priority>0.8</priority>
      <changefreq>monthly</changefreq>
    </url>
  - <url>
      <loc>http://tv-wipes.com/lang-it//tv-wipes.com/content/1-delivery</loc>
      <priority>0.8</priority>
```

What just happened?

Creating and keeping this file up-to-date will mean Google can easily keep up with the changes to your website and that is a good thing. You can also investigate submitting a site map to Yahoo and Bing.

PrestaShop search weightings

So how does the PrestaShop search system work? It works in much the same way as a real search engine. It analyzes the content of the shop and matches it to the words and phrases used by your visitors when they type in a search query. It then uses weightings, a sort of important criteria, to decide which results to give to the searcher.

The criteria considered include category, product, article, and even meta tags. So which is most important? PrestaShop does know what it is doing (trust me on that) and it has devised default weightings for each type of content. As you might expect with PrestaShop, these weightings are configurable. To get an idea of how it works, have a look at the screenshot below or log in to your PrestaShop control panel and click on the **Preferences** tab followed by **Search**.

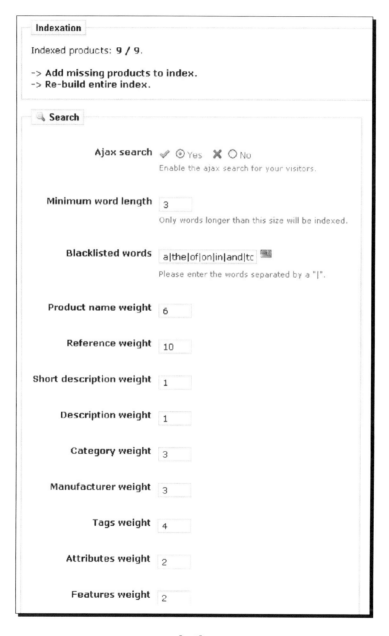

Let's run through the options. At the top you have a **Yes** or **No** option for **Ajax search**. This refers to the cool manner in which the search results are displayed as you type. If you thought your customers were likely to be using old web browsers or you were using one of the older PrestaShop templates discussed in *Chapter 2*, then you can choose **No**. Otherwise you might as well leave it on **Yes** for the user-friendly and rather nifty effects.

Minimum word length is just what it says. You can define a minimum word length for PrestaShop to start bothering with words. Three is a good minimum, so words like "at", "a", "is", and "by" are ignored. This is almost always a good idea.

The next option—**Blacklisted words**—allows you to specifically name a list of words that are ignored. If you sold products like "c5", then you would obviously need to allow two-letter words in your search results. You could then specifically define the two-letter words you didn't want included here—such as "at", "a", "is", and "by".

Next is a list of content areas and a box to type your chosen weight for that content area. The higher the number the more important that content area is considered. Having shown you how to change the weightings, do consider that PrestaShop developers know what they are doing, but they might not know what you are doing. That is why I have brought these search options to your attention. As usual think and plan what is important on your sites and make changes, if needed.

Speaking to new audiences

Using extra languages in PrestaShop is easy, apart from the need to be able to write and speak another language. And in some but not all ways, PrestaShop solves the problem for you.

You might think that to sell to customers in another language, you need to speak that other language. This is not necessarily the case. Of course, if you want to write detailed articles that are accurate and understood by readers of another language, then you need to write in that language.

In this quick section, we will look at just how easy it is to switch your store's default content to another language without knowing how to speak it. We will look at how you can create translations for key parts of your website, and finally we will explore a somewhat imperfect but still worth considering quick and simple translation option.

Switching languages

This is great. PrestaShop has very kindly created versions of its software in many languages. Your first option is to download and install PrestaShop in the language of your choice. Here I am assuming that you have already downloaded and set up PrestaShop in your language but now want to add another.

It is because PrestaShop has already done the work to make it available in so many languages that it is quite easy to add another language. But what do I mean by adding another language? All the content you create remains the same. But all the default writing can be changed by the customer to any language that you choose to allow them to install. What this means is that all your blocks, modules, buttons, checkout instructions, and more will—at the click of a button—change languages.

In some cases, this will be enough to get a sale from somebody who speaks that other language. But not always, and we will go a little further with the next tutorial. For now, here is how to allow your customers to change the default language in the shop front.

Time for action – enabling a second language

It is very simple to vary these instructions to install whichever language you want.

1. Click on the **Tools** tab, then on **Languages** and **Add new**.

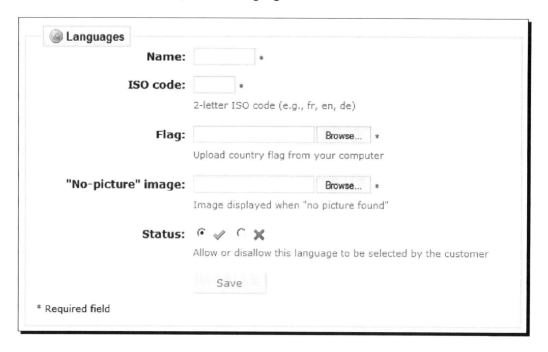

2. Now to fill the form in. The name should be straightforward: French, German, Swahili, or whatever.

3. Every country has an internationally recognized country code. To find the one for your second language visit `http://www.iso.org/iso/country_codes/`. Enter it in the **ISO code** box.

4. Next, browse to a graphic of the flag for that country. A handy website very kindly makes some available here: `http://www.famfamfam.com/lab/icons/flags/`. Upload it and move on.

5. In the box **"No-picture" image**, you need to provide a graphic that PrestaShop will use when no product image is available. If you always provide an image, this can be anything. If you regularly have missing pictures, a "picture coming soon" in the language you are enabling will suffice.

6. Make sure there is a nice green tick in the **Status** setting and then click on **Save**.

7. But PrestaShop cannot speak another language yet! We need to download a language pack from PrestaShop. The language packs are on the same page as the main PrestaShop download. Go grab your language pack(s) now from `http://www.PrestaShop.com/en/downloads/`.

8. Now click on the **Translations** sub-tab. Scroll down to where it says **Import a language pack**. Browse to the language pack you just downloaded and click on **Import**.

9. Click on the **Languages** sub-tab again and make sure your new language is enabled.

10. Now click on the **Modules** tab, scroll down to the **Language block**, and install it.

11. Visit your shop front. Notice you have some little flags that enable your customers to click on and choose their preferred language. It is important you explore your shop front in detail. How widely used your new language is might depend upon the extent to which the language pack covers all aspects of your shop. Any translations that have not been done as well as any extra translations you want to make are talked about in the next guide.

What just happened?

You just went global! Well sort of. If your language pack did not translate everything you wanted, it is not the end of the world. If your product is niche enough, you might still get some sales. If you need to translate even more, then read on.

Now we can go on to explore how to add more translations for key parts of your PrestaShop.

Creating translations

To see the extent of the translations so far, click on **Tools** and then **Translations**, and in the box labeled **Modify translations**, click the flag of your new language. Now click the **Expand all fieldsets** or choose a specific one. You can see a complete list of all the translations.

For many languages there are upwards of 500 translations done for you—an example of the power of the open source community. Imagine the cost of paying someone to translate just a few languages. PrestaShop gives it to you for nothing and you don't even have to say thanks.

Notice that on this page, you can easily add or change the translations. However, there is one very significant area that is not translated at all! That is our product descriptions. The next *Time for action* section will go through doing this. But before we dive in, let's look at how we can translate from our native language to a new language.

Perhaps, obviously, it is handy if you have somebody who speaks both languages. But assuming you don't and assuming you don't want to get your wallet out, here is a cheap, not totally reliable, but potentially profitable trick.

Please note we will be using a translation service that is free but not totally accurate. If you are translating something where inaccuracy could cause a problem, don't use this method. For example, it is probably okay to risk details of a teddy bear getting mixed up in translation, but the firing instructions for a new range of rocket-propelled grenades would clearly be problematic.

After this guide, I will point out how this very simple method can be used to translate almost all aspects of your PrestaShop.

Time for action – translating product descriptions

1. Log in to your PrestaShop control panel.

2. Click on the **Catalog** tab and find the first product you want to translate. Click on the **Edit** icon and then click on the flag next to the **Title** box. Notice that since we've added a new language, you have an extra option to change the language.

3. Now we need to redo all the description and title fields in our new language. Let's go over and use Google Translate to help us. Visit `http://translate.google.com/#`.

4. Select your **from** and **into** languages in the drop-down box, and copy and paste, individually, the descriptions and titles you want translated. Click on **Translate**, and copy and paste the translations back into their respective fields in the PrestaShop product page. A quick tip: as already mentioned, this is far from perfect. Consider shortening and simplifying the product descriptions. Click on **Save** when you're done.

5. Go and look at your shop front, change to your new language, and check out the product description.

What just happened?

When we saved the product, PrestaShop kept the original product information and descriptions as well as all the new information and descriptions we provided for the new language. PrestaShop will show customers the product description relevant to their choice of language.

What is important to realize is that anywhere in PrestaShop you see a flag, you can click it and add a translation. Also, places like meta tags, categories, and even whole articles in the CMS can have translations added in this way.

You might be wondering why we should settle for such imperfection. Some would say amateurism, simply because it can work and it costs nothing to try. If you find you are getting significant numbers of customers from a particular country, then it might be time to show proper respect to their language and get your wallet out. Visit www.elance.com and investigate their outsourcing website. You can often get great deals on translation. But beware. There are great translators and not-so-great translators.

A quick alternative to all of the above

Go and visit http://translate.google.com/# again. This time type in the URL of your website and click on **Translate**. Like what you see? Click around some more. If you approve, why not offer this service to your customers at the click of a button, direct from your PrestaShop?

Note that for this to work, the whole site needs to be in the original language. So this is an alternative to all of the other guides in this section, not an enhancement.

Time for action – translating your whole website

Here is how to do it:

1. Revisit your home page via Google Translate. Highlight and copy the URL of your translated home page.

2. Click on the **Modules** tab and scroll down to the **Home text editor**. Click on **Configure**.

3. At the very top of your home page, add the flag of the language of your choice. Now highlight the flag in the editor and click on the link button.

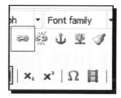

4. Paste the translated URL into the box shown below labeled **Link URL**:

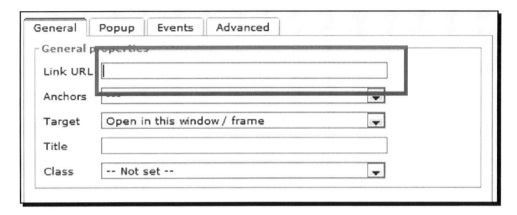

5. Save your new home page and visit your shop front and try it out.

What just happened?

Your customers can now switch to a completely translated version of your store. You can of course offer buttons for multiple language options.

Languages conclusion

As previously discussed, if you are successful with one or more new languages, it might be worth paying for professional translation. But why not go one stage further? If you find you have tapped a lucrative market in another country, why not start a website hosted in that country, with a domain extension specific to that country and using their language primarily? Have a look at *Chapter 9* and read about duplication if this is of interest to you.

Pop quiz – PrestaShop search

1. If you had a range of products, say teddy bears, and you wanted to make sure that the search results returned for teddy bear showed, at the top, a page that listed all the teddies in the teddy category and not just individual teddy pages, how would you do this?

2. How does the `robots.txt` file protect the private areas of your PrestaShop?

Summary

You might be getting quite excited about your new PrestaShop. The features and procedures that you have completed in this chapter together make for a very significantly optimized store. I have seen countless web stores, even some of the big names, that do not have anything like the SEO options that you now have enabled.

Now, it doesn't mean that this alone will suddenly bring a flood of thousands of visitors; it doesn't work like that. I can guarantee you that you have taken the very significant initial steps towards having a store that is approved of by both humans and search engines alike. And in a later chapter, we will turn on the tap to begin the eventual flood of visitors. SEO should definitely be an ongoing project and I recommend further reading. A good place to start is a website that discusses SEO in a specifically PrestaShop context. Check out `www.presto-changeo.com` and have a read of the SEO tips and tricks. Also visit the PrestaShop forum at `www.PrestaShop.com` where they have a section dedicated to all things PrestaShop and SEO.

Specifically, we covered:

- ◆ Choosing the best keywords: Deciding upon an overall keyword strategy
- ◆ Meta tags: What they are and how to benefit from them
- ◆ URLs: All about canonical and friendly URLs
- ◆ Writing and displaying great articles
- ◆ Other SEO stuff: Aliases, sitemaps, `robots.txt`, and search weightings
- ◆ Adding new languages to our PrestaShop

Now it is time to look at more customization options as well as some of the lesser-spotted PrestaShop features.

5
Tools, Newsletters, Extra Income, and Statistics

This chapter will cover as many PrestaShop features as possible. There is, as I have said, so much to PrestaShop. This is an attempt to bring as much of it to your attention as possible.

First we will explore the Preferences and Tools tabs and then go on to some more great stuff like newsletters and product notifications. Then we will look at Google AdSense. This is a way of making extra income through advertisers with just a couple of clicks.

Then we will take our first look at statistics. I say our first look because we will just introduce the concept and set them up. In Chapter 9, we will see how to start using the statistics you gather. We will set up the fabulously rich PrestaShop statistics features and the free-to-use Google Analytics.

Hold on to your chair, as we are going to:

- Look at the most useful things on the **Preferences** tab
- Explore the best stuff on the **Tools** tab
- Set up a newsletter and notifications system
- Talk about running an e-mail marketing campaign
- Set up PrestaShop statistics
- Set up Google analytics

So let's get on with it...

Exploring the Preferences and Tools tabs

The two tabs that you will probably use most, apart from **Modules**, are **Tools** and **Preferences**. The options available under **Tools** and **Preferences** are very diverse. Some you might never want to use and others will do wonders for your business.

What follows is a whirlwind tour of some of the options under **Tools** and **Preferences**. Each option described tells you quickly where it is and what it does. For brevity, I have left a few lesser (in my opinion) options out, and for sanity, I will not mention any that we have already looked at. So here goes...

Useful Preferences

These are the best things you will find under the **Preferences** tab that have not been covered already and will not be covered later in the book.

PS directory

If you need to install PrestaShop in a subdirectory (`www.yourshop.com/adirectory`), perhaps because you are adding a shop to an existing website, then specify the directory here.

Terms of service

Do you want to force your customers to accept your terms of service before they can complete the checkout? If you have a product range or service where this is essential, then obviously you should choose **Yes**. But if there is no good reason, then choose **No**. People don't like "signing" agreements and this could lose you sales.

Cart re-display at login

Have PrestaShop remember customers who had products in their cart but didn't buy them. Sounds like a good idea to me because you might get a sale from it.

Timezone

Select the time zone of your customers. If you are an international store, choose the most common one: for example, the Greenwich Mean Time (GMT).

Contact

This is a sub-tab on the top left-hand corner. Fill out all the contact details for your store. PrestaShop will automatically add relevant information accordingly.

Meta-Tags

Here you can define meta tags for your standard pages, site map, contact form, and so on. Simply click on the Notepad icon next to the page you want to define and you know how to do the rest.

Products

This sub-tab has loads of options all to do with products and how they are presented. Have a look at all these options. Important ones include the following:

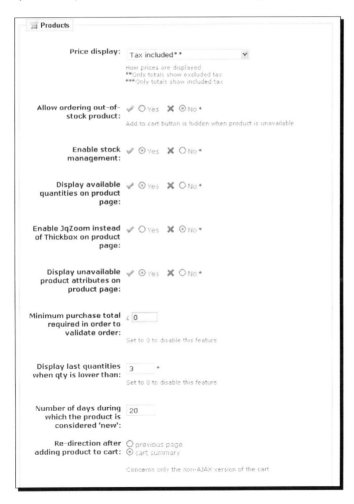

Price display

Do you want to display individual prices and total prices including tax, or without, or both?

Enable stock management for PrestaShop to keep an eye on stock levels. It will do nice things like sending you low stock warning e-mails if enabled.

Minimum purchase total

A minimum purchase total is required to validate an order. Enable this to enforce a minimum spend before customers can complete the transaction.

Number of days the product is considered new

Remember the **New products block**? Decide how many days a product is considered new and subsequently appears in the **New products block**.

Products per page

How many products do you want to appear per page when viewing a category? Keeping a low number like the default 10 is a good idea. But if you have a number of categories with slightly more than 10, it is sometimes worth increasing the number so that all the products appear on the first page.

If you have a category with, for example, 50 products, then it is a very good idea to spread them over multiple pages. But if you have a category with 13 products, then the default settings mean the three products on their own might be overlooked by your customers.

Unfortunately, there is no option to define the number of products per page for each individual category, so you need to choose a number that works well for all your categories. Did I just criticize PrestaShop? Sacre bleu!

Default order by

How do you want the products sorted when the category page is first viewed: alphabetically or in the same order as you created them? The customers can change this to whatever suits them, but you choose what you think their likely preference will be.

Default order way

Ascending or descending? This works in conjunction with the above: price high to low or low to high, A-Z or Z-A, category order or reverse category order?

Images options

All of the image options refer to the images that customers can upload if you have enabled image uploads for customizable products. So if your teddy T-shirt pictures need to be larger or should only be smaller than the size indicated here, then change it here. If you don't use customizable products, then leave this as it is.

Email

The settings on this sub-tab are usually best left alone. The default settings of **Use PHP mail() function** and **Both** are typical to almost all shared hosting environments. If, however, you were running your PrestaShop from a server on your PC at home, you could choose **Set my own SMTP parameters** and configure PrestaShop to use your ISPs e-mail service and your own e-mail address. When hosting with a professional host, you could also use the SMTP service provided by your web host, but in most situations, this would be an unnecessary complication.

Leaving the **Both** option selected will give your customers the choice of receiving simple text e-mails or formatted HTML e-mails.

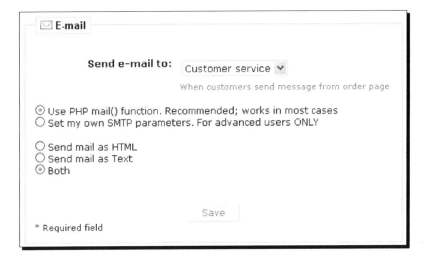

Image

Use these settings to customize the look and feel of your store.

Localization

Choose lbs, kg, or any other unit of measurement that suits you.

Database

As suggested by the warning message, stay clear of this tab until we discuss backing up your store in *Chapter 6*.

Top tools

Just about every tool has either been covered or will be covered in a specific section of the book. However, there are two tools that don't fall into any appropriate topic category. They are great for personalizing and customizing your admin control panel. These are Tabs and Quick accesses.

Tabs

Ever thought some of the tabs are in the wrong place? No problem. You can move and create as many tabs and sub-tabs as you like. So if you want to group different sub-tabs under different main tabs because that is convenient for you, then this is how to do it.

Time for action – customizing your tabs

As an example, we will move the main **Orders** tab and make it a sub-tab of **Customers**.

1. Click on **Tools** and then **Tabs**.

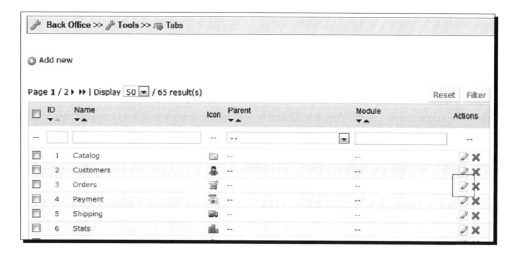

2. Click on the **Edit** icon of **Orders** in the list of tabs. You will find orders near the top. I have highlighted it on the image above.

3. We are going to change the **Parent** value from **Home** to **Customers**. This means that the **Orders** tab will be moved to a sub-tab of **Customers** instead of **Home** (a main tab). So click on the drop-down list and select **Customers**.

4. That's it. Click into the **Customers** tab and then the newly positioned **Orders** tab. Notice that all the sub-tabs of **Orders** have moved with it. That is because although you have only moved the **Orders** tab, it remains the parent of all its sub-tabs.

What just happened?

This feature might not be of any use to you. But imagine your business grows and you need to employ someone to perform one specific task. Perhaps you will need someone to write articles or do all the customer service and packing. You can easily create a single tab with all the features they need and then restrict their username to only that tab, avoiding the risk of them accidentally changing settings (which you don't want them to). We will look at this and other security features in *Chapter 6*.

Quick accesses

Remember the quick access drop-downs? Do they go where you want them to? Here is how to make more. I will make a quick access to the database backup facility, which we will use in the next chapter while making a copy of your store.

Time for action – creating a Quick Access

Here is how to do it.

1. Click on the **Tools** tab and then **Quick Accesses**.

2. Now click on the **Add new** button (the plus sign).

3. For the **Name** value, type **Database backup**.

4. For the **URL** value, type **index.php?tab=AdminBackup**.

5. Save your changes and try out your new quick access.

If you are looking to make your own quick accesses, then you are probably wondering how to get the value for the URL field. Go to the tab you are making the quick access to and copy the URL in your browser. Then delete everything before the `index.php` and everything from `&token`. I have copied the database backup URL below and highlighted the parts to delete so that you can see exactly what to delete and what to use:

```
http:/shop.com/adminpassword123456/index.php?tab=AdminBackup&token
=37a0e13f7
```

What just happened?

We made a Quick access shortcut to the database backup feature. You can make quick access shortcuts to anything that is useful to you. The database backup feature is something that should be used regularly and we will discuss it in *Chapter 6*.

Let's see how much you have learned, remembered, and what you can work out for yourself.

Pop quiz – Tools and Preferences challenge

Here are a number of questions all about what you can do on the **Tools** and **Preferences** tab. Just to make things more interesting, there are questions dealt with in previous chapters as well as this one.

Questions:

1. How would you configure PrestaShop e-mail messages to be sent from your personal ISP account when you are running PrestaShop on your own PC?

2. You are using PrestaShop 1.3, but you find a really smart 1.1 template. Can you use it?

3. We looked briefly at the database backup feature. Is backing up the database enough to ensure you have everything you need to recover from disaster?

E-mail marketing with newsletters

We will discuss marketing in *Chapters 8* and *9*. However, newsletters, or e-mail marketing, is a special case. That is why it is worth discussing it here before we cover other PrestaShop marketing options in *Chapters 8* and *9*.

E-mail marketing is not just another type of marketing. In my opinion, it is absolutely crucial to maximize the potential of any online business. E-mail marketing with newsletters is a kind of catchall to make all other forms of marketing worthwhile. What do I mean by this?

E-mail marketing can support every other type of marketing you are doing. Think about all the different sources your website will eventually receive its visitors from - search engines due to your SEO efforts (in the last chapter), paid-for adverts, link building, and social media marketing. If any of those phrases are alien to you, don't worry. They are all dealt with in *Chapters 8* and *9*. The point to grasp here is that all the other methods when used on their own are actually prone to failure.

Most people don't buy!

It's true. The vast majority of visits to your shop do not generate a sale. If you manage to achieve 10 percent, you have done incredibly well. Chances are the actual figure is nearer to 5 percent or lower. If we were working in a retail shop and 19 out of 20 customers we spoke to walked out with nothing, we probably wouldn't last long before we had to find another job.

So this means we are expecting to fail 95 percent of the time. Now assuming you have written a great sales copy, provided compelling informational content, set up your PrestaShop correctly and smartly, there is little more you can do on your site itself. And it is probably not the fault of your website that 95 percent of you visitors kept their wallets firmly in their pockets.

Why?

So why do 95 percent leave without spending? There are lots of reasons—they aren't ready to buy, they want to do more research or they are looking to find a better price or service, and there are many more reasons as well. And what makes things worse is that when the customers have put things right in their minds and they finally have their wallet out, they are unlikely to remember your website. So we have to, as much as possible, remove the element of chance.

What if you could constantly remind your future potential customer? What if you could help them arrive at a buying decision? What if you could improve your relationship and warm up your potential customers with interesting and relevant industry or product information? You guessed it, that's where e-mail marketing comes in. All the other forms of marketing bring people to your site—a small percentage will buy and e-mail marketing takes care of the rest.

Of course, you have to get the e-mail addresses of these people and their permission to be contacted. And when you send e-mails, they must contain high quality compelling content to sell them your products.

The stages of e-mail marketing

First we will look at how to start building a list of potential customers with the PrestaShop newsletter module. Then we will look at ways to build that list as quickly as possible, capturing as high a percentage of visitors as possible. Then we will look at actually sending product notifications through PrestaShop alerts. Next we will look at a range of methods—PrestaShop and some more—for actually managing your list of names and your e-mail campaigns.

Setting up the newsletter module

This is how we will begin to collect e-mail addresses of willing subscribers. This brief tutorial creates a simple form for customers to enter their details and start receiving your e-mails. As with most things in PrestaShop, this is a breeze. Follow the quick tutorial below.

Time for action – the newsletter module

A couple of clicks are all it takes.

1. Click on the **Modules** tab, scroll down to the **Newsletter block**, then click on **install**. Be careful to configure the **Newsletter block** located in the **Blocks** category and not **Newsletter** in the **Tools** category. We will look at the latter when we start sending e-mails/newsletters.

2. Scroll back down and click on **Configure**. Select the box for sending a confirmation. Then your new subscriber will get a very brief message confirming they have subscribed.

What just happened?

Go and have a look at the newsletter subscription block that your customers will see:

Now we can go on to explore other e-mail communications topics.

Switching on product notifications

Product notifications are different to newsletters but are a related topic. Switching on product notifications gives customers the option of receiving e-mails when out–of-stock products come back into stock. This works for actual customers who specifically request it, not newsletter subscribers, so it is still worth including new products and specials in your newsletters. We will talk more about newsletters in a minute. Now let's turn on product notifications.

Time for action – product notifications

Here is how to do it.

1. Click on the **Modules** tab, scroll down to **Mail alerts** and install it.

2. Scroll back down to the module and click on **Configure**.

3. Make sure all of the boxes are checked.

What just happened?

You just provided a useful service for your customers.

Back to e-mail marketing and newsletters for real. We will look at how to get lots of subscribers, create great e-mails, and then the different options available to send them. Another cool way to keep your shop in your customers mind is to allow them to configure their own reminder events. Have a look at www.presto-changeo.com and read about the Occasion Reminder module. Let's get on with building a list of subscribers.

Building a big list of subscribers

Now your subscription block is ready to roll. Let's look at a few ways of getting more subscribers out of our visitors.

Advertising your newsletter

Consider advertising your newsletter itself. That is, why not run some Google adverts saying "Get my free newsletter: All about fluffy teddies"? Of course, there are financial considerations to this option. It is worth considering for repeat purchase or high-margin products. Google AdWords is discussed in *Chapter 8*.

Compelling content

You might have already added some articles to your website. Why not revisit them and tweak them to include a suggestion of joining your newsletter? If they like your article they might want more.

Incentives

Offer something for free if they sign up to your newsletter. Mention the free gift in your articles and the home page or other prominent pages. Here are some ideas for what to give away.

What to give away

Think hard about your products, business, and industry. What would be really useful? If you are selling an information/music/video product, it's easy. Perhaps offer a sample chapter, song, application, or video. If not, why not create a downloadable PDF or a short video made on a webcam of the most compelling and useful information related to your products, business, or industry?

Here is another idea that might work for almost any business. Offer a free software download. Even if your website is not software related, you can almost always find great software that you can give away which has some connection with your industry. Visit www.sourceforge.net and find something suitable for your business.

If you're really stuck for incentives, offer a discount voucher. Consider this very carefully before doing it because it needs to be viable financially. But what better way could there be of making someone revisit your store?

Offering more via e-mail

Write a really great article. You can then offer it as a reward for signing up. The other way (though a bit sneaky, it does work)—write another cool article but only publish part of it. Then offer the conclusion or vital final bit of information when they subscribe.

Okay, let's assume we will have hordes of subscribers. We now need to make some newsletters worth receiving.

Creating newsletters

As with all your articles you need to write interesting content that people actually want to read. The same rules apply for writing a great article for your site, but a newsletter needs more than just an article. You could use one or more of the following.

Product Information

This is just what it says. The very best buys, newest additions, or hottest products from your industry.

Genuine news

Tell your readers about significant developments in the world of your niche. The 100th annual teddy bear's picnic or whatever is important to your visitors.

Company announcements

Upcoming sales, taking on new product ranges, or something as important are genuine reasons to contact someone who expressed an interest by signing up to your newsletter.

Designing your newsletters

You are probably beginning to see that this topic is getting quite deep and there are lots of possibilities that can't be discussed here. How about this?

If your shop covers a relatively unchanging niche, such as teddy bears, then you probably know enough to get going. Write a new article following all the guidelines from *Chapter 4*. Put your company logo at the top and a special offer or two at the bottom and read on about how to send them. You can grab a cool, free web page editor called **Nvu** to create your HTML newsletter. Get on over to `www.prestashop-book.com` and download a copy.

If, on the other hand, your niche is a dynamic one with enthusiasts or lots of opinion, then this is where you can really capitalize on a great newsletter. You can send multiple newsletters with a different focus on the main types and format and arrange them in many different ways to entice customers and maintain your readership. If this describes your niche, it is worth putting a bit more effort and thought into the design, content, and type of your newsletter. Get on over to `www.prestashop-book.com` and download a copy of my free e-book on designing and creating e-mail templates.

Now you have an idea of how to create a great e-mail newsletter. But how are you going to send it?

Sending newsletters

Of course, once you have created interesting content and formatted it beautifully, you need to send it. Here are a number of ways you can do this—some free and some requiring the dreaded wallet.

A quick word about spam

This is a complicated issue and varies greatly from country to country and in the US from state to state. In some places, you can do what you like; in others, you could end up in jail for breaking one of numerous communications or data protection laws. Here are a few rules:

- Never buy or borrow a list of e-mail addresses unless you are 100 percent certain they have been gathered legitimately and *all* the recipients have signed up for e-mails from third parties (you)

- Never add someone to your newsletter without their express, specific request

- Never use a person's e-mail after they have unsubscribed, no matter how much you think they might want to receive just one more

- Always include instructions to unsubscribe in every e-mail

You need to also be wary that even if you comply with all the laws and my guidelines mentioned above, where spam is concerned, an individual person's perception is all that matters. If a recipient thinks the e-mail you have sent is trash or doesn't identify it with the company he signed up with, even if they subscribed, they might click their **Mark as spam** button.

If this happens too often, then their ISP could mark your domain as spam. If you keep your content good and not too commercial as well as have a clear and easy unsubscribe process, then you should be able to avoid this.

Using a PrestaShop module to send newsletters

As you might expect, there is a PrestaShop module for sending e-mails to your subscribers direct from your PrestaShop admin area. This is a quick download and is as easy to install as any other PrestaShop module.

As you know by now though, I don't like spending money! This module costs 45 Euros. If you want utter simplicity and 45 Euros is not important to you, then you can go and buy the module from www.prestaworks.com.

If, like me, you don't want to get your wallet out, then read on. I will show you a number of ways to do it for free as well as point you in the direction of some pay-for services that can add extra frills to you newsletter campaigns. And because of the excellent PrestaShop facility to export a list of your subscribers, it is almost as easy as doing it through the PrestaShop module.

Using your web host to send newsletters

Most web hosts offer an e-mail marketing package or a script that you can add to your site. I have never seen one that is both adequate and free (included with web hosting). Most either lack features or come with significant costs per month. However, have a look before you get your wallet out.

A dedicated e-mail service provider to send newsletters

You can take out a new service with companies like Aweber (`www.aweber.com`) and MailChimp (`www.mailchimp.com`), and get a very easy-to-use and fully-featured service.

The big downside with these companies is that as your list grows, so does your expenses. For example, 2,500 e-mails a month could cost you $49. And if your business gets really big the charges get really big too. Go and have a look at what these companies offer, but think carefully before getting your wallet out.

A free e-mail system to send newsletters

Just what the doctor ordered! There is one that is fully-featured, fully–supported, and free. **PHPList** is one of the several but is probably the best open source e-mail list management software system.

You can install it on your web host and then work through all the phases of starting and running an e-mail marketing campaign using PHPList. It can help you build a list, create professional newsletters/e-mails, send them, manage replies, and give you statistical feedback.

PHPList is very extensive and therefore cannot be explained fully in a few paragraphs here. If you have decided that your e-mail/newsletter campaign is going to be an important part of your marketing strategy but you don't want to spend money on the likes of Aweber and require more functionality than most regular web hosts, then visit `www.prestashop-book.com` and download my free guide to get you up and running with PHPList in a hurry.

Getting your subscriber list

Whichever option you choose, you will need your list of subscribers. Here is how to get the list in a text file so that you can copy and paste them into your preferred sending method.

Time for action – accessing your e-mail list

We will use the PrestaShop admin area to create a `.csv` file that can be used to copy and paste all your subscribers into your preferred system.

1. Click on the **Modules** tab and scroll down to the **Newsletter** module. Now click on **Configure**.

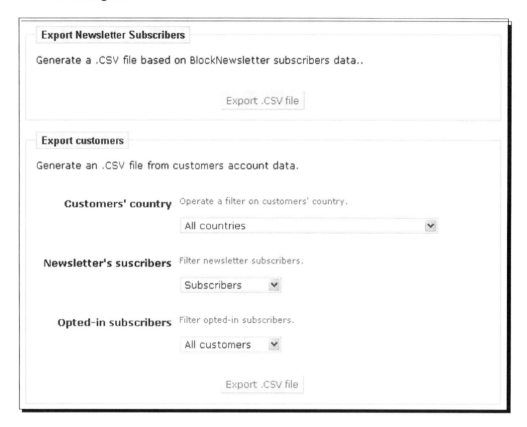

2. You have two buttons where you can click to export a `.csv` file.

3. The first will export a list of everybody who signed up using your newsletter signup block.

4. The second exports a list of everybody who has created a customer account. Notice here that you have some options for filtering/customizing the second list. You have the option to select a specific country or all countries. You also have the option to choose subscribers or non-subscribers from opted-in customers and newsletter subscribers. This is important. Never send newsletters to anybody who has not subscribed. You will get a bad reputation, end up on ISP block lists, and in some parts of the world you might even be prosecuted.

5. So select your country or all countries and then select subscribers in both drop-down boxes.

6. Now click on each of the **Export .CSV file** buttons in turn. The data is displayed in a new browser window. You can copy and paste from there or save it to a Windows Notepad document.

What just happened?

You now have a text file to use in your preferred e-mail system.

Now some people who visit your site, read your articles, and receive your free newsletter will never buy anything. Wouldn't it be nice if we could find a way of making a little bit of revenue from them? You can, with Google AdSense.

Extra revenue with Google AdSense

AdSense is the facility to put a snippet of code on your site that allows Google to place adverts relevant to the keywords on your page. When your customers click on an advert, Google pays you.

There are disadvantages to AdSense as well. When a customer clicks your advert, they go to another site and this site might be a competitor's. Oops!

My view with regard to this last concern is that if your site is set up correctly and your products and categories are described with proper sales copy, then this will only happen when you haven't got what the customer wants anyway. Customers know what they want, they know your site is not their only option, and most important, they know if they like what they see or not. So why not offer them an alternative that makes you money just in case you don't have quite what they are looking for?

I have read that putting AdSense on an e-commerce site is nothing less than stupidity. My experience says otherwise. Anyway, Amazon and eBay do it. I would rather be stupid and have a business like theirs (one day) than conform to industry expectations.

And why would PrestaShop include an AdSense module if it wasn't worth considering? You can decide what is appropriate for your website. If you want AdSense facilities, read on. If you don't want to install AdSense, then skip the next bit.

To sign up for an AdSense account, just go to `www.google.com/adsense/` and follow the instructions to create your account.

Creating the Google AdSense code

The first part of the plan is to generate the code that PrestaShop requires.

Time for action – creating the Google code

Here is how to get it.

1. Log into your AdSense account. Click on the **AdSense Setup** tab near the left of the page.

2. Now click on **AdSense for Content** at the top of the list of options. Make sure **Ad unit** is selected and click on **Continue**.

3. In the top **Format** drop-down, I recommend selecting **Banner (468 x 60)** which works well in PrestaShop.

4. Leave **Colors** and **Corner Styles** as they are and click on **Continue** at the bottom of the page.

5. Click on **Submit and Get Code**. Click in the code window to highlight the generated code. Then press and hold *Ctrl* and press *C* to copy the code to your PC clipboard.

What just happened?

You now have the Google AdSense code to use in the PrestaShop module. So when you're ready, read on.

Setting up Google AdSense in PrestaShop

As with just about everything in PrestaShop, implementing Google AdSense has been nice and easy. Follow the quick *Time for action* below to start earning from clicks.

Time for action – installing Google AdSense

Have your Google code from above ready to paste and read on.

1. Click on the **Modules** tab. Install the **Google Adsense** module—it is the first module in the list.

2. Click on **Configure**.

3. Paste the code created in the previous tutorial and click on **Update settings**.

4. Wait half an hour and visit your shop front to see the advert.

What just happened?

Your adverts will start running fairly soon. A quick word of warning, just in case you didn't read Google's terms and conditions. The one key thing to know is that you must *never ever* click on your own adverts. Google will pick up on this and will not give you many chances before it does something really annoying.

Setting up PrestaShop statistics

Now you are up and running (or at least you're in the starting blocks) and it is a good time to consider a way to measure the success of your site. If you can't take measurements, you won't know when you're doing things right or wrong. This and the next section will introduce two schemes for achieving this. First up, as the heading suggests, is **PrestaShop statistics**.

PrestaShop statistics, in my opinion, are unrivalled in free software. The depth of information and richness of presentation are literally second to none. As if this were not enough, PrestaShop statistics is an absolute breeze to set up.

That was yet another rant about the wonders of PrestaShop. You might at this point be wondering what my connection or hidden interest in PrestaShop is. Let me assure you that I have no vested interest whatsoever. PrestaShop genuinely is outstanding in many areas. I am just a strange guy who likes exploring the ins and outs of web software who stumbled across PrestaShop and liked it so much that I decided to write a book about it. Anyway, let's get on with the statistics section.

Graph and grid engines

These are the parts of PrestaShop that power the presentation of the statistics. Depending upon which engine you choose, the graph or chart you are using will be presented a bit differently. Or you could switch them all off and just view the basic manner in which PrestaShop presents things.

The way I suggest you find out is to switch them all on because you can flip between the different engines while viewing statistics and then decide what you like best. Then you can turn off all the ones that are unnecessary. We will do this in a *Time for action* section shortly.

Statistics modules

These are the different modules that present and collect statistics that you can use to find out interesting or useful information about your store. As with the engines, a good way of exploring these is to switch them all on, and then go to explore them. We will do this in the next *Time for action*. However, we will not go too deeply into how you can actually use them until we look at analyzing statistics in *Chapter 9*. For now we will just familiarize ourselves with what is available.

So let's do it.

Time for action – setting up statistics engines and modules

As I mentioned earlier, we will switch everything on.

1. Click on the **Modules** tab. Scroll down to the section headed **Stats Engines** and install the first one. Repeat this until they are all installed. There is no configuration required for any of these.

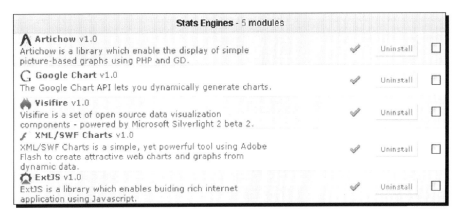

2. Now scroll down to the last modules section. It is headed as **Stats**. Install all the Stats modules. Don't worry about configuring any of them. Most of them don't have any options and the one that does can be left for now. It is much faster to check the boxes of the modules you want to install and then click on **Install the selection** at the very bottom of the page.

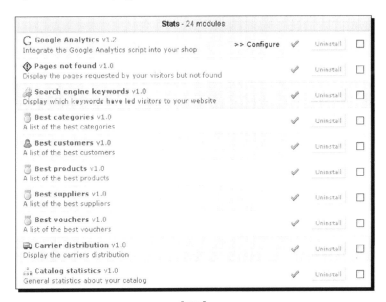

3. Click on the **Home** quick access drop-down. Notice you have a quick statistical summary on your admin home page.

4. Now click on the **Stats** tab. Notice there are lot of things to explore. That is what we will do now.

What just happened?

Now your website will begin to gather statistics and you can then make meaningful decisions based on what they tell you.

Exploring the statistics options

Let's have a brief explanation of the main options. I have included some screenshots because if your store has no customers yet, then you won't be able to see much.

Visitors online

See if there are people browsing your shop, what they are looking at, and most importantly, whether have something in their cart. This module can distinguish between a regular visitor and a logged-in customer.

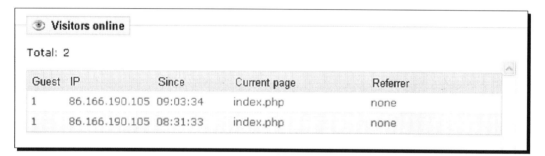

Pages not found

This lists URLs that people have attempted to access but were not found. This is useful for finding potential linking problems.

Search engine keywords

Find out which keywords brought traffic to your site.

Best categories

Just as it says—it lists the categories that do the best in your shop.

Best customers

Tells you which customers spent the most.

Best products

This option provides a league table of best-selling products as shown in the following screenshot:

Best suppliers

Says which suppliers supply the best-selling products.

Best vouchers

Vouchers you have created and how well they do. We will cover more on vouchers in *Chapter 8*.

Carrier distribution

A detailed look at the different carrier services your customers choose.

Catalog statistics

All the statistics you could think of to do with your product range.

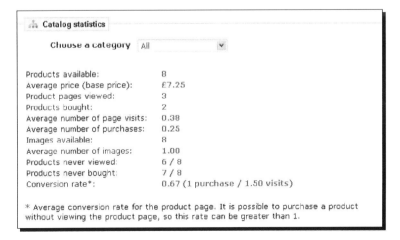

Software

Find out which web browsers, operating systems, and much more, that your customers use.

Geolocation

Get information about which country your customers come from.

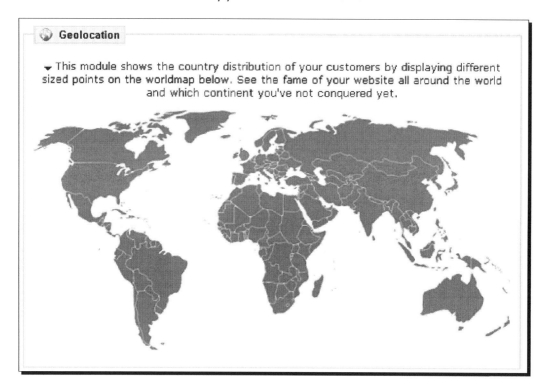

Newsletter

Statistics about signups to your newsletter we set up earlier.

Visitors origin

Tells you which search engines and websites sent visitors to you.

Registered customer info

This option will give you some useful customer demographics. These include age, sex, country, and currency.

Product details

This gives you a quick summary of products and stock levels.

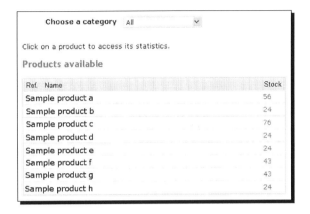

Customer accounts

This is useful stuff. It tells you how many registered customers there are from a particular time period and also how many customers gave up during registration or registered but decided not to buy.

Sales and orders

Gives lots of sales information.

Shop search

This provides a league table of search terms used in your shop and how often they have been used. This can be really useful for picking new aliases and other things as well.

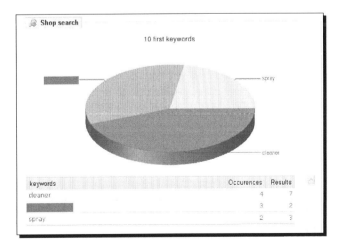

Visits and visitors

Helps you work out how many returning visitors you have by comparing the number of visits to unique visitors.

Installing Google Analytics

It has to be said that Google Analytics is really quite impressive. If you want to know (and as a switched-on web master, you should want to know) who visited your site, where they live, what operating system and browser they have, what pages they visited, how long they stayed, where they got the link to your site from, what websites are sending you visitors and much more, then Google Analytics is for you! And what does it cost? Absolutely nothing!

Getting a Google Analytics account

Go to `http://www.google.com/analytics/` and click on **Sign Up Now**. Follow the simple instructions to open an Analytics account.

This task with just about any other shopping cart system or any PHP website can be a challenge. The very nature and variety of PHP websites, especially shopping carts, means it is impossible for Google to give explicit instructions.

The budding e-commerce entrepreneur is often left trawling forums with contradictory comments or advice based on an old version of Analytics. And then there was PrestaShop.

Have a go hero – doing more with the thing

Have a go at this. Make sure you have signed up for Google Analytics already and then have a go at this challenge. Clear a space; make sure the kids are in front of the telly. Make sure you are logged into PrestaShop and your Analytics account. Now hold your breath. I am serious. Can you install Google Analytics in PrestaShop before you have to take a breath?

Time for action – installing Google Analytics

Just follow the instructions. Ignore Google's additional warnings and instructions. PrestaShop is different. Go!

1. In your Analytics account, click on **Add Website Profile** and type in your domain name.

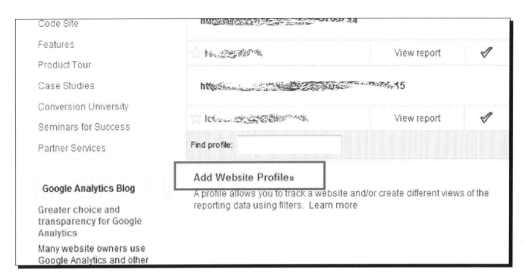

2. Note the **Web Property ID** in the **Tracking Status Information** box.

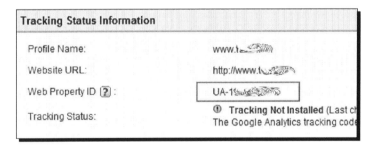

3. In PrestaShop, click on the **Modules** tab. Scroll to the **Stats** category and install the **Google Analytics** module.

4. Scroll back down to the **Google Analytics** module and click on **Configure**.

5. Enter your **Analytics Web Property ID** in the box and click on **Save**.

Breathe.

If this is not your book and your partner has a blue face and their head on their keyboard, please call an ambulance. Please note the publisher and the author accepts no responsibility for death or serious injury while reading this book.

What just happened?

Tracking has now been installed. Data will start to be gathered and you should have meaningful statistics in around 24 hours. We will cover much more on statistics in *Chapter 9*.

Using Google Analytics

Just log into your Analytics account and have a look. Click on some of the options and sub-options in the main left-hand menu. There won't be any data there yet, but as you can see there is an abundance of possibilities. In *Chapter 9*, we will discuss in detail a plan to make your PrestaShop a roaring success, with Google Analytics playing a big part in it.

Summary

We learned a lot in this chapter. It was probably the most diverse chapter. A sort of mopping up, if you like, to make sure we appreciate the diversity PrestaShop has to offer before we move on.

Specifically, we covered the following topics:

- We now have a very good knowledge of the **Preferences** tab.
- The **Tools** tab has been fully explored.
- We have a good understanding of e-mail/newsletter campaigns and our different options for implementing them.
- We have a range of powerful tools for analyzing statistics. We also looked at the range of data available but put off actually analyzing anything until *Chapter 9*.

Now how would you feel if after all this work your web host had a catastrophe and you lost the lot? That really would be a bad day! So without delay we will move on to the next chapter and look at security, backing up your store, and recovering from a disaster.

6
Security and Disaster Recovery

In this chapter, we will do everything possible to make sure our store is not the victim of a successful attack. Fortunately, the PrestaShop team takes security very seriously and issues updates and fixes as soon as possible after any problems are discovered.

We just have to make sure we do everything we can and also implement the PrestaShop upgrades as soon as they are available. All this is covered next.

It is also vital that we always have a recent copy of our store because one day, it is probably inevitable that our shop will die on us. It might be a hacker or maybe we will accidentally muck it up ourselves. A recent backup to handle this type of event is a minor inconvenience, because without one, it is an expensive catastrophe.

In this chapter, we shall:

- ◆ Look at ways your shop can be damaged
- ◆ Add users, profiles, and permissions to increase security
- ◆ Talk about and optionally implement SSL to protect your customers' private information
- ◆ Learn how to backup and restore your shop in case everything else fails
- ◆ Talk about upgrading PrestaShop and how this helps keep your business secure

So let's get on with it...

Types of attack

There are different types of security attacks. Here is a very brief explanation of some of the most common ones. Hopefully, this will make it clear why security is an ongoing and evolving issue and not something that can ever be 100 percent solved out of the box.

Common sense issues

These are often overlooked—make sure your passwords are impossible to guess. Use number sequences that are memorable to you but unguessable and meaningless to everyone else. Combine number sequences with regular letters in a variety of upper and lower case. Don't share your passwords with anyone. This applies to anyone who has access to your shop or hosting account.

Brute force

This is when an attacker uses software to repeatedly attempt to gain access or discover a password by guessing. Clearly, the simplest defense against this is a secure password. A good password is one with upper and lower case characters, apparently random numbers and words that are not names or are in the dictionary. Does your administrator password stand up to these criteria?

SQL injection attack

A malicious person amends, deletes, or retrieves information from your database by cleverly manipulating the forms or database requests contained in the code of PrestaShop. By appending to legitimate PrestaShop database code, harm can be done or breaches of security can be achieved.

Cross-site scripting

Attackers add instructions to access code on another site. They do this by appending a URL pointing to malicious code to a PHP URL of a legitimate page on your site.

User error

This is straight forward. It is likely that while developing or amending your website, you will mess up some or perhaps all of your PrestaShop. I did it once while writing this chapter. I will give you the full details of my slightly embarrassing confession later.

So with so many ways that things can go wrong, we better start looking at some solutions.

Employees and user security

If you plan to employ someone or if you have a partner who is going to help in your new shop, it makes good sense to create a new user account so that they have their own login details. Even if it will be only you who needs to use the PrestaShop control panel, there is still a good argument for creating two or more accounts. Here is why.

First we will consider a scenario, though a slightly exaggerated one:

◆ Guns4u.com

Guns4u wants to offer articles about how to use its products. The management, probably correctly, believe that in-depth how-tos about all its products will boost sales and increase customer retention.

The diverse nature of their products makes employing a single writer impossible. For example, an expert on small arms is rarely an expert on ground-to-air ordinance. And a user of laser targeting equipment probably doesn't know the first thing about ship-based artillery.

This is quite a problem. The management decides they need a way to allow a whole team of freelance writers who can login directly to the PrestaShop CMS. But bearing in mind the highly dubious backgrounds some of these writers will have, how can they be trusted in the PrestaShop control panel?

◆ Users of Guns4u.com

Suppose you employ somebody to write articles for you. You don't really want them being able to play with product prices or payment modules. You would want to restrict them to the CMS area of the control panel. Similarly, your partner might be helping you wrap and pack your products. To avoid accidents you might like to restrict them to the **Customers** and **Orders** tab.

Now consider this scenario. Even you, after reading this book, can make a mistake. It is a really good idea to create at least one extra user account for you. I always make myself a wrapping and packing account. I use it all the time and it is reassuring to know that I can't accidentally click anything that can cause a problem.

This type of user security is common in large organizations. On a company intranet, employees will almost always be restricted to areas of the company system to which they need and nothing more.

Below is how to create a new user account and then after that we will look at profiles and permissions to enforce the restrictions and permissions suitable to us.

Okay, let's create a new user.

Time for action – creating users

As you have come to expect, this is really easy.

1. Click on the **Employees** tab and then click on the **Add new** link.

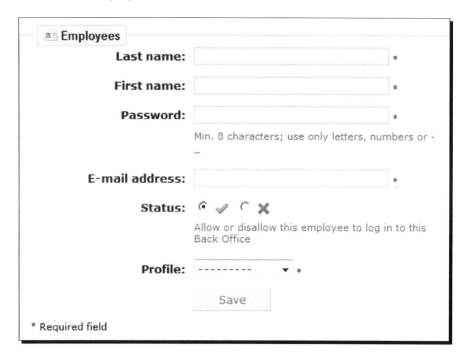

2. Enter the **Last name**, **First name**, and **E-mail address** of your new employee or user.

3. The status box enables you to allow or disallow access to the new employee. Unless you have a reason for creating an account and not letting them use it, select the check mark (**Allow**). If you have reason to want to stop your new employee or user accessing your control panel, simply come back here and click on the cross.

4. In the **Profile** drop-down box, choose **Administrator**. This will give the new user full access. We will investigate when this is a good idea and when you might like to change this, if you would like to add our freelance writer next.

5. Click the **Save** button to create the new user account.

What just happened?

The new user can now log into the control panel and perform any task.

Profiles

Profiles and the next topic, *Permissions*, are very closely linked to users. A profile is like a position. You can create a profile and assign responsibilities and restrictions. The administrator profile created by default can do everything in the control panel. As we discussed previously, this might not be the ideal situation for you.

What we will do now is create a new profile called "customer service". In the next section on permissions, we will assign the appropriate permissions to this new profile. Allowing all users with the customer service profile to access everything they need to do their job but restricting their access to anything that is not part of their job, significantly reduces the possibility of accidents or, dare I say it, malicious actions, by a disgruntled employee or someone who gains access to their account.

Time for action – creating profiles

With a couple of clicks, we will now create a profile:

1. Click on the **Employees** tab, then **Profiles** sub-tab, and subsequently the **Add new** link.

2. Type **Customer Service** or whatever your first profile will be called.

3. Click on **Save** and read on about permissions.

What just happened?

Now we have created a user profile to which we can assign users.

But to make the profile meaningful and worthwhile, we will now assign appropriate permissions to it, which are explained in the next section.

Permissions

In the *Time for action* that follows, we will assign the permissions that might be appropriate to an employee with customer service and packing responsibilities. First we will take a look at the options in general for permissions.

Permissions and their levels

There are four types of permissions—**View**, **Add**, **Edit**, and **Delete**. PrestaShop controls access by allowing you to assign these types of permission to any of the tabs and the sub-tabs.

You can restrict members of a profile from viewing any tab(s) you like. So you might not want the customer service profile to change anything on the **Payment** tab. No problem, you can totally remove that tab for users of a profile. In the Guns4u freelance writer scenario, you would want to create users who can only access the **CMS** tab. You would do this by removing, or as we will see in a bit, not adding any permissions except for the **CMS** tab.

So to stop a profile from adding and removing products, you need to remove the **Add** and **Delete** permissions from the **Catalog** tab. They could then edit product descriptions but not add or remove products themselves.

The depth of information we have just discussed is almost certainly adequate for any new shop, even if you are an existing business owner and you intend to hand over the running of your PrestaShop to your staff. The key with permissions, profiles, and users is planning. Take time to consider your company structure, which users should have access to what, and create a profile for each. Then read on to configure permissions for those profiles.

Now since we have looked at the different permissions, you will easily be able to decide which are most appropriate for the different profiles you want to make for your shop.

Time for action – configuring permissions to profiles

Of course, the permissions and levels that I suggest in the *Time for action* are just my views. You will know best what is most appropriate for your business. Let's get on with it then:

1. Click on the **Employees** tab, then the **Permissions** tab, and select the **Customer Service** or whatever profile you are configuring from the drop-down box.

2. Take time to examine the tabs and their options. Notice that if you click a checkbox, you instantly get a message from PrestaShop saying it is configuring your permissions.

3. Try adding permissions from one of the tabs. For the freelance writer, I would just append the view functionality to the **Tools** tab and the **View**, **Add** and **Edit** functionality to the **CMS** tab. The reason we need to assign **View** to **Tools** is because otherwise the **CMS** tab will not be visible.

4. Go back to a user's sub-tab in **Employees**, edit the user, and assign the profile you have just amended to the user. Now log in as that user and see the changes taking effect.

5. Now log in again as the administrator and make the rest of the changes you decided upon. Here are my suggestions for a *typical* customer service profile, as can be clearly seen in the screenshot of the **Permissions** screen:

Search	☑	☐	☐	☐
Catalog	☐	☐	☐	☐
» Tracking	☐	☐	☐	☐
» Manufacturers	☐	☐	☐	☐
» Suppliers	☐	☐	☐	☐
» Attributes and groups	☐	☐	☐	☐
» Features	☐	☐	☐	☐
» Image mapping	☐	☐	☐	☐
» Tags	☐	☐	☐	☐
» Attachments	☐	☐	☐	☐
Customers	☑	☐	☐	☐
» Addresses	☑	☐	☐	☐
» Groups	☑	☐	☐	☐
» Carts	☑	☐	☐	☐
Orders	☑	☐	☐	☐
» Invoices	☑	☐	☐	☐
» Delivery slips	☑	☐	☐	☐
» Merchandise return	☑	☐	☐	☐
» Credit slips	☑	☐	☐	☐
» Customer messages	☑	☐	☐	☐
» Statuses	☑	☐	☐	☐
» Order Messages	☑	☐	☐	☐
Payment	☑	☐	☐	☐
» Currencies	☐	☐	☐	☐
» Taxes	☐	☐	☐	☐

» Vouchers	☑	☐	☐	☐
Shipping	☐	☐	☐	☐
» Carriers	☐	☐	☐	☐
» States	☐	☐	☐	☐
» Countries	☐	☐	☐	☐
» Zones	☐	☐	☐	☐
» Price ranges	☐	☐	☐	☐
» Weight ranges	☐	☐	☐	☐
Stats	☐	☐	☐	☐
» Modules	☐	☐	☐	☐
» Settings	☐	☐	☐	☐
» Search engines	☐	☐	☐	☐
» Referrers	☐	☐	☐	☐
Modules	☐	☐	☐	☐
» Positions	☐	☐	☐	☐
Employees	☐	☐	☐	☐
» Profiles	☐	☐	☐	☐
» Permissions	☐	☐	☐	☐
» Contacts	☐	☐	☐	☐
Preferences	☐	☐	☐	☐
» Contact	☐	☐	☐	☐
» Appearance	☐	☐	☐	☐
» Meta-Tags	☐	☐	☐	☐
» Products	☐	☐	☐	☐
» Email	☐	☐	☐	☐

What just happened?

You have now created your first profile. It should be simple to create as many profiles as you like. Don't forget to assign your users to their appropriate profile as well.

Pop quiz – security

1. Can you think of a good reason why you assign permissions to profiles and then profiles to users, instead of assigning permissions directly to users?

2. Taking into account the different types of attack and other things that can go wrong, what do users, profiles, and permissions protect against?

3. How can we protect users' logins from being sniffed out by people listening for information?

SSL—Secure Sockets Layer

SSL is a cool system or, in tech speak, a protocol for allowing encrypted communication over the Internet. The need for this is obvious when you think about the type of information that must be given and received in even the simplest transaction. A customer's personal details and credit card details are the most obvious of these types of information.

By encrypting (making incomprehensible to all but the intended recipient), you can take your customers' money and personal details without worrying that their private details are intercepted by a third party.

Regular encryption relies on the sharing of a decrypting key. A decrypting key, simply speaking, is a mathematical formula for making the incomprehensible comprehensible again. SSL uses a method known as public key cryptography that allows a website, such as yours, to give an encryption key to your customer's web browser, which encrypts the confidential information before sending it. The SSL web server then has a private key known only to itself, which can descramble the information and retrieve your customers' confidential information.

Shared SSL, dedicated SSL, or no SSL

Shared SSL is usually free. Dedicated SSL, on the other hand, will certainly cost you a few pounds per month.

Almost any web server could be configured to be an SSL server. In most hosting environments, you would be offered a shared SSL server for free. This is where you have your communications rerouted through an SSL-enabled server. The problem is that the SSL server has a different address from the server your website is actually hosted on. PrestaShop is not designed to easily use a shared SSL server.

If, however, you must have SSL and absolutely do not want to get your wallet out to pay for a dedicated SSL certificate, then have a read of this article in the PrestaShop forums: `http://www.prestashop.com/forums/viewthread/19232/`.

Be warned that it is a bit on the technical side and involves editing the PHP code that makes PrestaShop tick. Yuck!

Do not despair! If you want or need SSL without the technical hassles, then you will need to contact your web host and arrange to buy a dedicated SSL certificate for your website. You shouldn't need to do anything technical. Just pay, wait for it to be set up, and then follow the easy tutorial explained next. PrestaShop will then use `https://` instead of `http://` before any relevant page on your website and your customers will be protected.

So SSL sounds like a good idea. But it is not an absolute must. If you are using PayPal to take payments, then all your customers' financial details are dealt with on the PayPal website anyway. And they use their own SSL server as you would expect. Just consider that the name and address of your customers will be entered on your website. Is this a security problem? Will your customers object to their names and addresses being retrieved unencrypted? Only you can decide.

Another potential drawback of not using SSL is that your login to the control panel will be left unencrypted. Do you use wireless Internet? Perhaps in a busy location with lots of other wireless users, it is possible for somebody to obtain your username and password. Then they can do whatever they like with them.

The other consideration with SSL is that more and more customers look for the `https://` when going through checkout. And most web browsers display a nice graphical padlock and maybe some other reassuring embellishments like green address bars. So even if in your opinion you don't *need* SSL, it might be worthwhile even if it is just for show.

So decide whether you want shared or dedicated SSL, or none at all. Read the next tutorial after setting up SSL with your web host if you are going to use it.

Setting up SSL in PrestaShop

This is so easy. Many shopping carts require editing of the PHP code in multiple files, even for dedicated SSL. Again, well done PrestaShop! Perhaps you can make shared SSL easy as well in a future revision.

Time for action – setting up SSL in PrestaShop

Let's do it.

1. Click on the **Preferences** tab.

2. For the fourth item in the list of options (**Enable SSL**), select **Yes**.

3. Scroll to the bottom of the page and click on **Save**.

4. Now go to your shop front, and click on **Log in** on your account or similar and notice the **https://** at the front of the web address in your browser.

What just happened?

Your customers' vital details are now encrypted by SSL. If you are going to use PayPal as your payment provider, then the customers' financial details are kept secure by PayPal, even if you opted not to use SSL on your website.

Making a copy of your store

We have taken a number of steps to protect our PrestaShop, but what if it all goes wrong anyway? It is still possible, although much less likely, that you will get hacked. It is also possible that we might accidentally spoil our own PrestaShop. If you promise not to tell anyone else, I will give you an example of a self-inflicted disaster I had.

While working on this chapter, I was playing with the **Permissions** features. I deleted a few tabs and then with a single inadvertent click I deleted the **Employees** tab! The permissions page went blank and there was no way to restore all the tabs that I had deleted. I can't put in print what I said when I realized my mistake.

But I had a copy and the page was up and running again in 10 minutes.

A lesson to be taken from this incident is to create a new profile and user for you. Call it *Junior admin*, and then if you do something dumb like I did, you can log in as the administrator and put it right.

So our objective for this section is to create an offline, untouchable, and easily usable backup. Then, no matter what happens, you will be able to get your business up and running in around 10 minutes. And, no matter how talented and resourceful a hacker might be, I guarantee that he or she won't be able to get remote access to a CD stored in your locked cupboard!

Introducing the backup process

Two main areas will be covered in these step-by-step tutorials. Coming up next, we will back up the PrestaShop database. The database is separate to the files in your web space on your web host. It holds information that is accessed by the code contained in the PrestaShop files.

The second part of the backup process is obtaining a full copy of the PrestaShop files. This is nice and simple, but we will still do it step by step to make 100 percent certain that we are never left with a problem that can't be fixed.

Frequency

So how often should you make a backup? It all depends on the frequency of change to your store. Let's say you get ten purchasing customers a day. If you backup every week but suddenly get hacked just before you do a backup, you would lose the details of 70 customers and their orders. In most businesses, this would be quite a dire situation.

Now when you first open your PrestaShop, you might not get an order for some weeks. So does this mean an infrequent backup would be okay? Maybe yes. But when your PrestaShop is new, you are probably making more regular configuration changes. Some or all of those could be lost if you hadn't run a recent backup.

Only you can answer the question of how often to do a complete backup. What is sensible will depend upon the frequency of change to your PrestaShop files and database. I will show you how to take backup that is fast and trouble free, although there isn't really any reason not to do it daily. Obviously though, it is up to you.

Backing up your database

PrestaShop has a handy database backup utility. This makes backing up your store a breeze. Here is how to do it.

Time for action – backing up your database

Log into your PrestaShop control panel and read on.

1. Click on **Tools** and then on the **DB Backup** sub-tab.

2. Now click on **Create new back-up**. Wow, that was quick! We are almost done.

3. Now click on the link that says **You can now download the backup file** and save the file to your hard disk. If your files on your web host are destroyed, your PrestaShop database takes the backup, and unless you have downloaded them, these are destroyed with them. Always download each backup file after creation.

4. Click on **Back to list** and you will notice that PrestaShop keeps a nicely ordered list of the database backups you have made. Just be aware that PrestaShop doesn't keep a record of whether you have actually downloaded the backup file. So the previous step is really crucial.

What just happened?

You now have a backup of your PrestaShop database. It shouldn't have taken more than a minute. We will look at how to use your database backup soon.

Backing up your files

You probably already know how to do this, but as it is so crucial, we will go through it step by step.

Time for action – backing up your files

We are going to use FTP, so have your web host's FTP username and password handy and then read on.

1. Open an FTP window on your web space containing the PrestaShop files.

2. Open a second Explorer window in a folder where you want to keep your backup files. You can use a dedicated FTP application as mentioned before.

3. Highlight all the files on the web server and drag them to the **Backup** folder. It might take some time for the download to finish, but obviously you don't need to be there to watch it.

4. Sometimes the download fails. It is very difficult to ascertain exactly where to resume the download, and the safest policy when this happens is to start the whole download again. If the download fails on a regular basis, just get into the habit of copying the folders one at a time. This does demand much more of your attention, but you can easily be doing something else in between folders.

5. To be absolutely sure your backup is safe, copy it to a CD or DVD.

What just happened?

You now have a complete usable backup. With the one caveat of your FTP download probably failing, there is only a very tiny demand on your time even if you do this daily.

Now let's look at how to use your backup in the event of disaster.

Using your copy

Using your backup is not too tricky, and because of the importance of the topic, we will go through it a step at a time.

Restoring the database

To do this, we will need to get a little bit more technical than when we took a backup of your database. We need to use a database tool provided by our web hosts. It is called **PHPMyAdmin**.

Many web hosts provide access to databases hosted with them through PHPMyAdmin, but in the unlikely event that yours doesn't, then contact them and ask for the equivalent. It should then be fairly simple to interpret the following instructions.

As every web host is different, I will mention potential shortcuts and some potential problems (with solutions) that are web host-dependent. What is fairly sure is that at some point you will need access to a web-based program provided by your web hosts, called PHPMyAdmin. Hence we will look at that first.

Time for action – how to restore the database

Log into your web host's control panel. Find PHPMyAdmin. In all of the hosts I use, it is accessed by viewing the list of databases and then clicking on **Edit** or **Manage with PHPMyAdmin**. Then a screen very similar to the next screenshot is shown by clicking on the **Edit** link relative to the PrestaShop database. All the functions that we carry out in this tutorial will be performed on that specific database.

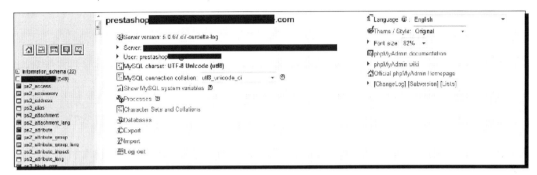

When you have located PHPMyAdmin or your web host's equivalent, read on.

1. Open a new browser window or tab. In your web host's control panel delete the database.

2. Recreate the database using the same name, username, and password. A potential problem here is that some web hosts do not let you choose the name of a database. Don't panic, just create a new database and proceed with whatever name they give you. An extra step that I point out near the end of this tutorial should solve the problem.

3. Extract the compressed database backup on your hard disk so that you are left with a file named `something.sql`.

4. Go to your PHPMyAdmin and click on **Databases**, and you will see the screen change to display a row of tabs across the top. They look like the ones in the following screenshot:

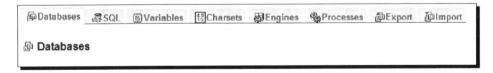

5. Click on the **Import** tab. Browse to your extracted database backup and select the file. You will also need to click on the **Go** button on the PHPMyAdmin page. A few seconds later your database is restored.

6. If you created a database with the same username and password, you can skip the rest of this tutorial. If not, you have a bit more to do.

7. In your backup files, you need to open a file from the `config` folder using Windows Notepad. The file is named `settings.inc.php`.

8. There you will see a list of database configuration parameters. Simply copy and paste your new database name and server address to overwrite the old ones. Save the file and read on.

What just happened?

You now have a perfectly restored database.

Restoring the files

This is much simpler and quicker than restoring the database. Very simply we need to replace all the files on the web server with the files from our backup.

Time for action – how to restore your files

1. Open an FTP connection to your web server.

2. Delete all the PrestaShop files on your web server.

3. Upload all the backup files. Be sure to upload in the exact same structure as they existed previously. For example, if you stored the backup files in a folder, don't upload the folder they were stored in as well.

4. As with backing up your files, if you get errors when dragging all the files and folders at once, retry doing the process a folder or two at a time. Don't forget the "loose" files that reside in the main directory and not in any of the PrestaShop folders.

5. Visit your shop front and the PrestaShop control panel to see if they are working.

6. Breathe a sigh of relief.

What just happened?

You have just deployed a backup of your store.

Assessing what went wrong

The first thing to do is check if you have the latest version of PrestaShop. Upgrading is covered in a minute. Other than that, the causes of a hack attack can be difficult to assess. Take a look at the upcoming *Have a go hero* to learn and think about some extra precautions to prevent a reoccurrence.

Have a go hero – securing your newly restored shop

So what if the security problem arose because the hacker had your database username, address, or your admin password? How can you stop exactly the same thing happening tomorrow?

Answer:

1. Create a new database with a different, name, username, and password through your web host's control panel.

2. Import the backup file to the new database just as you did for the original. Then in your PrestaShop control panel click on the **Preferences** tab then the **Databases** sub-tab.

3. Now enter the details of your new database. Be sure to get it exactly the same. Click on **Save**. Your hacker must start again discovering your database details.

4. Now click on the **Employees** tab and then the **Edit** icon and type a new password. Click on **Save**.

5. If the hacker used your password, he now needs to start again.

Upgrading PrestaShop

PrestaShop from time to time will add new features and enhancements. Of course, it is great to be able to add these improvements to your shop. The main reason to keep up-to-date at all times is because the updates include security fixes, that is, changes to PrestaShop that make it less likely and harder for a malicious person to mess up your hard work or compromise your customer's security.

Time for action – how to upgrade PrestaShop

Keeping PrestaShop up-to-date will keep us secure against all the known threats.
So let's do it.

1. Make sure you have a full backup of your store, files, and database in case this goes horribly wrong. And it can.

2. Log into your PrestaShop control panel. If there is an update available, it will be shown near the top of your admin login page. If not, you could revisit this tutorial when there is.

3. Click on the **Download** link and save the upgrade. Yours will probably have a different version number to the one in the screenshot.

4. Extract the download and you will be left with a `prestashop` folder full of subfolders and files.

5. Rename your main `prestashop` folder and leave it on your website. Call it `prestashop_old`. We do this so that in a few steps time we can easily copy back some files to the new folder. You can perform this step in your web host's control panel or by opening an FTP window, right-clicking, and selecting **Rename**, and then renaming it to `prestashop_old`.

6. Now recreate an empty folder with the same name as your original `prestashop` folder (the one you just renamed).

7. Upload all the files and folders within the `upgrade` folder to your folder where PrestaShop was originally. You now have the latest versions of the PrestaShop files on your server. But what about all your configurations?

8. Copy the /img directory from your old folder to the folder with the upgraded files.

9. Copy the /modules directory from your old folder to the folder with the upgraded files.

10. If you have installed any new themes, copy the /themes/newtheme directory from your old folder to the folder with the upgraded files.

11. Compare the contents of the old and new .htaccess files in the main directory. Add any parts in the old file, which are not present in the new file, to the new file. Don't simply copy it across because the upgrade might include some amendments. Simply copying across would remove these changes.

12. Copy your sitemap.xml file from the old files to the new.

13. Copy the file config/settings.inc.php from the old folder to the new.

14. Run the installer and do things just as before but select **update** on the first page. PrestaShop knows you are updating by the presence of the settings.inc.php file. When you're ready, type www.yourshop.com/install.

15. On the next page of the updater, you will see this warning. If you followed this guide, you have already done so. Click on the **I certify** button followed by the **Next** button.

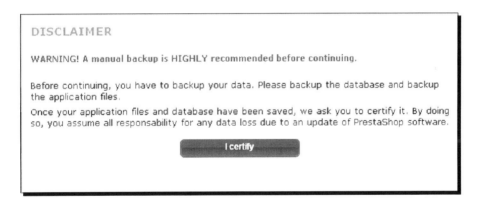

16. When you're done, just as before, delete the install folder and rename the admin folder.

What just happened?

You now have the latest version of PrestaShop up and running.

Okay, I admit it. That wasn't pretty. Upgrading PrestaShop is a little bit of a chore. It is one of the few areas where other shopping carts do a little better. But it's not so bad either. Half an hour's work every couple of months to get the latest features and security fixes shouldn't really be a huge problem.

Have a look at this quick challenge to do with upgrading PrestaShop.

Have a go hero – keeping your store live while upgrading

While all the various processes are going on, during an upgrade, your shop is offline. When brand new, this is probably not a problem. But what about in a year or two when you are serving hundreds of customers at a time? Being offline is obviously unacceptable!

How would you perform the upgrade without affecting your stores availability? (A clue is that it involves temporarily having two sets of working files using the same database.)

The answer is, simply perform the upgrade in a new folder, perhaps call it `prestashop_new`. Now you can copy across your settings as before but this time from a live folder. When you run the installer, don't forget to type `www.yourshop.com/prestashop_new/install`. When you have finished, rename the original folder to `prestashop_old` and rename `prestashop_new` to the name of your original PrestaShop folder, pointed to by your domain name.

This chapter in a nutshell

There are lots you can do to protect your PrestaShop. But there is always a way that a determined attacker can find a flaw with your security. Do everything you can; in fact, I suggest you seek further reading on general web security. A good starting point is an excellent article I found via the PrestaShop forums. Here it is:

`http://www.smashingmagazine.com/2010/01/14/web-security-primer-are-you-part-of-the-problem/`

But remember you are never totally secure. Always have a very recent backup ready to use.

Summary

We learned a lot in this chapter about malicious attacks, user-caused problems, how to avoid them, and how to recover when all else fails.

Specifically, we covered the following topics:

- The most common types of malicious attacks and some problems that can be caused by legitimate users
- User security using groups and permissions
- SSL for our customers and our own privacy
- Keeping PrestaShop up-to-date and safe from known attacks by upgrading our PrestaShop to the latest version
- Creating and using a backup

Now that we have this essential information under our belts, it is time to look at how we actually get money from our customers and the different ways this can be achieved with PrestaShop payment modules.

7
Checkouts and Shipping

Here we will configure and set up anything and everything to do with taking money. This will include the actual mechanism for getting customers' money from their account to yours as well as a number of important related topics.

In this chapter, we shall:

- Choose and set up a payment provider
- Look at alternative payment methods
- Take a look at sales taxes
- Discuss and implement gift vouchers
- Learn how to accept foreign currencies
- Look at the multitude of different ways to set up shipping options for your customers to choose from and make sure they get charged correctly.

Here we go then...

Introduction

There are a number of interrelated issues with regard to payment handling, some of which are not obviously apparent. This is one of those times when I recommend reading about payment providers and the different installation processes and currencies, perhaps the whole chapter before actually signing up to anything or installing any modules.

Which payment provider should I use?

This is an interesting question. The two big players that we will cover specifically are Google Checkout and PayPal. There are a few comparisons between them that should help you choose the best option for you. First, a few words about merchant accounts.

Merchant accounts

A merchant account is where you use a company, sometimes called a "gateway", to handle the actual transaction, but the customer's payment is deposited directly into your account. This sounds great and in some ways it is, but it's not all good news. Another advantage is that you are probably less prone to being defrauded by a customer. This is because regular credit card chargeback rules apply. Although they are there to protect the consumer and not you, they are not as easily abused as they are through Google Checkout and especially PayPal.

The big downside with having your own merchant account is cost. Rates vary and many gateways and banks have low introductory offers, which make it difficult to accurately calculate the real ongoing cost, but here is a typical example of costs after special offer periods for a typical UK business. You would need to pay the monthly charges and transaction charges of a business bank account, the monthly charges and setup charges required by the bank for the merchant account, and the monthly and transaction charges of the gateway company. A quick calculation using a main UK bank and a well-known company as the gateway came to over a hundred UK pounds per month and several hundred setting them up.

The other downside is that the technical requirements—how they interact with PrestaShop—of the various gateways are different and there is not always a handy module to do the job. So programming knowledge or getting your wallet out is often required.

So why would anyone use a merchant account? I already mentioned the payments direct to your account, but the percentage charge per transaction is also usually significantly low. But, of course, you have to consider the monthly costs before you have even taken a single payment. This means merchant accounts don't usually add up for a new business.

If you are expecting a very high turnover very quickly and you want the slightly more retailer-friendly chargeback conditions, then get your wallet out and get a merchant account. If not, then read on about Google Checkout and PayPal.

PayPal or Google Checkout

Both companies allow you to sign up and get trading with a few clicks and without cost. Both companies have a PrestaShop module, which makes setting up your checkout almost as easy as adding any other module. There are some differences that will probably sway you in one direction or the other.

SSL requirements

To use Google Checkout, you must use SSL. Google will not handle payments and communicate with PrestaShop without it. Shared SSL is fine, but that (as we spoke about in *Chapter 6*) does involve some technical jiggery pokery. So a small monthly investment to buy a dedicated SSL Certificate might be necessary. PayPal does not require you to have an SSL certificate.

Cost

At time of writing, Google Checkout was slightly cheaper. Both the per-transaction costs and the percentage of sale value charge are slightly lower. So your handling costs with Google Checkout are lower.

Getting your money

Google Checkout can pay you monthly or daily, you choose. This might sound quite good because you obviously want your money as quickly as possible. What I found was that monthly was a bit too infrequent and daily was awkward for accounting purposes. Leaving my customers' money for a whole month was awkward for maintaining cash flow and daily squirts of varying amounts of money was a major pain.

PayPal allows you to decide when to withdraw your money. So you can wait to the end of the month if you are not selling much because you are just getting started or do it weekly or more frequently, whichever is best for you. PayPal does charge for withdrawals under £50, and, as you might expect, it takes a few days from request to receive your funds.

Flexibility

Google Checkout and PayPal can take payments from almost anywhere in the world. However, Google Checkout can only take the payment in your country's native currency. This means that a customer from the US could buy something from a store in France but would have to pay in Euros.

PayPal can take payment in most major currencies, which can make your customer feel more comfortable about a purchase and will perhaps be more likely to complete it. You can specifically configure PayPal to accept other currencies or just tell PrestaShop to accept them (more on this later), and when a transaction is made in a new currency, PayPal will confirm with you whether to take it or not.

Chargebacks

Google Checkout and PayPal offer protection to your customers. The precise terms and conditions are a bit of a minefield and I am not qualified to go into it in depth, but I can give you some feedback based on experience.

Google Checkout has a chargeback process that could be considered comparable to that of the major banks. PayPal, on the other hand, is significantly biased towards your customer. If a customer contacts PayPal and claims non-delivery, PayPal will immediately freeze your funds. They will not discuss it first. If a customer complains to PayPal that goods are significantly not as described, they will do the same.

It will then be up to you to prove otherwise. You will enter into an electronic arbitration system on the PayPal website. And PayPal will decide the outcome. They will not discuss it with you. There will be no human contact and their decision is final. The frozen funds could be permanently removed from your account.

Go and have a look at www.paypalwarning.com and you'll see thousands of horror stories.

In a nutshell, you need to consider the needs of your business. If you sell the type of products that are not repeat purchase, are low margin, and prone to fraud, then seriously consider Google Checkout. By prone to fraud I mean the sort of goods that are easily resold for cash. Consumer electronics are a good example.

However, if you have a high-margin product where you are building a base of loyal repeat-purchase customers, then the convenience and ease of PayPal could still be right for you. And of course, PayPal's bias towards the consumer is quite well-known. This could mean that the fact consumers feel protected means they are more likely to shop with you and most of them, of course, are honest.

Friendliness

If you get any technical issues with Google Checkout, you have to discuss it via e-mail. With PayPal, perhaps surprisingly, you can get telephone technical support.

However, don't expect PayPal or Google to discuss a dispute with you. They will act in whatever way is best for them and that will be the end of the matter.

Conclusion

If you are wondering which I use, the answer is both (see *Chapter 9*). So there is no best payment handler, but there will be a payment handler that suits you best.

Decide from the pros and cons what is best for you and read on...

Have a go hero – turning a negative into a positive

Please don't let this section put you off PayPal and Google Checkout altogether. After years of trading and having set up around a dozen shops, I still haven't moved on to a merchant account. PayPal and Google Checkout are too convenient. Just take steps to protect yourself.

Q) If you have a customer who gets a chargeback claiming non-delivery what can you do?

A) Always get a proof of posting. If an order is not cost-effective to track, get a proof of posting. You can often claim from the delivery service. The very fact you have documentation of a dispute on PayPal is evidence that a parcel never arrived.

You can often claim up to an agreed maximum per package for the lost mail. And here is the good bit: you can often claim the retail price. So if you resupply the product to your customer and avoid a refund, you actually make more money than if the package had got there without getting lost!

Also, by making a claim, the postal service will often investigate. If there is a person making regular fraudulent claims, you will add evidence to the case against them. I have received feedback twice in the last few years where legal action has been taken. Once action was taken against a defrauding "customer" and once action was taken against an employee of the delivery service.

Check the specific details of your delivery service. If you don't like it, look for a new one. If you can't afford to lose the package, then you need to pay for tracking. If the margin is too small to pay for tracking, reconsider your prices or product range.

Using PayPal

What follows is a really brief discussion and tutorial to get your PrestaShop connected to PayPal so that you can start taking payments. It is brief because that is all that is necessary.

PayPal account

Visit www.paypal.com and you will be redirected to the PayPal site that is appropriate for your country or region. Sign up for an account if you don't already have one and make sure to choose the premier account. PayPal will want to verify your credentials with a few procedures that might take a few days. So sign up as soon as possible in order to keep in the running for passing my 7-day challenge.

Setting up your PayPal checkout

Once you have a Premier PayPal account, you need to configure PrestaShop and your PayPal account to talk to each other.

Time for action – installing the PayPal module

Here is how to do it:

1. In your PrestaShop control panel, click on the **Payment** tab and then install the **PayPal payment** module. Notice there is also a module called **PayPalAPI**. This is NOT the one we need here.

2. Now click on **Configure** next to the PayPal module you just installed. Here is a screenshot of what you will see:

3. PayPal business e-mail simply refers to the e-mail address used on your PayPal account. So put that in there.

4. Select **No** for **Sandbox mode**. We want to do this for real.

5. The next option needs a short explanation. **Banner image URL** refers to the address on your web server of an image that represents your company. If you put one in, then PayPal will put your company logo at the top of each page when your customers are proceeding through the PayPal checkout process. Nice touch but not essential. As mentioned previously, consumers feel safe on PayPal and leaving this option blank will not do you any harm. If, however, you do want to use this feature, be sure to use an SSL address. This is because the PayPal pages are SSL secure, and if you link to an image that is not SSL secure, the user's browser will give a security warning. This could put off the whole transaction. If you purchased a dedicated SSL certificate, the banner URL for your default banner you uploaded in *Chapter 2* will be: https://yourdomain.com/img/logo.jpg.

6. Now let's configure your PayPal account. Log into it and click on the **Profile** tab. From the list of options click on **Notifications**. Scroll down and put a tick, if there is not one already in the three boxes pictured in the following screenshot:

Payment Notifications	Email
I receive money with PayPal	☑
I request money with PayPal	☑
I receive PayPal Website Payments and Instant Purchase	☑

7. Go back to the main profile page by clicking on the **Profile** tab again. Under the **Selling preferences** column, click on **Website Payment Preferences**. Make sure **Auto Return** and **Payment Data Transfer** are set to **Off**. These settings are turned off because PrestaShop communicates directly with PayPal to configure these options. Do not be concerned if you think these settings should be on.

What just happened?

You told PrestaShop to use PayPal. You then gave it the payment e-mail required by PayPal. You optionally customized the PayPal payment pages with your store logo and then we clicked a few boxes on the PayPal website to make sure all is well. PrestaShop does the rest for you. How nice!

Using Google Checkout

Here is how to do it. A little bit more to it than with PayPal but not much. The slightly lower fees should make the tiny bit of extra work worthwhile. Make sure you have SSL set up on your store before continuing.

Google Checkout account

Go to the Google site for your country or region. Click on **Business solutions** and then **Checkout** and sign up for a Google Checkout account if you do not already have one.

Installing the checkout

Have your Google Checkout account open in a tab on your browser and your PrestaShop control panel in another. We will be clicking back and forth between the two.

Time for action – how to set up Google Checkout payments

The first thing to mention is that Google offers a "sandbox mode". This is where you can connect to Google Checkout and try everything out but in a mode where no actual financial transactions take place. This is quite handy. As our objective is to get up and running quickly, we will talk about setting up the real mode. If you want to use the sandbox mode first, the instructions are identical. You would just enter the details of your sandbox account instead of your real account. You can get a free sandbox account from `https://sandbox.google.com/checkout`.

There is nothing particularly technical here, but there are a number of steps that need to be done just right. So let's do this.

1. Click on the **Payment** tab. Install the Google Checkout module. Scroll back to it and click on **Configure**.

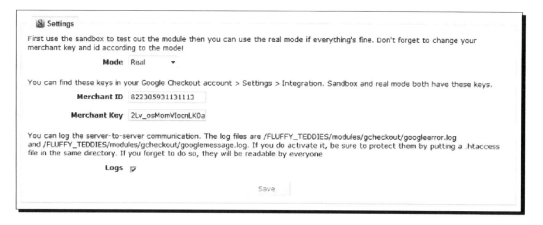

2. Set the **Mode** to **Real**.

3. On your Google Checkout account home page, and in the top right-hand corner is your **Merchant ID**. Copy and paste this into the **Merchant ID** box.

4. On your Google Checkout account, click on the **Settings** tab. Then, from the list on the left, click on **Integration**. On the right-hand side, you will see your Merchant Key. Copy and paste this into the **Merchant Key** box on the PrestaShop Google Checkout module configuration page.

5. Disable logging by removing the tick in the **Logs** checkbox. Logging is beyond the scope of this book, and without additional action, it might present a security issue.

6. In the information box, at the bottom of the PrestaShop Google Checkout module configuration page, there is a URL in bold. This is your API callback URL. This is where Google Checkout communicates with your PrestaShop to talk about orders and payments. Copy this URL in full, including the HTTPS right to the end.

7. In your Google Checkout account, on the **Integration** page we were on a few steps ago, paste the URL into the box labeled **API callback URL**.

8. Just below this box, check the option **Notification as XML**. This denotes the protocol that PrestaShop and Google Checkout will use to communicate.

9. Save the settings in your Google Checkout account and your PrestaShop Google Checkout module configuration page.

What just happened?

Google Checkout and PrestaShop will now talk to each other. When a customer wants to place an order, PrestaShop will hand the last part of the process to Google Checkout who will take the money. Google Checkout will update your **Customers** and **Orders** tabs with the order details and all relevant information about the transaction.

While you are logged into Google Checkout, you might like to click on the **Financials** link on the left. Check whether your bank account details are correct and choose the frequency of payments from Google Checkout to your bank account.

Other payment methods

All these other payment methods rely on you, your customers, or both taking action. All PrestaShop does is offer a little guidance. For example, with Bankwire, PrestaShop cannot tell you that the payment has been made. And it cannot tell you if a cheque has been cleared. All this must be done manually.

I include a brief description of the next three payment methods mainly to highlight the availability. If one or more of these methods suit your business, then great, use them. But consider the business principles discussed at the end of *Chapter 8* before making any of these methods a cornerstone of your business. I only usually use such methods as a favor to a customer who requests it.

Cheque

From experience, this is probably the most common form of payment after a conventional online payment. There are a number of reasons a customer might want to pay by cheque. As an example, there are still millions of people who love the idea of the Internet to browse and research but wouldn't use their credit card online unless they could travel up the telephone wire with it to keep it safe.

Cheque is a good solution. Enable the cheque module in the usual place, click on **Configure**, and you can specify who to make cheques payable to and where to send them. PrestaShop will communicate this information to customers wanting to use cheque as payment.

Most of my cheque orders are from customers a bit like I have described above. I have also received orders from companies where they like to be invoiced and then pay by cheque. This is a bit of a manual thing to handle but has brought the biggest, most profitable, orders that any of my shops have had. It can be well worth it. You decide what is best for your business. Remember you can change your mind with the click of a button.

Cash on delivery

The cash on delivery module doesn't really do anything other than make the option available during checkout. You would obviously need to use a carrier that can handle cash on delivery. There are lots of potential offline security problems here but worth considering for special cases like if you are going to sell pizzas.

Bank wire

This is where the customer makes a payment directly from their account to yours.

Click on the **Payment** tab and then install the **Bank Wire** module. Notice that a fairly non-specific description of what is required is provided. This is because banks in different countries require different types of information to receive payments. And some banks within the same country sometimes have different requirements.

Contact your bank and find out what is required for somebody to send a payment directly to your bank account. Don't be fooled into thinking an account number and branch number (sort code) are sufficient. Very often you will need to provide BIC, Swift, or IBAN numbers as well.

And don't forget to check whether the payment has arrived before sending the order. You see how this payment method could quickly become awkward or confusing to operate. I suggest using it in special cases. Perhaps you could use this method for a really good customer who insists upon this type of payment, for a really good order, or as an occasional favor to someone who requests it.

Sales taxes

Depending upon the country, state, or region you operate from and your type and volume of business, you will have different taxes. Also, different products have varying tax rates and exclusions as well. I hope you think it is reasonable for me to shrug responsibility for explaining what your tax rate(s) is.

PrestaShop have made it really easy to apply the appropriate tax rate regardless of what it is, if you have to apply tax at all. Find out your appropriate rate and look at this quick tutorial to set the rate in your PrestaShop.

Time for action – setting up PrestaShop to handle sales tax

Here we go.

1. Click on the **Payment** tab and then the **Taxes** sub-tab.

2. Click on **Add new**; enter the name and rate of tax.

3. Click on the boxes where the tax applies and **Save** your new tax.

4. Take a look at the screenshot below:

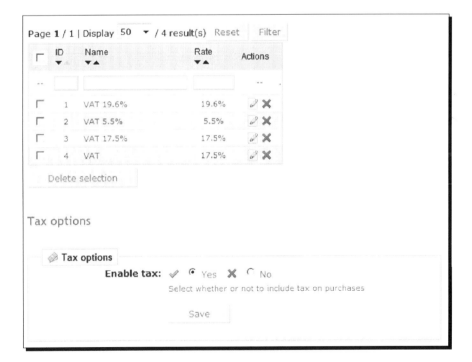

5. Click on the red cross to delete any taxes that are not appropriate to you.

6. Finally, make sure the **Enable tax** box is ticked. Click on **Save**.

What just happened?

It is really important to get this right. It is hard to run a business from jail. But that doesn't necessarily mean you have to get your wallet out. Most tax authorities offer free advice over the phone and face-to-face. Look them up and give them a call.

Now we can go on to explore currencies.

Currencies

Do you want to encourage customers from other countries to shop in your store? You could produce a foreign language version of your website. This was covered in *Chapter 4*. A really quick and easy way to encourage purchases from countries other than your own is to offer your products in foreign currencies.

There are three quick stages in doing this. First, we will add the currencies you want to use.

Adding a currency

If you want to use Euros, US dollars, or GB pounds, then PrestaShop is already set up to do this. You can skip this tutorial and read about setting currency rates.

If the currency you want to use is not one of these, then read on.

Time for action – adding a currency

Here is how to add a new currency to your PrestaShop:

1. Click on the **Payment** tab and then on **Currencies**.

2. Now click the **Add new** button. The following is what you will see:

✏ Currencies

Currency: [ ] *

Will appear on Front Office, e.g., euro, dollar...

ISO code: [ ] *

ISO code, e.g., USD for dollar, EUR for euro...

Symbol: [ ] *

Will appear on Front Office, e.g., €, $...

Conversion rate: [ ] *

Conversion rate from one unit of your shop's default currency (for example, 1€) to this currency. For example, if the default currency is euros and this currency is dollars, type '1.52' 1€ = $1.38

Formatting: X0,000.00 (as with dollars) ▾

Applies to all prices, e.g., $1,240.15

Decimals: ○ ✓ ◉ ✗

Display decimals on prices

Blank: ○ ✓ ◉ ✗

Include a blank between sign and price, e.g.,
$1,240.15 -> $ 1,240.15

Save

* Required field

◈ Back to list

3. And this is how to fill out the boxes:

Property	What to put in the box
Currency	This is the actual name of your currency. Write here as the native user of the currency would expect to find it: British pounds, Euros, and so on.
ISO code	This is the internationally recognized code for currency. Dollars is USD, British pounds is GBP. To find out what yours is visit any major news site and check out the currency rates for the day. The ISO code will be quoted here.
Symbol	£, $, and so on.
Conversion rate	Leave this until the next tutorial.
Formatting	This is simple but important. When you present prices, do you want the symbol to appear before or after the price?
Decimals	For normal price formatting, click on the tick. You will have prices displayed like this $29.49. Or click on **No** if you wanted to remove the decimal places and have prices displayed like this: $49
Blank	Leave a space between the currency symbol and the amount? Or not.

4. Click on **Save** and read on.

What just happened?

You now have a new currency in your store.

Read on to find out about setting the conversion rate.

Setting currency rates

You can Google currency exchange rates or look them up on all the major news websites. Have the exchange rates for all the currencies you wish to accept to hand and read this quick tutorial.

Time for action – setting a currency rate

Here we go.

1. Click on **Payment** and then its sub-tab currencies. Quickly make sure the default currency is set correctly because all the rates we set will be used in the calculations against your default currency.

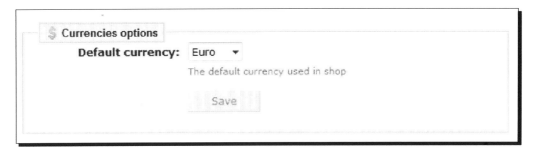

2. Click on **Edit** next to the currency you want to set the rate for. Note this is the same screen we saw when adding a currency. This time we will look at actually setting the currency exchange rate relative to your default currency. Here is an example. If your default currency is Dollars and you want to set the rate for Euros, go to www.google.com and type **usd to euros** in the search box. Google shows you an up-to-the-minute conversion rate.

3. Copy and paste the rate into the box labeled **Conversion rate** and click on **Save**.

What just happened?

Of course, the exchange rate is changing all the time. It is perfectly acceptable to set the rate a little higher and then just check it occasionally. We will look at auto-configuring the conversion rate next. This might or might not be for you.

Auto exchange rate updates

Down the very bottom of the currencies' page is a button to update currencies now. So why didn't I tell you about this 10 minutes ago, you might well ask.

Quite simply because:

- The likely possibility that you want to increase the conversion rate for some or all currencies is not auto-configurable
- If the ISO is wrong, it won't work
- It can be just plain wrong
- Sometimes it doesn't work at all

But with those points in mind, it can be a time-saving tool. Now you can do it always. I auto-update occasionally, then make a quick check on Google for approximate agreement and then, if required, go in and manually raise the rate a little.

Now we can go on to explore or discuss another key aspect of the topic.

Vouchers

Vouchers are good for lots of things. You can sometimes give them as a refund when the customer does not qualify for a money refund. You can keep the customer's goodwill and their money. You can distribute or advertise them to encourage sales. I like to offer them as an incentive to sign up for my newsletter.

There are no ends of imaginative ways you can use gift vouchers. So let's learn how to create and distribute them now. In the next chapter, we will use gift vouchers as part of a broader campaign to launch your store and beat my 7-day challenge of opening your store and getting your first sale within seven days.

Creating a voucher

First of all, we need to define the parameters of our voucher—when it can be used, who can use it, how much, and a bit more as well.

Time for action – creating a voucher

Follow this quick tutorial to create a voucher:

1. Click on the **Payment** tab and then on the **Vouchers** sub-tab. At the bottom of this page, make sure that the vouchers are enabled.

2. Now click on **Add new** and you will see the voucher creation screen. A screenshot followed by a table of what to put where follows:

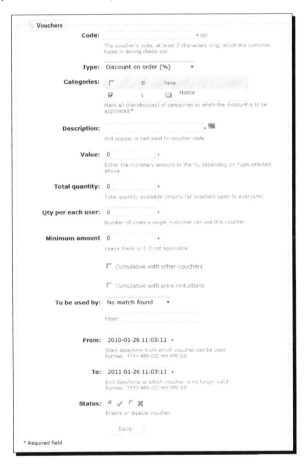

Voucher option	Explanation
Code	This is the code that must be entered at the checkout by the customer in order to get the discount.
	It is worth giving meaningful names to your vouchers so that you can track their usage and success using PrestaShop statistics features.
	But not too long because that makes it awkward for your customer to use.
	Perhaps JAN10% or AMMO5%. You get the idea.
Type	There are three types to choose from in the drop-down box.
	You can select a percentage of the sale, an actual cash amount, or give free shipping.
Categories	Tick all the product categories you want this voucher to apply to. If you have a category that has a particularly low profit margin, you might like to exclude it.
	On the other hand, you might want the voucher to apply to one category specifically. Such as the Guns4u Ammo category.
Description	A simple explanation of what the voucher is: "10 percent off on everything in January" or "5 percent of all ammo".
Value	This is referring to the type that you selected previously. So if you selected % of the sale, the number you put in here will be the percentage discount. If you chose an actual cash amount, then the number entered here will be the actual cash discount the customer receives.
Total Qty	You can enter a maximum number of transactions that can occur.
Quantity per each user	Do you want to restrict each individual customer to a maximum number of discounted transactions? Often you would want to reward people just once, perhaps for their first purchase or for signing up to a newsletter.
Minimum amount	Define the minimum order value this voucher can be used on or leave blank for no restriction. This might be particularly relevant for vouchers with a cash discount.
To be used by	The most common option here would be "all customers". If you define customer groups, perhaps wholesale and retail, you could define which group specifically the voucher is for.
From	A start date for your voucher.
To	The last date on which your voucher can be used.
Enable	Here you can turn the voucher on or off.

3. Click on the **Save** button and move on.

What just happened?

Now that you have a voucher, people can enter the voucher code during the checkout process and get the discount you specified. PrestaShop makes sure all your specifications, like valid dates and quantity per user, are adhered to. If you suddenly realize a mistake has been made, you can quickly disable the voucher.

But how does your customer know about the voucher?

Giving the vouchers to your customer

To give a voucher to a customer, all you have to do is give them the code. PrestaShop can then take care of the details based on the parameters you defined when creating the voucher. But distribution of vouchers goes a little bit deeper.

I like to create a structure of vouchers to encourage as many different customers to make as many purchases as possible. Consider running a number of voucher promotions simultaneously. I will give you an example of a voucher structure in a moment, but obviously you must consider what would work and be profitable to your business. Hopefully, my example will give you some ideas if not the precise format for a multi-voucher promotion.

- **5 percent off on everything**: A small percentage amount available to absolutely everyone on a one-off basis. Distribute this on relevant forums, social media, and your home page and on Google AdWords. There's more in the next chapter about these and other promotional ideas.

- **10 percent off on everything**: Consider a bigger, more significant, one-off discount for signing up to your newsletter. It is often okay to give away a bit more of your profit in return for constant contact with your customer. Remember the value of e-mail marketing when you do it right. You could get multiple sales without any discount if your customer signs up for and enjoys your newsletters.

- **Free Shipping when you spend**: Consider offering free shipping, perhaps permanently, in return for larger-than-average orders. Look at or estimate your customers' average spend per order. Then consider a value at which to offer free shipping that encourages customers to put an extra item or three in their basket. Remember to have lots of great add-on and accessory options. You can advertise this anywhere and everywhere.

- **10 percent off category X**: Always keep promoting something for customers who don't qualify or have already used other vouchers. A discount on a specific category will encourage customers to make additional purchases at the same time as non-discounted ones.

Whatever you decide is best for your shop—take your time to do the math. There is no point selling anything if you don't make what you need.

Shipping options

Shipping is a surprisingly wide and deep topic. When I opened my first e-commerce store, I was very surprised at the complexity involved in adding a shipping charge to an order. So here are a couple of ways you might be able to avoid any complexity-not to save us a few minutes or hours configuring your shipping options because if your specific business situation demands it, then that is what you obviously have to do. But if even we are baffled by the vast array of shipping configurations, then what will our customers think? Will it lose us some customers?

In the vast majority (but not all of my stores), I use one of the two following super-simple shipping configurations. If one of these work for you, then I recommend using it. If not, what follows from my super-simple shipping configurations are a summary of the PrestaShop shipping configuration options.

Super-simple shipping configuration options

Is it possible, with your product range specifically, to build the cost of shipping into the product? I have heard arguments against this because it can make the product look more expensive without close examination. My view is that customers are not stupid. As long as you make it plain and shout about the fact that shipping is included in all your prices, then customers will actually appreciate the upfront cost. It can even be a really great feature of your store. 90 percent of my stores are all products and free delivery on all products.

♦ To configure free shipping in PrestaShop, click on the **Shipping** tab and change all the figures you see in the following screenshot to zero and save it:

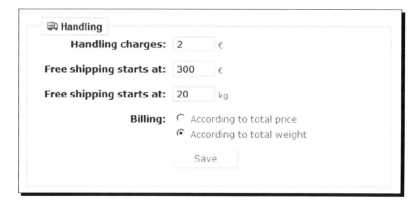

♦ Another option is to configure PrestaShop for free shipping as earlier, and then consider adding a flat postage rate for any product. This can be done through the same mechanism shown previously by changing the handling charges to whatever you want your flat fee to be and then changing **Free shipping starts at** to **0**. So if you don't want to load the shipping cost onto the product but want to keep things super simple, add a flat fee onto every purchase.

Common shipping scenarios

The PrestaShop shipping configuration options does a good job of removing some of the complexity of shipping configuration. However, necessarily it is still very in-depth and it could easily take up a couple of chapters on its own.

My objective here is to show you exactly how to configure a couple of common scenarios. So if you like, skip ahead and follow the tutorial that is most appropriate for you. If, on the other hand, you want a deep and full explanation before you decide, then read all the different options because, in the last section on configuring shipping, *Shipping configuration in depth*, I will give you some good ideas of how to do almost anything you like.

If you are looking to set up a shop that sells products of varied values and weights to different geographic locations and want to vary the shipping cost according to all of these factors, then read the three specific scenarios as an introduction and then study the *Shipping configuration in depth* section, including the Guns4u case study.

As promised, let's start with some relatively simple and common scenarios.

Shipping calculated by sale value

This method gives you the flexibility to define ranges of price. The ranges can be as narrow or as wide as you like. You can then, with a few clicks, assign a shipping price to each range. PrestaShop will then charge customers shipping according to the total value of their order.

Time for action – configuring shipping by sale value

This is how to do it:

1. Click on the **Shipping** tab. Put zero in the handling charge box unless of course you want a handling charge on top of the delivery charge. Clear the box labeled **Free shipping starts at** for the weight (**kg**) because we are not interested in weight at this stage. Finally, put a value you want free shipping to start at, if any, in the box labeled **Free shipping starts at** for the price (**€**).

2. Now we will define some price ranges. Click on the **Price ranges** sub-tab and then on **Add new**.

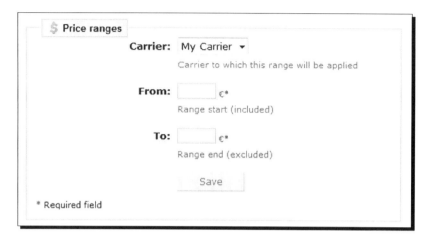

3. Type in the starting value of your first order value price range. Almost certainly the **From** price will be **0**. Enter the upper limit of the first range. So if you wanted to charge a specific amount of shipping for orders from 0.01 to 49.99, enter the value **50.00**. Click on **Save**.

4. Now click on **Add new** again. Enter the starting value of your range in the **From** box. This should be the same as the **To** value from the previous range. This is because the actual value you enter in the **From** field is inclusive, but the value you enter in the **To** field is not inclusive. So if you define the second range as **From: 50** and **To: 100** then the following will apply. All orders up to 49.99 will be in price range one and all orders from 50.00 up to 99.99 will be in price range two. Click on **Save** when you're done.

5. Define as many ranges as you need to. On the last range make the **To** figure higher than you expect an order to ever be. This way you will have defined a range for any potential order. If, in Step 1, you entered a value where free shipping starts, then your highest ranges **To** value should equal the value at which free shipping starts.

6. Now that we have created some ranges, we will now assign a shipping cost to each range.

7. Click on the **Shipping** tab and scroll to the bottom of the page. You can view a summary of the ranges you just made. In my following example, I used three ranges: **0€ to 50€**, **50€ to 100€**, and **100€ to 250€**.

8. Simply enter the delivery price of each order value range and click on **Save**.

9. Go and put a few things in your basket and see how it works.

What just happened?

You have now defined your shipping costs based on the value of the customer's order. You can define the ranges as widely or as narrowly as you like.

Configuring shipping by weight

This method gives you the flexibility to define ranges of weight. The ranges can be as narrow or as wide as you like. You can then, with a few clicks, assign a shipping price to each range of order weight. PrestaShop will then charge customers for shipping according to the total weight of their order.

Time for action – how to configure shipping by weight

The first thing to do is tell PrestaShop what each of your products weighs so that it can do the sums. So let's get on with it:

1. During the setup of your products, we discussed the weight property of the product configuration page. If you didn't define the weight then but have now decided to calculate shipping by weight, then click back into your products and configure the weight before continuing. Refer back to *Chapter 3* for details.

2. Click on the **Shipping** tab. Put zero in the handling charge box unless of course you want a handling charge on top of the delivery charge. Clear the box labeled **Free shipping starts at** for the price because we are not interested in order price in this tutorial. Finally, put a weight you want free shipping to start at, if any, in the box labeled **Free shipping starts at** for the weight.

3. Now we will define some weight ranges. Click on the **Weight ranges** sub-tab and then on **Add new**.

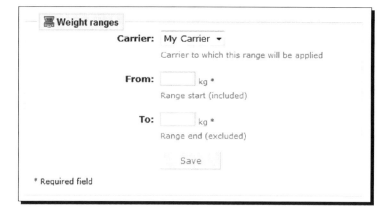

4. Type in the starting value of your first order weight range. Almost certainly the **From** weight will be **0**. Enter the upper limit of the first range. So if you wanted to charge a specific amount of shipping for orders from 0.01 kg to 4.99 kg, enter the value **5.00**. Click on **Save**.

5. Now click on **Add new** again. Enter the starting value of your range in the **From** box. This should be the same as the **To** value from the previous range. This is because the actual value you enter in the **From** field is inclusive but the value you enter in the **To** field is not inclusive. So if you define the second range as **From: 5** and **To: 10**, then the following will apply. All orders weighing up to 4.99 kg will be in price range one and all orders from 5.00 up to 9.99 will be in price range two. Click on **Save** when you're done.

6. Define as many ranges as you need to. On the last range, make the **To** figure higher than you expect an order to ever be. This way you will have defined a range for any potential order. However, if, in Step 1, you entered a value where free shipping starts, then your highest ranges **To** value should equal the value at which free shipping starts.

7. Now that we have created some ranges, we will assign a shipping cost to each range.

8. Click on the **Shipping** tab and scroll to the bottom of the page. Make sure that **According to total weight** is selected. You can then view a summary of the ranges you just made.

9. Simply enter the delivery price of each weight range and click on **Save**.

10. Go and put a few things in your basket and see how it works.

What just happened?

You have defined your shipping costs based on the weight of your customer's order.

Now we can go on to explore the PrestaShop shipping configuration options in more depth.

Shipping configuration in depth

Have a think about this scenario.

Guns4u is the web outlet for a major arms reseller. Guns4u has a very wide range of weapons, from small arms to inter-continental ordinance, with various warheads as well as state–of-the-art missile defense systems.

So the need for a more flexible shipping solution is apparent. For example, a small private customer ordering a small box of ammunition to be delivered will raise very different costs depending upon where it must be delivered.

If you also consider that products of similar weights could actually cost very different amounts to deliver because of what they are then this needs to be catered for as well. Perhaps a Kalashnikov compared to a Plutonium fuel rod. Clearly, the latter needs much more sophisticated and costly transport.

Can PrestaShop be configured to offer a solution?

Part of the solution lies in offering multiple shipping options. It is possible to have multiple carriers and then define each carrier to use a different shipping method.

You can create an extra carrier. Click on **Shipping**, then on **Carriers**, and then on **Add new**.

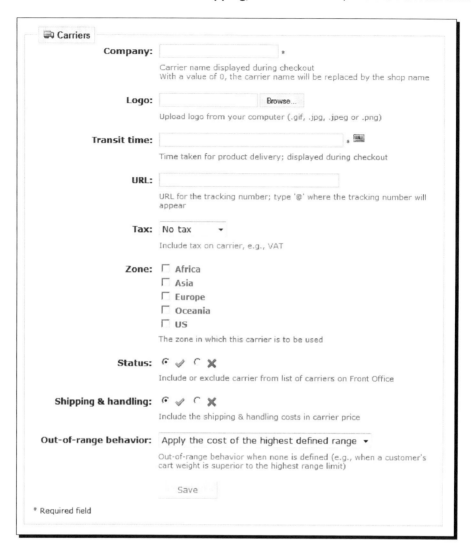

Notice the top field in the previous form—**Company**. This is not necessarily for the actual company, it can also be for a description of the service. For example, in the Guns4u example, we could create a carrier called "Radioactive substances distribution". This enables us to make it clear to our customers what the carrier is for. We can then define order value or weight ranges specific to this carrier. This is achieved after creating our new carrier by defining a weight or order value range in the normal way but selecting our new carrier in the drop-down box as we do so. See the following screenshot:

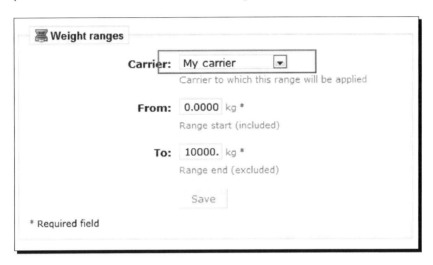

Notice also in the **Add new carrier** form the option to define availability by continent. So you could create multiple carriers with different price or weight ranges, perhaps called "Small arms Europe", "Small arms Africa", and so on.

As you can see things can get complicated. Forget Guns4u for a moment and consider a large online retailer like Amazon. Think about the vast range of weights, order values, product types, and destinations, not to mention the choice of different speeds within all these other possibilities.

The key to a successful shipping configuration, likc that on Amazon, when a very simple price, weight, flat fee, or free model will not do, is planning. If you must introduce multiple carriers, think carefully about what to call them and how to configure them, because your customers, not us, need to understand them in order to spend money.

If it is not necessary to create new carriers in PrestaShop, then don't. Let's suppose we use regular mail for order weights up to x and a courier for x and over. Do we need to create two carriers in PrestaShop? The answer is that if a single carrier, perhaps "Our carrier", can have weight ranges defined that charge what we need to, then don't create a new carrier in PrestaShop. A simple explanation of when you use regular mail and when you use a courier on your **Delivery and Returns** page would probably be much better.

Gift wrapping and recycled packaging

On top of all these shipping options, there are two more. They can be both money makers and credibility builders. If you offer a product suitable to be a gift, why not offer a gift wrapping service and charge for it? If you have a product that is available in full packaging or a more minimalist, environment-friendly form of packaging, why not offer that too?

Time for action – setting up gift wrapping and recycled packaging options

Here is how to do it.

1. Click on the **Preferences** tab and scroll down to what you can see in the next screenshot.

2. Click on **Yes** or **No** for gift wrapping.

3. Enter a price for the service.

4. Enter a tax rate, if any.

5. Click on **Yes** or **No** to **Offer recycled packaging**.

What just happened?

By offering gift wrapping and recycled packaging, you can save costs, increase turnover, and please your customers. This can all be done at the same time with just a couple of clicks.

Pop quiz – a refresher

1. How does SSL make your password safer?
2. How are your customers' credit card details protected when using PayPal, even if you don't use SSL?

Your PrestaShop so far

Phew, that chapter was a big one! But it is well worth knowing how advanced and in-depth your options are.

Are you starting to get a little bit excited? Your shop is ready. It is connected and configured for real customers. Goodbye 9-5, hello e-commerce business.

Summary

We learned a lot in this chapter about checkouts, currencies, taxes, and shipping.

Specifically, we covered:

◆ How to choose and connect the best payment provider for your business
◆ Some alternate payment methods
◆ How to take multiple currencies and configure sales taxes
◆ How to set up simple and efficient shipping options

Now that we've reached this stage, we will do a few quick checks on your checkout, get some family/friends' sales to make your shop look used, and then give the final push to your first small wave of real customers. All that and more will be covered in *Chapter 8*.

8
Get Set...

This chapter is all about the final preparations. It's a quick dry run through the process of making a purchase followed by the first steps in a diverse marketing campaign that we will expand upon in the next chapter.

In this chapter, we shall:

- Create a customer account and place an order
- Look at the PrestaShop customer loyalty scheme
- Look at how to get some feedback on your products using the PrestaShop comments module
- Tell the search engines about your cool new shop
- Look at a multi-pronged marketing campaign, including vouchers, forums, social media, and Google AdWords
- Cover some functionality on the Customers and Orders tabs that we haven't covered already

So let's get on with it.

Before we look at the first element of the campaign, let's be sure that everything is working properly.

First of all, let's get ourselves a customer. Here you will need the good will of a friend or relative. We are going to ask them to make a purchase. You can obviously refund them once the transaction is complete. I am also going to suggest that you lend or give them some of your products for them to use. The reasons for this will become clear as we proceed through the chapter.

Creating an account and placing an order

You can create an account on behalf of your willing volunteer or you can ask them to create it for themselves. The important thing for us here is to pay close attention to the details of the sign up process. We are looking to see if we have missed something. Does it look easy and intuitive? If you're willing volunteer is doing the form filling, did he or she find it straight forward?

Time for action – creating an account and placing an order

Here is how to do it. I will go through this tutorial as if you are doing the clicking.

1. Browse through your store and add a couple of products to your cart. Click on the cart link and see what it looks like. Does it all look straightforward and intuitive to you?

2. Click on the **Check out** button and create an account as prompted.

3. Click on the **Next** button and review the shipping summary page. Does it appear as expected with the right shipping options? Click on **Next**.

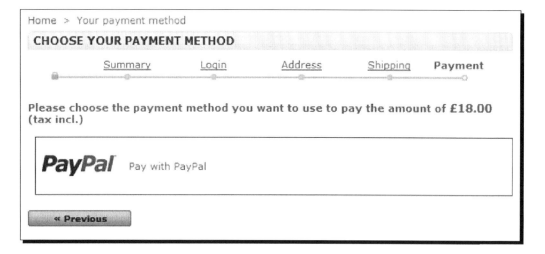

4. Click on the payment option PayPal, Google Checkout, or any other option that you have set up. If you chose to offer cheque, bank wire, or cash on delivery, then I suggest you do not choose them here. It will be useful (as we will see later in the chapter) to see how PrestaShop integrates with your chosen payment provider, and we will discuss how to handle the orders as well.

5. Complete the transaction through your preferred payment provider.

What just happened?

Now we know that the whole process is up and working. We understand first hand what our customers need to do in order to spend money in our store. We are now much better placed to serve them and turn them into long-term big spenders. We will use this account to do a few things in this chapter.

Let's look at a PrestaShop feature to encourage repeat business.

Repeat business with customer loyalty scheme

The customer loyalty scheme is great. If you have enough margin in your products, consider giving a little bit back to your customers in return for some repeat purchases. This works especially well if your customers have lots of stores to choose from and you sell repeat purchase items.

The best way of learning about how the loyalty scheme works is to set it up.

Time for action – setting up your loyalty scheme

Here is what to do:

1. Click on the **Modules** tab and scroll down to **Customer loyalty and reward** scheme. Install this module.

2. Scroll back down to the **Customer loyalty and reward** scheme and click on **Configure**. You will see something similar to the following screenshot:

3.   Most of the fields can be left at default. Here is an explanation of the interesting or important ones. First, in the **Ratio** field, enter the number of US dollars ($), British pounds sterlings (£), or Euros that a customer must spend to earn a point.

4.   Underneath this option, you have to enter the value of a single point as a decimal fraction of your chosen unit of currency. Do the maths carefully for this value. As an example, if you leave the default of $10 per point and the value at 0.2 per point, then for every $10 your customer spends, they will get 20 cents. If this is not generous enough, you can reduce the required spend per point, say, to 5. Then they would get 20 cents for every $5 spent. Or it can be your strategy to encourage a high average spend and then reward it by being a bit more generous. You can make the customer spend $50 per point but then give them a $5 value. Think carefully about what will work for you.

5.   Enter what you want the voucher to be called in the **Voucher details** field. Leave it at **Loyalty**, or call it something else such as **Fluff points** or **Thanks vouchers**. It is arbitrary: leave it as it is or choose something that you like.

6.   If you need to temporarily stop discounting, then just click on **No** (the red cross) next to **Allow discounts**.

7.   The **Points are awarded when the order is** field is self-explanatory. The default value of **Delivered** is probably a good option. It means that the discount will become available when you mark your customers order as delivered. But you can choose others.

8.   The **Points are cancelled when the order is** drop-down is important because it stops customers from accumulating points when they get refunds or cancel an order.

What just happened?

You now know how to offer a loyalty reward scheme.

Getting some product comments

You now have somebody who is using your products, and it is time to ask them what they think of these products. You can also ask for feedback on what they think about your store. You can ask them to log in to their account and leave some product comments. Alternatively, you could create the comments on their behalf.

All about comments

I strongly recommend that you do not invent comments. These comments are really easy to spot and will be obviously lacking in integrity. This is not the path we want to start on right at the beginning of our new business. However, filling out some genuine comments on behalf of a genuine user of our products is probably fine.

The benefit of this is that, again, you see how the process works and just as importantly your future customers will have comments to view. This makes your site look more established as well as being useful and reassuring to a customer's decision making.

How to get some product comments

Get the feedback from your willing volunteer. And then follow this quick guide.

Time for action – getting some feedback for your products

This is really easy.

1. First of all, we need to enable product comments. Of course, if you think product comments are not suitable for your store, then you don't have to do this. However, the benefits are great, so think carefully before skipping this guide. Log in to your admin control panel.

2. Click on the **Modules** tab, and very near to the top install the **Product Comments** tab. Now scroll back down and click on **Configure** next to the module you have just installed.

3. Select whether you want to validate comments before publishing them. This option is useful if you are nervous of what people might say.

4. The next two options about Criterion are optional. For each product, you can create a grading criterion. Let me explain. Your customer will be able to choose up to five stars. You can suggest and specify a criterion for these stars (for example: 'Please choose 1 star for poor or 5 stars for great'). You can then, in the next box, assign specific criterion to specific products. As I said, this step is not necessary; however, if you have a product range that would benefit from a specific criterion, then specify it here (for example, a site such as Guns4u.com would use Accuracy or Range).

5. Click on **Save** and visit your shop front. Browse to the first product you want to leave a comment for. Notice the new tab at the bottom of the screen. Click on it.

6. Leave a rating in stars (be honest) and a product comment. Click on **Send**.

7. Now go back to your admin control panel, click on the **Modules** tab and then click on **Configure** next to the **Product Comments** module.

8. Notice that you can approve or delete any of the comments. Obviously, it is not good practice to delete a comment just because it is imperfect. However, if the comments are unfair, untrue, or abusive, then I would say that you are perfectly at liberty to delete it. Approve your comment, and go back to the product page to see the effect on the **Comments** tab.

9. Create and approve as many comments as you can.

What just happened?

You now know the experience your customers will have when writing comments and you have a good, ethical way to get some comments in your store before real customers start shopping.

Now we will look at adding a juicy incentive for all your visitors.

Putting a discount voucher on the front page

We already know how to make a voucher. Here, we will create a voucher for a very specific purpose: getting some sales as soon as possible and winning my 7-day challenge.

Creating the voucher (reminder)

The **Vouchers** sub-tab is on the **Payment** tab. The things to consider here are the precise values to create your voucher.

I would suggest a percentage, rather than a cash value, because we don't know what sort of order values we might get. I would suggest a modest percentage but one big enough to be enticing—maybe 10 percent if your profit margin can take it.

Set the total quantity quite high. Then the voucher will continue to be available until you disable it. Set the **To be used by** value to **All customers**. Define a start and end date—I suggest, maybe a month.

I would enter something such as 'Store opening offer' for the voucher description and a simple, memorable code that the customer enters at the checkout.

Showcasing the voucher

Here I assume you have already created your voucher using the guidance provided above and, if necessary, referring back to the previous chapter.

Time for action – putting your voucher on the home page

Do you remember the **Home text editor** module? We will use it here to showcase your opening offer voucher.

1. Click on the **Modules** tab, scroll down to **Home text editor**, and click on **Configure**.

2. Make sure to put your voucher, as described next, before the fold. That is, when a visitor arrives at your home page they should see it without scrolling.

3. I suggest entering a very short introduction to the voucher (probably one sentence only, such as 'Have a look at this great opening offer'). Then, below that, I recommend a graphic of a gift voucher. If you're feeling arty, you could create one in Gimp. If not, visit www.dreamstime.com and pick up a high quality, enticing voucher graphic for around US$ 1. Below this graphic, in big bold letters, enter the voucher code.

4. Click on the **Update the editor** button and visit your home page to check you approve of the layout.

What just happened?

Everyone who visits your home page now has a reason to explore further—a discount.

We now have a great shop. We know it works, we have entered comments to make it look used, and we have an enticing, special opening offer. It is time to tell the world we are here.

Registering with the search engines

Some of the search engines might have found you already. Certainly, once other sites start to link to you they would find you anyway. However, just to be absolutely sure, we are considered for inclusion with all of the major search engines. We will spend a few minutes registering with them.

Registering

Registering with these major search engines will mean you have covered over 95 percent of all searches. Spend time registering with the smaller ones later, if you like, but at this stage I suggest this is more than sufficient.

Time for action – registering with the search engines

We will look at Google first, then Yahoo!, and then Bing.

1. Go to `http://www.google.com/addurl/` and fill out the very simple form. Also consider signing up for Google Webmaster Tools, and explore the options and statistics that it provides.

2. Next, for Yahoo!, visit `http://siteexplorer.search.yahoo.com/submit`. You will need to register first, but it is worth the effort!

3. Finally, visit Bing at `http://www.bing.com/webmaster/ WebmasterAddSitesPage.aspx`. You will need a Windows Live ID. But if you don't already have one, it is free to create.

What just happened?

You might get your site indexed immediately, it might take months. Don't worry too much about it because there is no way to influence the search giants other than creating great, unique content. And, of course, we have already done that.

Now let's look at getting your first sale.

Marketing your site

The information in this part of the chapter is designed to be digested in full and used fairly simultaneously. If you want to act on each section individually, to dip your toe in, that's fine, but my intention is to help you start a campaign that brings you your first wave of paying customers.

It is also important to realize that the brief burst of activity described here is not the end of the matter. We will look at some ways to get visitors and links to your site. However, be sure to read *Chapter 9* to turn what you do here into an ongoing, effective campaign.

Let's get on with it then.

Posting in forums

There are chat forums for just about everything these days. Enthusiasts love to talk and get their opinions known. Enthusiasts are often the best customers, but they can also be the harshest critics. So forums can be a very powerful way of reaching large audiences and to raise the profile of your PrestaShop business, but if done wrong, it can do great harm.

Finding the forums

Do a bit of searching by using terms related to your industry with words such as chat, forum, and help. Don't rush off and join the first forum you find. Make a list of as many as you can. Now go back and choose the ones that you think are the ten best.

Choose by the number of members and the relevance to your specific industry. Now create an account with each of them and read on about posting to them.

In the unlikely event that you can't find any or many good ones, why not start one by yourself? Grab my free PDF on how to start your own forum for free. Visit www.prestashop-book.com.

How to write good posts

You do not necessarily have to be an expert in your field, as most forums cater to users of many skill levels. However, it is very important if you are not an expert to try and pretend that you are, or if you do consider yourself an expert, not to overstate your level of knowledge.

Write at your skill level

You will certainly damage your reputation if you attempt to come across as more of an expert than you really are. So if you don't fully understand a topic of conversation, but want to join in any way, come clean about your level of knowledge. For example, you could start a reply to a post with "I'm no expert but if...". You can give an opinion, even one that disagrees but in which you are pointing out that perhaps you are wrong. If you're right, you will come across as polite, and if you're wrong, you will not be the target of potentially embarrassing replies.

Criticism

People don't like being criticized. If you absolutely must point out that somebody is wrong, do so very delicately.

Don't shamelessly promote yourself

If you sign up for a forum and then post "Hi come and check out my new gun shop", you will be doomed to failure. At the very least, other members will make a mental note that you are a self-promoter and will take what you say with caution. More likely, your post will be removed and you might have your account deleted.

The way to promote your business is to get involved in conversations about your industry that you are genuinely interested in. You will gain respect, and you never know when the conversation might naturally take a course towards an opportunity to mention your shop. Take the opportunity if it arises, but don't keep mentioning it unless the conversation makes it completely natural to do so.

If the forum allows and it is natural, as discussed, to do so, include a link (if not, your web address would suffice).

The one exception to all of these rules is when the forum has a category specifically intended for promoting your business.

So what is the point of all these conversations if you never, or rarely, get the opportunity to shout about your PrestaShop?

Creating forum signatures and profiles

When you join a forum you get the option of creating a profile. The precise format of a profile varies from forum to forum but usually includes some or all of the following:

- A bit of blurb about you and any business you might be involved with.
- A link to a website.

- A picture to represent you—why not use your store logo?
- Options about receiving private e-mail and messages from other forum users.

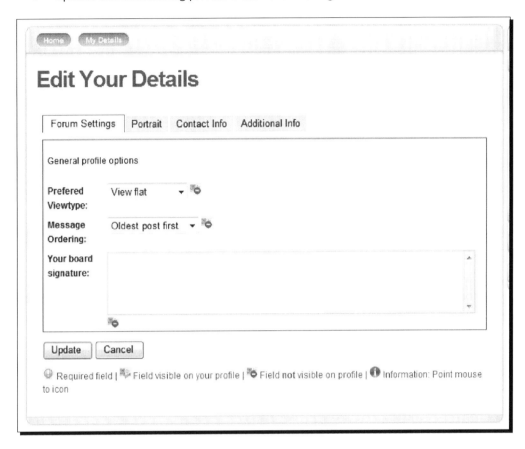

So perhaps you should fill in the information about you and your shop, enter the link to your business, add your shop logo to represent you graphically, and make sure your communication options are as open as possible.

Several things have been achieved here. Your shop logo will appear on all of your posts. The logo is usually a clickable link to your profile, which then exposes the link to your shop and information about it and you. This means that search engines will pick up inbound links from related content and forum users seeing your logo can click on it and quickly click through to your store.

Also, the image makes it plain to everyone who is interested in exactly what your business is and gives them easy access to contact you. Some people might even see your presence on their forum as an opportunity to discuss special terms for a purchase—just what the doctor ordered!

Be aware though that when it is obvious that you are a shop it is even more important to not be pushy about products. If you were a private individual, it would be fine to jump up and down and promote a product. However, when you are in an obvious position to benefit from a shameless promotion, nobody will believe you.

Now, if somebody else does genuinely promote a product, then that's an opportunity to join in and get your profile some exposure in the posts. But don't say anything that is an obvious self-promotion. Just your profile's presence is enough. If people are interested in the product, and see your logo, they might just make a couple of clicks and make a purchase.

Forum marketing conclusion

Humility and genuine respect for the feelings and reputations of others on the forum are the keys to initially blending in. Regular, but not excessive, activity will eventually gain you some prominence. Creating a full and professional profile will benefit you from direct visits from forum users as well as potential improvement on related keywords with search engine rankings.

Promoting your store using social media

Social media, at the moment at least, seems to be the big thing on the Web. There are many social media sites that allow anybody to join and communicate with millions of members. This is obviously an opportunity not to be missed. However, it is very easy to end up on the wrong path. It is very easy to waste time, and it is also possible to do your business more harm than good.

To address these potential pitfalls and to make sure that you get the most benefit possible with the smallest time investment I have created a whirlwind guide to two of the biggest social media sites. I aim to point out the big benefits of each and the most likely stumbling blocks, as well as some specific methods and actions that work on each platform.

If you want results in as short a time as possible, then read on.

Twitter

Twitter is my favorite because is so quick and easy. The very nature of Twitter makes it really easy to build your network. On Twitter, you build a team of 'followers'. You can also be a follower of other Twitter users. If you want significant, fast results, Twitter could be for you. However, as with all social media relationships, quality informational content (called tweets in this case) is still vital to lasting success. Here are some quick dos and don'ts.

Branding your profile

Make sure that your Twitter page looks represent your brand and products, and has your domain name boldly shown. Also, in the settings, be sure to link to your home page.

Following others

It is a good idea to follow some other Twitter profiles. This is the essence of a network on Twitter. If you want people to read your information and follow your links in your tweets, then you need people to follow you. However, there are many advantages to following others.

For example, you can get really fantastic, really topical information by following people interested in and knowledgeable about your industry. In the unlikely event that there is nobody on Twitter who fits the bill, you have a massive opportunity to become that person. Another advantage of following a respected, and popular, user is that you can comment on their tweets. This, along with the fact you appear in their list of followers, means that more people have a chance of finding you. The holy grail of this type of relationship is when the respected user decides to follow you! And when they start replying to your tweets, it will bring even more viewers and potential new followers to your Twitter home page.

A lightning guide to tweeting

Every tweet should be meaningful on its own or add something to the conversation. Just remember that everything you say is public. If you send a direct message, then even that could be repeated publicly. Don't reveal anything private about yourself, and if you want to be popular on Twitter don't spoil anybody else's day by revealing private information about them.

Regular tweets

Just answer the question: "What are you doing now?" Make sure you are tweeting relevant industry information: "I am considering a new range of teddy bears for my shop. Do I want the giant golden teddy? Or is small best?"

A quick glance at almost any twitterer and you will see that they tweet a lot more than just answering the question, "What are you doing now?" Make up your own questions and answer them, for example, "What is the very latest innovation in your industry?" Answer the question and most importantly give your opinion about it in a single tweet.

It takes some refining of your text, but it can almost always be done. "What is the biggest upcoming event in your industry and what do you think about it?" For example: "Looking forward to the teddy bears annual convention this Fall—no way I am going to miss it—anyone else coming?"

Asking a question begs a reply. And as we know replies are good for business. There is no end of topics that can be thought up for even the smallest niche. Sometimes the topic could be an ongoing one that could justify many tweets over time. For example: "Just looking in to how these wonderful Russian teddy bears are manufactured. Did you know they start with stuffing made from Siberian wool?", "The lining is hand stitched blah blah...", and so on. You get the idea. Never lose focus on making it relevant to your audience. Be consistent, but not too frequent, and keep it uncommercial (see *Sales tweets* section a bit further on).

What's your frequency Kenneth?

What tweeting frequency is right for you will depend upon how frequently things change and how dynamic your industry is. Test out different frequencies and look at what popular people in your industry are doing. What you can do quite legitimately is link to a very closely related article on your website. This is perfectly acceptable and would not put off followers. Just make sure that the article you link to is entirely relevant and not a product page.

Broadcasting

All your regular tweets should be relevant and personal, from you. So even when talking about an event, for example, the focus is on you and how the event relates to you. The exception to this rule is when you just want to broadcast something really significant. For example: "Fire at Siberian stuffing plant kills three and puts teddy production back by six months".

This is a tweet that people might be interested in but something that is not personal. And, if the timing is right, broadcast tweets will get you lots of attention. But they should not be the standard format of your tweeting. Impersonal all of the time is uninteresting. Pick your broadcast tweets carefully and make sure they are relevant and topical, even more so than your regular tweets.

Humour

If you've got it, flaunt it. Jokes are great, and there are plenty of jokes on Twitter. A good joke can keep your followers keen. But if you haven't got it, it's probably best to leave the jokes to someone else.

Questions

Questions are great. Asking for peoples' opinions often provokes a reply and an appearance on someone else's timeline. By all means ask for help but keep it occasional. The best type of question is asking for opinions. If you ask for an opinion you can get responses without being socially indebted. Also, if you are lucky (or smart) you might provoke a discussion, lots of replies, and the publicity that goes with it. The sort of opinions you can ask for are almost limitless. Ask about industry, business, products events, personalities, organizations, or anything else relevant. Ask for feedback on a new article, product, or site layout. Almost anything is valid.

Achievements and events

Done something great, new, or interesting? Think your followers will care? Then tweet it. Attended an industry event, visited a competitors store/site, had a nice lunch, Tweet it. Anything is valid. Just remember the guidelines that it must be worth reading. So if you regularly tweet valid information about your field of expertise then the occasional, informal nicety is cool and a nice contrast. But don't overdo the trivial.

Replying and re-tweeting

Can't think of anything to say? No problem. Find somebody who can. Search for the phrases you are interested in and find something relevant to post a reply to. This will tell all your followers what you are looking at. And who knows, the other person's tweet might inspire something original from you. And if you're really stuck, just re-tweet (copy) someone's message. Be sure to give credit to the other person. You can do this by adding an 'RT @otherpersonstwitterusername' to the beginning of the message.

Sales tweets

The simplest and most subtle, way of promoting your site is by adding a link to your home page with occasional tweets. The tweet does not have to suggest a purchase or promote a product, it simply says what you want to say and links to your home page so that people can click and see what you are all about.

More direct, but still fairly subtle, is to ask people for an opinion on a very specific aspect of a product or service. Ask for feedback on the product itself, the way you have described or photographed it. Perhaps ask people their suggestion for a selling price or just say "How much would you pay for this teddy?"

You can do this with an existing range or use the same process to get feedback on potential new ranges before you purchase stock. This could generate some useful feedback and even some pre-orders.

If you're really stuck, promote your business by offering a discount voucher. Consider this very carefully before doing it because it needs to be financially viable.

Tell your followers about special offers—be careful here. If you send out a tweet to a group of trusting followers, be absolutely sure that it is genuinely and undeniably SPECIAL! If it isn't, you will lose credibility and probably followers as well. There are loads of people on Twitter sending out "special offer" tweets to rubbish, spam, or pornography. Don't get tarred with the same brush.

Twitter summary

Build a following by following other quality users, interacting with them, and by sending your own quality tweets. You can probably see a trend developing here, it is the same with all web content—quality, useful, and don't ram your products (too hard) down people's throats.

Facebook

Facebook is more technically endowed than Twitter. The features and fancy gadgets on Facebook are far too numerous to go into any greater depth. However, there are a few really key places you can market yourself and one really important thing you must never do on Facebook.

Avoid spamming

Whenever you post to your wall or send any other type of message all of the recipients have the option to report it as spam. If too many people do this, your Facebook account is likely to be deleted.

So although I do recommend building your network as wide as possible, I don't recommend sending commercial messages to your entire group. However, there are a number of communication channels where you can get a bit commercial and you shouldn't get reported for spam. In addition, anyone in your social group will be able to see these channels when they look at your Facebook profile.

Therefore, by building the biggest network possible but only marketing through very specific, targeted channels, you avoid the spam problem and reach a wide and targeted audience. A brief discussion of my top three Facebook features for targeted communication now follows.

Start a group

There is a group for just about everything on Facebook. Have a look at the menu bar that Facebook neatly locks at the bottom of your browser window. Hover your mouse over the icons on the left-hand side. Click on **Groups**. You can use the search by typing in a keyword and looking for a very specific group or click on **Browse Groups** to see the huge range, volume, and diversity of groups. Click on **Browse Groups** and we will explore a little.

Anybody can create a group and the group could be targeted at anything. When a group is created, its creator defines certain criteria. This includes whether the group is open, closed, or secret. If a group is open, you guessed it, you can join. If it is closed, you have to request to join, and if it is a secret, you will know nothing about it.

Secret groups are all cool and funky for conversing with college buddies, but probably have limited use in the world of marketing, so we will say no more about them. When you visit a group page, you will quickly see what they are all about and if you want to join.

Join groups relevant to your industry, join in and make new friends. Start your own group for a really powerful, targeted marketing channel.

Start an event

Events are exactly what they say. Anybody can create an event page. The event page can then be visited by Facebook members and they can interact with it. They can learn about the event, register attendance, or put themselves down as a maybe. The manner and amount of interaction is determined by the creator of the event page. Event pages, like regular pages, turn up on the profiles of people who have registered an interest in the event as well as on the profile of the person who created the event. Events can be anything from a presidential election to a walk in the park or a special discount day on a website. Are you beginning to see the potential here?

Start a page

Pages, as the name implies, are web pages you can visit, or create, within the Facebook site. They, like any other web page, can be about almost anything.

When you find a page you like, you can click on a button to become a fan. You can also 'share' a page with a friend to give them the opportunity to view and become a fan of the page. When you, or anyone else for that matter, is a fan of a page, the page's image appears fairly prominently on your profile page. This gives further visibility to the page when people are visiting their friends' profiles, as you do on Facebook. So where are all these pages? Click on the cool Facebook toolbar in the bottom left-hand side and browse and create pages. Start building your fan base of targeted Facebook users.

Social media conclusion

If social media is something you want to get into in great depth, or if any of my suggestions or explanations were not detailed enough, then for more information on social media marketing download my free PDF from www.prestashop-book.com.

Now we can go on to explore another marketing method.

Google AdWords

Google AdWords is great. It's not free but it is very easy to spend as much or as little as you like. Great manuals have been written on Google AdWords, and I do recommend further study on the subject.

But setting up the basics is so quick that it would be a crime not to add AdWords to our suite of marketing tools right away. The next chapter will talk about refining your AdWords campaign. This lightning tutorial will help you set up a campaign, limit your costs to a level you are happy with, and perhaps get your first order.

Setting up a campaign

Head on over to your country's Google and click on **Advertising Programs** and then **Google AdWords** and sign up for an account.

Time for action – Google AdWords made quick and simple

You might be prompted to create a campaign when you sign up. Either way, follow this guide for the fastest route to getting well-targeted visitors on your PrestaShop.

1. Click on the **Campaigns** tab in your AdWords control panel.

2. Click on the **New campaign** button.

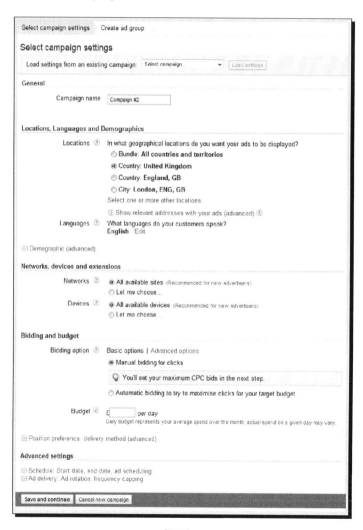

3. Choose the geographic locations where you want your adverts to run. Leave the defaults **All available devices** and **All available sites**. This means your adverts will appear in search results and on partner sites, like AdSense publishers. The important box here is the budget per day. I would put a bare minimum in here. You might be surprised how quickly you get some clicks. You won't know until you try. You could even put £1 in here if you are concerned. You can always increase the amount later or disable it completely.

4. Click on **Save** and continue.

5. Name your campaign—I suggest a name that stands out. As this is a first attempt in order to familiarize ourselves with AdWords, and to get some quick customers, it is almost certain you will want to come back and amend or delete this campaign. Why not call it 'Test'?

6. Next write your advert. The headline should grab attention. The two description lines should very clearly and specifically tell people what they will find when they click. This means you are more likely to only pay for visitors with a genuine interest in your shop. For simplicity, put the same thing in URL and Display URL, `www.yourshop.com`. The following screenshot shows a sample advert:

> Start an e-commerce shop
> Prestashop for beginners
> Learn how to make money online
> www.prestashop-book.com

7. In the **Keywords** box, enter all of the most relevant two-word and three-word phrases about your products. We discussed keywords in *Chapter 4*. You can put the same keywords in here. We will look at refining, optimizing, and adding keywords in the next chapter. For now, just get the most relevant ones in.

8. In the search box, enter a value per click you are prepared to pay. Consider that possibly only a small percentage of visitors will make a purchase. So the cost only needs to be a modest percentage of the profit you might make on a sale.

9. Click on **Save ad group**. That's it!

What just happened?

Hold onto your keyboard, the visitors will be arriving any moment. If you want to increase or reduce your maximum cost per click, then click on the **Keywords** tab and then on **Max CPC**. A pop-up box will appear and allow you to enter a new value. To change the advert, click on **Ads** and then click on your advert. To cancel everything, click on **Adgroups**. On the left-hand side, by the adgroup name, you can click on the little green button to pause or delete the campaign.

Have a go hero – optimizing for Google AdWords

Google charges per click based on a number of factors. Probably the most significant is how well the keywords that you bid for and the keywords in your advert match the content of the page your advert points to.

1. How could you make maximum use of the previous search engine optimization to keep your cost per click as low as possible and also make sure that your customers see the most relevant page on your website?

2. Create an ad group for every product and category. List the keywords relevant on your site and divide them up into the most relevant ad group. This will mean that the content for the page will closely match the keywords you are bidding for. This will make your clicks cheaper and the customers who click on your adverts will go directly to the product the advert refers to. The key as ever is planning. There will be more in the next chapter.

Handling orders and checking payments

Any day now you're going to get an e-mail from PrestaShop saying you have a new order! When you have stopped dancing around the room read on to learn about handling orders and much more.

Creating order messages

As you will see shortly you have the facility to quickly send messages, via e-mail, to your customers by accessing their order. Considering that many of the messages will be identical, wouldn't it be useful to write those messages in advance and then, with the click of a button, send the message of our choice? Well you can.

Time for action – creating messages

Here is how.

1. Click on the **Orders** tab. We have two sub-tabs that mention messages. The first tab, **Customer messages**, is where PrestaShop stores up all of the sent and received messages. We are creating messages and want the **Order Messages** sub-tab. Click on it now and then click on the **Add new** button.

2. We are presented with a nice, simple form asking for the name of our message and the actual message itself. I suggest creating a message called 'Dispatch notification'. Type a brief and friendly message informing the customer that their product has been dispatched. You might like to create multiple versions of this message, perhaps for orders with different delivery methods, or times, or some other reason specific to your business.

3. Save the message and then create as many messages as you think you will need. You can, of course, come back at any time to create a new message for a situation you didn't anticipate. Messages that you might like to create as well as the dispatch notification are things such as "Thanks for the cheque/bank wire". Perhaps you have special orders or fluctuations in stock that require you to notify a customer when their order or part order has arrived? Note that the "Thanks for your order" messages are done automatically by PrestaShop.

What just happened?

We have composed some pre-prepared messages that we will use when processing customer orders. These can be a great time saver by avoiding lots of typing. It also helps us avoid errors and keeps our customer contact consistent.

Statuses

Statuses keep our customers informed of the state of an order. They can view order statuses in their account. Statuses are very useful to us for managing our shop as well. PrestaShop creates a number of default statuses for us. These will probably suit the needs of most shops. But this next tutorial will introduce statuses and show you how to add or edit them should you want to.

Time for action – Statuses

Here we go.

1. Click on the **Statuses** sub-tab.

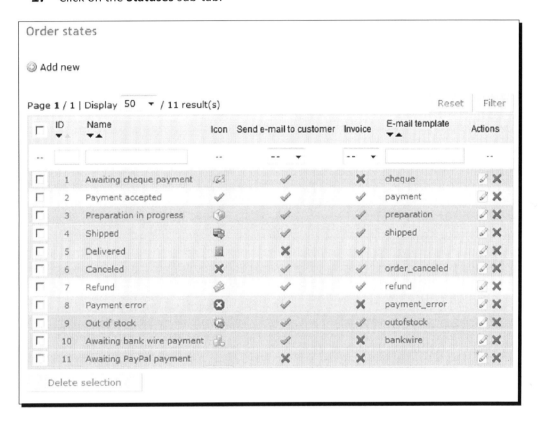

2. Take a look at all of the order statuses available to us by default.

3. Let's have a look at one in detail. Click on the **Edit** icon next to one of the statuses.

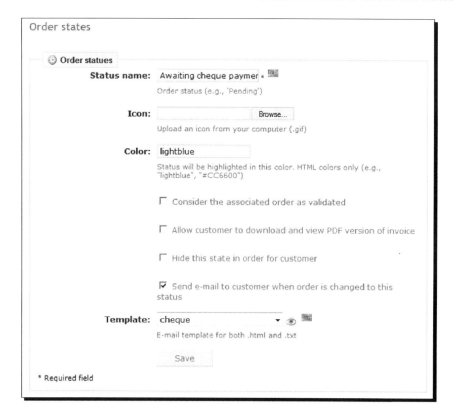

4. Here is an explanation. As you can see, I have clicked on the **Awaiting cheque payment** status. I could, if I wanted to, browse to find a graphic to represent that status. I can see that the highlighted color when an order has this status will be light blue. The next four checkboxes give you options related to the customer. Probably the most interesting option is the **Template** option. This defines the e-mail template used to send a message to the customer when an order reaches this state.

5. Click on the little eye icon to view the e-mail the customer would receive.

6. Click back to the list when you're done.

7. In the unlikely event you do not have enough status options click on **Add new** and you will see the same form we were just looking at. Fill it out to match the new status you are after.

What just happened?

We looked at statuses, and how to view at them in detail, including the message that a customer will receive. In the next two sections, we will actually make use of and change statuses as well as send some of the messages we created previously.

Checking Payments

Click on the **Orders** tab and if you processed a sale from your willing volunteer you will see the order there. Notice the **Paid** status, in the status column.

This is all well and good, but how can we be sure we have the money? It is always worth double checking that a payment has actually arrived and has not been reversed or cancelled. Also, note that with Google Checkout the customer's card is merely verified and is not actually charged until the order is processed.

I suggest logging into your PayPal or Google Checkout account to verify that the list of orders you have in your PrestaShop control panel matches with the payments received in your payment provider's transaction list. When you are satisfied that all is well, read on.

Processing an order

For this next guide, we will assume that the order is in stock and ready to be shipped. If the situation for you is different, then simply select the appropriate status for you. Note that Google Checkout terms and conditions say that you should not set the order to processing or charge until you are ready to actually ship the order.

Time for action – how to process an order

Let's process our first order:

1. Click on the **Orders** tab and then click on the order that you want to process.

2. Click the drop-down box to change the status of the order as shown in the following screenshot. For example, if you are packing the order and about to go to the post office, select the **Shipped** status.

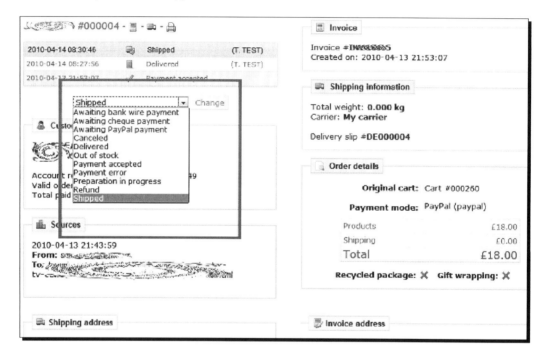

3. Scroll to the bottom of the order detail page and click on the send message link as highlighted in the following screenshot:

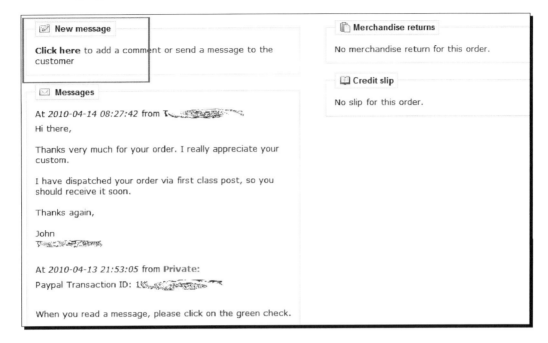

4. Select an appropriate default message to keep the customer up to date or to write a new message.

5. Wrap the customer's order or do whatever you need to fulfill the order. Notice that there are two addresses: invoice and delivery. Often these are the same, but not always. If they are different, be sure to send to the delivery address.

What just happened?

Now when you receive your first customer order it can be a moment of joy and not one of panic.

Let's look in more detail at the **Customers** and **Orders** tabs to see some of your options.

More about the Customers and Orders tabs

Here is a whirlwind tour of the **Customers** and **Orders** tabs, covering the most useful functions that have not been covered so far.

Groups

Groups are potentially very useful. Not surprisingly, you can create groups and then add your customers to specific ones. The purpose is the interesting bit. You can then assign discounts to groups and then all of the members of that group would qualify for that discount.

Time for action – creating and using groups

Perhaps a common group might be wholesale and retail. Here we will create a group called Wholesale, give the group 10 percent discount, and then add some customers to it.

1.   Click on the **Customers** tab, then the **Groups** sub-tab, and then **Add new:**

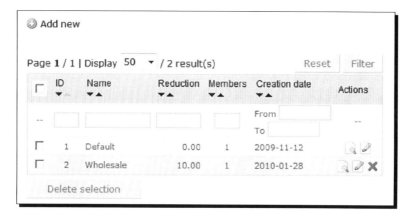

2.   Enter **Wholesale** in the group name box and enter **10** in the percentage discount box.

3.   Save your new group. Notice in the list of groups that there is the new wholesale group and a default group. In this scenario, the default would be our retail group.

4. Now click on the **Customers** tab again and then the **Edit** icon on one of the customers. Can you see the little checkbox highlighted in the following screenshot?

5. Select the checkbox to add the customer to the wholesale group and then click on **Save**.

6. The customer will now enjoy any discounts assigned to the wholesale group.

What just happened?

We now know how to use the groups feature and have looked at one possible use for it.

Customers

You just saw how we edited the membership of a group via the **Customers** tab. You can also view a list of all the customers via this tab. Notice the empty boxes above each of the fields in the table of customers? I have highlighted them in the following screenshot:

We can use the empty boxes to enter dates, names, partial names, and so on. Then we can click on the **Filter** button to see a new list of customers based upon the filtering requirements we specified.

Also, try clicking the magnify icon at the end of a customer's name and look at the full customer detail summary that pops up.

Carts

The **Carts** tab is a very useful tool. We can see at a glance the carts that were created in our store and when. Note that it is very distinct from **Orders**. Lots of carts being created that don't lead to orders could be an indication of a problem—perhaps something the customer didn't like that put them off, and it is probably worth investigating.

We can click on any of the carts and get an expanded description of it.

Invoices

There are two main uses for invoices. First, our customers might want one, especially if they made a purchase for their business, and second, it is good practice to keep a copy for yourself for accounting purposes.

Time for action – Invoices

Make sure that you are logged in to your admin control panel and read on.

1. Click on the **Orders** tab and then the **Invoices** sub-tab.

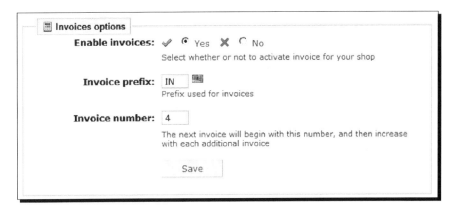

2. In the **Invoices options** panel, shown above, select **Yes** to enable invoices for your customers.

3. In the **Invoice number** box, you can specify the number of the next invoice to be generated. This is a great cheat for hiding the fact that your shop is brand new. When your first-ever customer gets invoice number 5456753, they will have no idea how special they really are.

4. Look at the section labeled **Print PDF invoices** shown in the following screenshot:

5. Specify a date period, perhaps the beginning to the end of a month.

6. Click on the **Generate PDF file** button and you can easily print off all of your customer invoices for that month.

What just happened?

We saw how to enable and disable customer invoices as well as print off invoices for our own records.

Merchandise return

Here you can enable merchandise return as well as specify the number of days after order that this is acceptable.

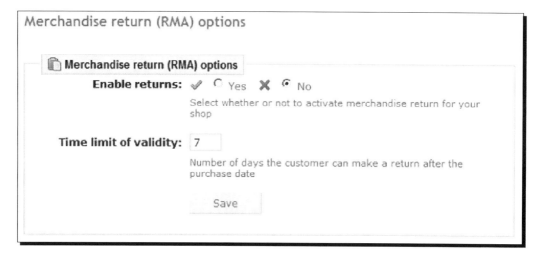

Once this is enabled, you can then assign return statuses on you orders screen. This includes waiting for package, package received, refund given, and return denied.

Pop quiz – refresher questions

Have a go at these:

1. I have a new product and I absolutely must shout about it NOW. Where is an appropriate outlet?

2. What type of products and shops benefit from a customer loyalty program?

3. How do forum posts without links in still potentially help your standing with the search engines?

4. How else could you market your site for free?

Summary

Now you know everything you need to know to make money from your e-commerce business. Specifically:

♦ We created a customer account and used it to test the checkout, write some product comments, and practice processing an order

♦ We now have a PrestaShop customer loyalty scheme

♦ All of the major search engines know about your great new shop

♦ We have looked at the beginnings of a marketing campaign on forums, blogs, social media, and Google AdWords

♦ We looked at some extra functions of the **Customers** and **Orders** tabs that weren't covered by the rest of the chapter

However, the most important information is in the next chapter. Learn how to grow your new small business into a massive e-commerce empire. Find out the big secret to turning a successful small business into a massive one and explore why you would even want to anyway. *Chapter 9* has all this and more.

9
Go... To the Future

Welcome to the last chapter. This is the chapter that can make the most difference to your new business. The really simple tools and ideas that we discuss here are the key to turning your nice little PrestaShop into a thriving e-commerce empire, if you want to.

In this chapter, we shall look at:

- Why we do this anyway
- Analyzing, optimizing, and adding
- The big secret
- The future of e-commerce and PrestaShop

So let's get on with it.

"Why are we here?"

My science teacher used to boom this question across the classroom and scare half the class into paying attention. But it is a good question and well worth thinking about.

What is critical, especially in this type of business, is to understand what we are trying to achieve. It is necessary because a deep understanding and certainty of purpose will guide our actions. Although our PrestaShop might be just about done, our business must have a real and clear purpose, and path, in order for us to achieve the maximum we can with our newfound knowledge.

So why did we open a PrestaShop? Why did you buy this book? For some of you, it might be simple curiosity about PrestaShop or perhaps e-commerce in general. I am guessing that for the majority of us, it was to start a business. And for any number of good reasons, you specifically chose PrestaShop.

But why did you want to start a business at all? Well, that's obvious you might say—to make money. But why make money? To pay the bills. It is probably obvious what I am hinting at. You may think there is some impending lecture on home or work balance—I promise it won't be.

However, I hope you have considered exactly what you would like to provide for yourself and your family through this business. In particular, are you doing this for the thrill of an online business? That's fine, I am. Or are you just looking at an online business to provide you with the means to give yourself and your family what you deserve? That's fine as well, me too.

I just wanted to point out one or two things that might not be immediately obvious.

The power of e-commerce and a passive income

You have, at this stage, an opportunity for a little bit more than just paying the bills. I am not suggesting that we should, all or any of us, try and be extremely wealthy entrepreneurs. There isn't anything wrong with that though. I am not suggesting we should, all or any of us, be big business people and dominate our markets, although that is OK as well.

I am not even suggesting that we should consider e-commerce, PrestaShop, or any other e-business tool to be anything more important than just that, a mere tool. But it would be negligent of me, having strung you along for more than 200 pages, not to double check if you fully realized the power and potential of what you just started.

The busy billionaire

I admire people who work hard. And to have a successful e-commerce business, you have to work very hard indeed. But unlike a high-powered job or conventional self-employment, a self-built e-commerce offers the opportunity for income without the massive time constraints and life-dominating commitment required by most other businesses and by every form of employment.

I am not trying to describe an income that is necessarily big, although it can be, but an income that you control and not one that controls you.

The rest of this chapter will go on to explain how to use PrestaShop in conjunction with other tools to grow your income, but with only a very minimal time commitment. Starting a business like this should not be the precursor to a full-time job. In fact, just the opposite can be true.

What I am trying to get to is this: PrestaShop, when used efficiently, can be the start of a significant passive income. That is, an income that keeps coming in, even when you are not actually working on it. Don't believe me? Read on.

Perpetual analyzing, improvement, and marketing

The key theme here is in the word perpetual, meaning, continued without interruption. Marketing, optimizing, and improving your website is not a one-off job. It has to be done on an ongoing basis—it is never finished. That's the bad news. The good news is it doesn't have to take long, just so long as it is done on a regular basis. And as your website becomes more established, I would suggest that the amount of time you spend on optimization can decrease as long as the frequency is maintained. This is good news and sits well with our plan for a passive income.

First of all, let's look at how we can measure the performance of our PrestaShop.

Analyzing statistics

In *Chapter 5*, we set up the PrestaShop statistics modules as well as installed Google Analytics. Now we will look at how you can use them to understand some areas for change and improvement in your PrestaShop. It is also worth pointing out that quite often the statistics gathered by Analytics will overlap what has been gathered by PrestaShop. However, as we will see, both do have unique statistics that the other doesn't. First of all, we will look at the built-in PrestaShop features.

PrestaShop statistics

Look at the huge menu of stats options in the next screenshot. We very briefly looked at them in *Chapter 5*. Here we will try and deduce how to make practical use of them. Try and glean useful information that can then be used to make changes and improve our stores. You can access the menu by clicking on the Stats tab. The menu is located down on the left-hand side.

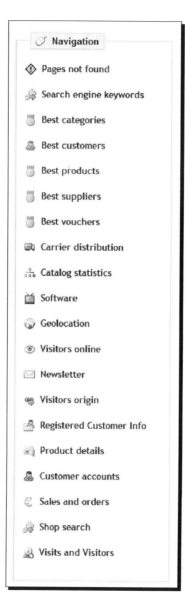

The actual statistics themselves are very straightforward, but sometimes their meaning is less obvious. We will cover perhaps the most commonly useful stats, but what is useful to one business might not be to another. Be sure to think about all of the information PrestaShop gathers for you and how you might be able to use it.

Pages not found

First up is **Pages not found**. When we generated your `.htaccess` file in *Chapter 4*, we gave instructions to the web server to visit a page called `404.php` whenever a visitor tries to visit a page on our site that doesn't exist. This statistic then records the details of pages that visitors tried to visit that don't exist and how often it happened.

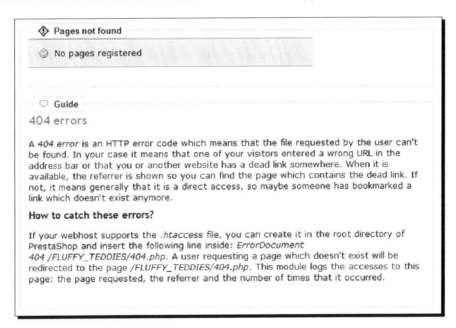

What you are aiming for is to get the message shown in the screenshot above. **No pages registered** means there were no pages that couldn't be found. If you have one or more pages not found, it is probably a really good idea to find out why and fix it.

A common cause of pages not found is broken links (that is, you have made a link on your site and mistyped the URL). Perhaps you created a link in an article to `./teddybearf` when it should have been `./teddybears`. This would cause an entry in the **Pages not found** statistics. Another cause is where the page was real but was for some reason removed. Then when visitors click on links to the page, which should otherwise have not been removed, you will get the details of it here.

When a customer comes across a broken link, it is highly likely they will give up on your site. So check the **Pages not found** statistics regularly and fix or remove links that cause problems.

Best products, best categories, and catalog statistics

These three statistics pages can be used in conjunction with one another. Why not go and have a look at the **Best products**, **Best categories**, and **Catalog statistics** now. The **Catalog statistics** are shown in the following screenshot:

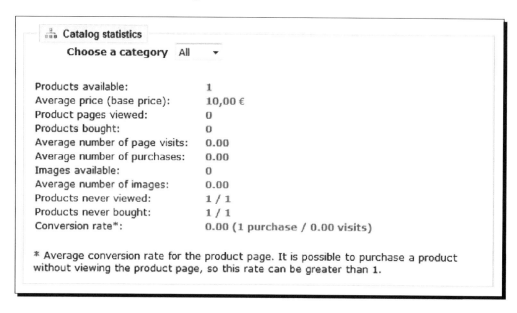

On the **Best products** page, there is a wealth of information. See the following screenshot:

On the **Best categories** screen, we can see a narrower range of statistics, but they tell us about a broader range of subjects (a whole category of products). See the next screenshot:

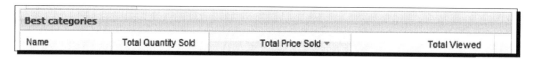

From this information, we can see the best selling categories and products, which of course is interesting, but we can deduce something much more useful as well.

On the **Best products** page look at the **Qty sold** and **Page viewed** column. From these two figures, we can see how effective our product offering is. Have you received 200-page views without a sale? There is probably a problem.

Is the price good? If it is, then how full is the description and how clear are the images? If you pass the last two tests, consider taking a look at your sales copy and referring back to *Chapter 3*, and see if you are using the best possible sales copy.

A "good" conversion rate varies dramatically from industry to industry, but if you are getting five sales in every 100 page views, you can probably give yourself a pat on the back. But if yours is lower than this, do not despair; it might just be normal for your type of product.

You can use the same technique to judge the effectiveness of categories, including the category page and all of the products in the category combined. Use exactly the same technique, but this time use the figures from the best category page. You will often find the number of sales per view is lower for the category than the product page.

Now look at the **Catalog statistics** page and you can see the average sales and page views across the whole store. Page views to sales, at any level, are a really good benchmark to measure your success. It is much more worthwhile to measure your improvement than try and compare with somebody else's figures or even the figures I just gave. The figures I gave are just a very rough guide.

If you think you could improve, we will look at a plan for continuous improvement in a bit.

Shop search

This page is simple. It shows you the search terms being used in your search box. This is obviously distinct from the search terms being used on the search engines, and we will come to them when we look at Google Analytics.

The terms that people use to search your shop can tell you many things. For example, if people are searching extensively for a particular term or two, it means they are finding your site easily, but perhaps the specific item or article they are looking for is proving more elusive.

Visit your shop front and try out the search term. Does it take you to the page you expected? If not, you probably need to look at your meta tags and search weightings, discussed in *Chapter 4*. If it does give you the expected page, great! But that is not necessarily the end of the matter. If people are using a search term a lot, could it be worth making the thing easier to find? Perhaps, feature it on the home page, have it added to your tag cloud, or make the category more prominent by moving it up the category list order. All these things should not definitely be done, but should be considered. Don't rush off and do it now. Make a note and we will look at when to schedule such tasks soon.

PrestaShop statistics summary

The statistics features that are useful to you will not be the same as those that are useful to everybody else. Try and get familiar with all of them and then apply your knowledge of your industry to make them useful to you.

Google Analytics

Log into your Analytics account and look at the huge menu of Analytics options. Here we will try and deduce how to make use of them. Try and glean useful meaning from the data that can then be used to make changes and improve our stores.

Like Google AdWords (more soon), Analytics is a massive topic. I will cover perhaps the most useful features here. However, if you are finding that using these features is getting results, then I would definitely recommend further study. For example, you can link Analytics to AdWords to fully explore how viable your AdWords are. But that goes beyond the space we have here. Let's get on with it.

Visitors

The following screenshot shows the number of daily visitors to a website. This is interesting and of course we should strive to increase it. Here it displays just a month. However, you can change the date range with the buttons in the top right to whatever you like.

If you are a brand new store, a short date range can be very telling. When you have been open for a while, extend the overall date range and look for a steady upward increase.

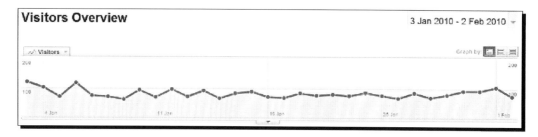

Log into Analytics, select your site and click on **Visitors**. We will discuss some of the mines of precious information you can dig up on the **Visitors** tab.

You have options like new versus returning. This tells us how many of our visitors are repeat customers and how many are new. The actual figures are imperfect because the technology is also imperfect at detecting return visitors. But it is a very good guide.

Not enough return visitors? You need to give people a reason. Perhaps the customer loyalty scheme discussed in *Chapter 8* can help or a discount voucher may be sent out to existing customers. If there aren't enough new visitors then you need to employ all the marketing tools that you can. Have a look at the following screenshot comparing new and returning visitors:

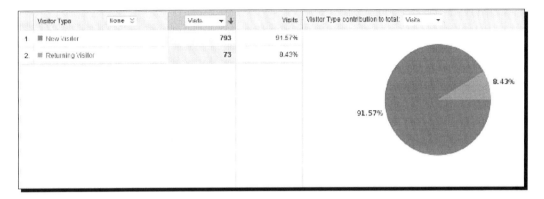

You can also click on **Customer Loyalty** and see a full breakdown of the number of customers who visited once or more.

Length of visit is a great indicator. It will show how long people stayed in great detail. How many stayed for 0 to 10 seconds, 11 to 30 seconds, and upwards. Your aim is to get people to browse your site for as long as possible. If you are getting a high percentage of your visitors leave in under 30 seconds, then look in detail at which pages they are viewing (and not liking). Then try and work out why and fix it.

Have a look at your map overlay. It allows you to hover your mouse pointer over different regions of the world and see where your visitors live. If you're getting lots of visitors from countries you don't ship to or from countries that speak languages you don't cater for, it might be time for a rethink.

The options under **Visitors** are immense and exploring them is highly recommended. We will look at how to best spend time searching for and using statistics soon.

Traffic sources

Traffic sources refers to the manner that our visitors arrived as opposed to the geographic location talked about earlier. The options are links from other sites, the different search engines, and people who typed a URL or clicked on a bookmark. Have a look at the following screenshot:

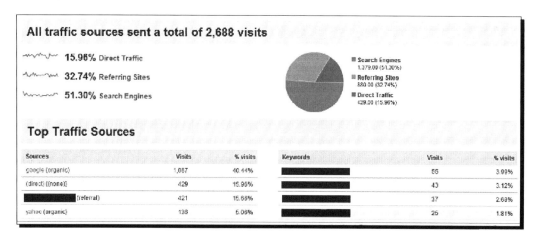

If you don't have many referrals from other websites, then you need to get marketing on the forums, blogs, and social media. If you find that any of the major search engines are missing completely, then did you register? Check back to *Chapter 8*.

Under **Traffic Sources**, you can also click on keywords and see mountains of information about the keywords that search engines sent visitors to your site from. This can be very revealing. Are they what you expected? Do you need to refine your search engine optimization discussed in *Chapter 4* or do you need to start writing articles and creating product categories or product descriptions for a whole new set of keywords?

	Keyword	None	Visits ↓	Pages/Visit	Avg. Time on Site	% New Visits
1.			69	1.38	00:01:25	97.10%
2.			60	1.62	00:01:10	96.67%
3.			37	2.35	00:02:01	83.78%
4.			36	1.58	00:01:13	97.22%
5.			34	1.68	00:01:01	97.00%
6.			32	1.56	00:00:41	3.12%
7.			31	1.97	00:01:09	87.10%
8.			26	2.04	00:01:50	88.46%
9.			26	1.08	00:00:03	96.15%
10.			24	1.92	00:02:04	87.50%

Have a think, but don't rush off and do anything major until you have read the rest of this chapter.

Content

Content, as the title suggests, gets down to the specifics of each page. Have a look at the next screenshot that shows the simplest use of Content statistics: how many entrances to your site came from each page?

	Page	None ⌄	Entrances ↓
1.	/		973
2.	/index.php?main_page=page&id=23&chapter=0		328
3.	/index.php?main_page=page&id=1&chapter=0		286
4.	/index.php?main_page=index&cPath=6		232
5.	/index.php?main_page=page&id=63&chapter=0		107
6.	/index.php?main_page=page&id=2&chapter=0		85
7.	/index.php?main_page=page&id=2...		77
8.	/index.php?main_page=product_info&cPath=6&products_id=6		53
9.	/index.php?main_page=index&cPath=6&zenid=5337a284349eb6ea4c0f6bb...		42
10.	/index.php?main_page=index&cPath=152		41

See which pages had the most views overall. These are the ones that must be made as perfect as possible. The best sales copy, the best images, or if it's an article, make sure it is linked to the appropriate product pages. However, don't change too much because the page could lose its popularity if you change too many keyword attributes. A screenshot of the most popular content page on Analytics is as follows:

Top Content

Pages	Page Views	% Page Views
███████████████	3,024	39.13%
███████████████	324	4.19%
███████████████	258	3.34%
███████████████	255	3.30%
███████████████	247	3.20%
███████████████		

You can see in the previous screenshot that the top page on that site gets almost 40 percent of the page views. Clearly, this must be a top priority for optimization.

Google Analytics summary

As with the PrestaShop statistics, the Analytics features that are useful to you will not be the same as those that are useful to somebody else. Try and get familiar with all of them and then apply knowledge of your industry to make them useful to you.

Improvement

Hopefully, the discussion on statistics will enable you to identify potential areas for change. But perhaps the most enhancing and updating will be done based on your knowledge of your industry or how it is changing. For examples, read on.

Optimizing your articles, product descriptions, and category descriptions

You should constantly be updating your articles to keep them current. If something changes in your industry that affects something in one of your articles, then change it. You might be surprised at how quickly the search engines pick up on it. Thought of a better way to describe a product? Then update that too. Can you improve your grammar in any way? Can you use your statistics to change or optimize the density or actual keywords that you use? Did you find a new great image to use somewhere on your site? Constantly updating and amending your content keeps it fresh and scores big marks with search engines and humans.

Optimizing your AdWords campaign

We need to continually optimize our AdWords campaign. By optimizing, I mean trying new keywords, deleting poorly performing keywords, and varying the amount we pay for keywords. Also, as mentioned in *Chapter 8*, we need to create Adgroups, certainly for each product category and possibly for each product. This can take a lot of time and you probably don't want to do it in one go. Read about it to devise a routine in a bit.

Here is a lightning tutorial. First, we will add some keywords, then delete some, and finally we will vary the maximum price we are prepared to pay per click.

Time for action – optimizing Google AdWords

Make sure you are logged in to your AdWords account and read on.

1. Click on the **Campaigns** tab and then click on your campaign name. You should see something similar to the following screenshot. From this screen, we can manage all aspects of our campaign:

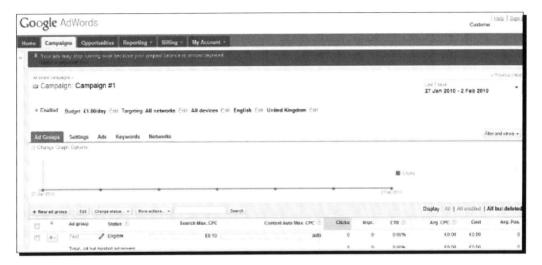

2. Now click on the **Keywords** tab and then the **Add keywords** button. You will see where you can add your new keywords. Add one new keyword or key phrase per line in the box shown in the next screenshot:

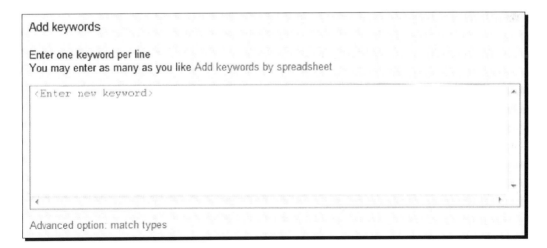

3. When you are done, click on the **Save** button. Your keywords are added and you are returned to the main campaign screen.

4. Now we will stop some keywords. Notice that your keywords each have a little green circle next to them. Click on this green circle and select the pause icon. Your keyword will no longer be used to generate your advert. Take a look at the following screenshot. Notice one keyword is paused and the other is running:

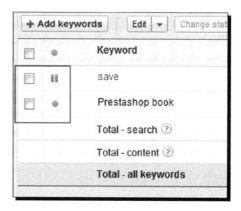

5. Now we will look at varying the maximum cost per click. You can do this in two ways. First, you can set a default maximum for a whole Adgroup so that any keyword not specifically set will have this default as its maximum. Second, you can specify it by an individual keyword so that more profitable phrases can have their maximum cost per click set accordingly.

6. Here is how to set the maximum cost per click for each keyword. Simply go to the **Max. CPC** column and click on it in line with the keyword you want to change. A little pop-up box, like the one shown in the next screenshot, allows you to enter your maximum cost per click:

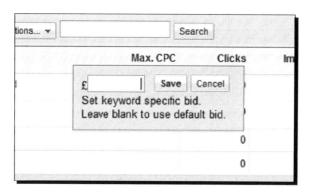

7. To change the default maximum cost per click, click on the **Ad Groups** tab. You can change your default maximum cost per click by clicking on the **Max. CPC** column in line with the Adgroup you want to change.

What just happened?

We have seen how to make changes to our AdWords campaign. Google AdWords is a huge topic. You only have to look at all the different tabs and buttons, let alone all the different tracking systems that you can configure. AdWords is only right for some businesses. Some of my stores can get great value clicks and it is well worth me buying all the clicks that I can. On others, the amount I need to spend just doesn't make sense, so I don't do it.

You will hopefully be able to decide if Google AdWords is, or might be, right for your business. If it is, I would definitely recommend further research. What we have done here really is just a tiny glimpse at the workings and measurement possibilities. A good place to start is on the AdWords site itself. Log in to your AdWords account, click on help in the top right-hand corner. Scroll to the bottom of the window that pops up and there you will find a whole load of information resources.

These include getting started, beginner's guides, and a learning centre. A word of warning: all of the resources are provided by Google themselves and you will never get the advice that your business might not be suitable for AdWords.

Let's talk about adding new articles.

Adding new articles

Always be looking for new topics to write articles about. Once your articles have been indexed by the search engines, you might be amazed how responsive they are. I have added new articles and found them in search results just hours later. And this can be true on sites with fairly modest profiles.

So if there is something important, topical, or controversial in your industry, write about it and make sure it is linked with your other relevant articles. Having said what I have, don't write articles for the sake of it. If it is not genuinely relevant, don't bother. If a once-relevant article has become irrelevant, take it down. It is not a competition about quantity but quality and relevance.

Marketing

We have already talked about many different forms of marketing. The main point to make here is that these forms of marketing should also be perpetual. If you log in to your industry forum once every six months and post a hundred messages, you will be judged as a self-promoter and there will be no benefit to your business. If, however, you post a small number of relevant messages or replies once a week across all the platforms, you will reap enormous benefits over time.

It is the same with your e-mail marketing. If you send an e-mail a day for a week, your subscribers will be reaching for the spam button. However, sending one well-constructed newsletter per month (or whatever frequency is right for you) will bring new customers and repeat customers.

You know how to make changes to your AdWords campaign. This too is best looked at on a perpetual basis at a frequency relevant to your specific business. So if you are getting 60 percent of all your sales via AdWords, then you should look at it with a higher frequency than if you only have a small spend with small returns.

Devising a routine and sticking to it

Think about all the things we have talked about. Perhaps make some notes and read on.

Time for action – making a plan

This quick guide will help you create a monthly plan for perpetual improvement of your website. The key is to be as efficient as possible and take up as little time as possible, but at the same time making sure that nothing is neglected.

1. Write a list of all the different marketing activities you are involved in and next to that the frequency with which you think you should be doing them. Next to that, write the amount of time (in hours) you think it will take.

2. Write a list of all your optimization activities that you expect to engage in and, as earlier, the frequency and expected time you will take for each.

3. Now do exactly the same as the previous step, but this time as an estimate for adding new content. This includes articles, categories, and products.

4. Now estimate the amount of time, probably quite frequently, you will set aside for customer service and handling orders.

5. Now using that information, write out a monthly plan showing the days divided into one-hour slots so that you can see the spare time you have.

6. Your final plan should show a very small amount of time, perhaps each day (for me it is an hour per day), for customer service and packing. You will probably have a frequently recurring block. For me it is half a day per week that I spend on marketing, optimizing, and adding. The vast majority of your monthly planner will hopefully, at least for now, be empty.

What just happened?

The result should show vast empty spaces to spend as you please. If you have achieved your financial objectives, this time could be spent just doing what you please. If, like me, you have not achieved this yet, you could spend the spare time working on new projects. More soon.

It is worth mentioning that while writing this book, I spent no more than a few hours a week across all my stores. But my income went up! The amount of time you spend developing your PrestaShop is not the most important, but what you actually do with the time is.

Now that we have the management of our websites down to a tee, we can look at what we might like to do with all our newly found spare time.

The big secret

So you have a working e-commerce business and you know how to develop and increase profitability. We have also discussed how to do this with the smallest time commitment possible. Starting an e-commerce business should not be about becoming a full-time, online equivalent of a shelf stacker, checkout operator, and store manager all rolled into one. It is about getting technology to go to work for you.

There comes a time when any business will begin to reach its full potential, and just as important as that, the development and improvement cycle we discussed earlier takes time, perhaps years. What if you are not making all you want from your store yet? What if you have successfully replaced whatever income you previously had, but you now have a taste for success and you want more? What should you do?

Just do what every successful business has always done. But first, a bit about conventional business.

High street retail

Walk down any shopping street or any modern shopping mall in almost any town or city around the world and you are faced with a wall of recognizable brands. McDonalds is an obvious example.

In 1954, a milkshake machine salesman called Ray Kroc was fascinated why one particular hamburger restaurant in California, USA was so much more successful than any of his other customer's restaurants. There were a number of elements that made the McDonald brothers' restaurant better than others, but that is not the point of the story.

Ray Kroc made a deal with the McDonald brothers and started to open more burger restaurants using their successful formula. Every new restaurant brought a significant increase in sales but without the initial risk and time commitment of the first. Why? It had been done before he knew it worked, and he knew, eventually from experience, how to get up and running very quickly and avoid all of the pitfalls. Ten years later, there were 700 McDonald's restaurants.

So how does this help us? You have reached this point, so you already know how to open an e-commerce business. You know how to run it without a significant investment in time. So what are you going to do next? I struggled to open my first e-commerce store. It took months, and it looked rubbish and I mean rubbish. But guess what? It worked because I used open source software that was already tried and tested by thousands of other businesses and people purchased my stuff. Not much, but a bit.

So I opened another. This time it was a bit smarter looking, took only a few weeks, and was a little bit more successful. Can you think what I did next? Yes, I opened another one and it was even easier than the last one. And I didn't stop there.

For those of you who have completed my seven-day challenge, congratulations! For those of you who took a bit longer, much longer, or are still waiting for your first customer, don't worry about it, keep going. Keep refining your PrestaShop and don't wait for it to be a hit before you open another one.

Duplication

The technical term for copying a successful business over and over is duplication. Think about McDonalds again for a moment. Why did it work for them? Two important factors were that first, people liked it, and second, when people went to another town or city they saw the golden arches and recognized it as a brand they liked. This, of course, is how all of the big names on the high street succeed with duplication—brand awareness. And brand awareness is where my suggested model of duplication is completely different from that of the high street.

If you walk through a mall, you see all the usual suspects. Go and look at their online presence. Here they usually only have one main web store. Why? Simple, because as we talked about just now, people are drawn in by brand awareness. On the high street or shopping mall, they are drawn in by location and brand awareness. On the Internet, having five Circuit City computer store websites won't work. They are only successful because the name and perhaps the domain name are very well-known.

This can't help us because we don't want to spend loads of money building brand awareness. So how are we going to duplicate our business?

Look at it like this

When I was a very young boy, I used to love going to the local corner shop to buy a quarter of Cola Cubes. Sometimes I would be sent on a short errand to get a loaf of bread or a pint of milk. Other times, we would all go in the car and get a whole load of things because we didn't have time to go to the supermarket that week. That little corner shop was a busy, bustling, and thriving business. It was a part of our local community and a big part of my small world back then.

As I got a little older and travelled further afield, I noticed there were other corner shops. Not always on actual corners but the same type of thing. They would all specialize in something slightly different, but still have a core range of everyday products. There was one that had a great range of toys, another books, another baked goods, and so on.

And eventually I realized these places existed in their thousands all over the UK. And those similar businesses existed in their millions across every continent in the world. The point is that they were all successful businesses in their own right. How did they all succeed so close to one another? Perhaps the obvious answer is that they all served their own specific community, defined approximately by distance to the next corner shop.

An analogy to explain

It is true that the independently owned, small-store business is in something of a decline, at least in the UK anyway. But only because the big companies are buying them up or replacing them, not because that type of business has no demand. Big companies can use their financial might to monopolize this market just as they did the high street, malls, and out-of-town sites. It is hard, if not impossible, to compete.

But on the Web the rules are very different and the advantage, I believe, is with the small business. Here is why. Tesco has the largest share of the UK supermarket business with hundreds of stores around the country. They also have an incredibly successful online presence—www.tesco.com—that delivers shopping to their customer's home. So if it is so successful, why don't they open another website doing the same thing and multiply their business? Perhaps www.tesco-two.com. I checked and the name is available. Simply because all that would happen is that if the site was successful it would only get business from the existing www.tesco.com. There would be no new customers because Tesco's online business, like the other big names, is entirely dependent on their brand awareness. Here lies the first major difference between our duplication model and theirs.

When we create another store, it must be different from the last—with a new domain name, new product and category descriptions, perhaps a slightly varied range, and perhaps even new prices. By creating an apparently unique business, we are potentially doubling our income. Why does this work for us but not for Tesco or other big businesses?

I am well aware that at this point I have created more questions than I have answered. This works for us and not the big boys because we do it ourselves in a fraction of the time and at a microscopic percentage of the cost to them. With their unwieldy, inflexible size they cannot specialize in niches. They would need designers, buyers, marketing, staff, managers, and the list goes on. We need a spare day or two and $5 a month for hosting if that is the case.

The return on such an investment would be too slow for a shareholder-owned organization. And the one thing that the big boys will never have, which is essential to make a success of this type of business, is a person with the passion for the products and a commitment to its success. Money can never buy this.

What about all these corner shops?

So why did I go on about the corner shops? What have they got to do with it? Simple; think about search engine optimization for a minute. It is a bit unclear to say the least. What keywords, what density, page structure, formatting, meta tags or not! It makes my head spin.

Big organizations and others with only one main website have to get it right—exactly right, or their business will fail. They have to spend fortunes researching keywords, buying Google AdWords, paying affiliates, and the list goes on. Most of these tasks rely on employing expensive outside agencies or in-house "experts" because they have no choice but to get it right. And guess what happens when Google or another of the search engines changes its ranking formula? They start again on an endless frantic circle of trying to convince the search engines they should be at the top.

Yes, we must optimize and refine as discussed earlier. However, if we have a dozen stores all feeding off of slightly different keywords and phrases, all with their own slightly different structure, formatting, and density, then any change in the search engine ranking formula is just as likely to benefit some of our stores as it is to be detrimental to others. We win. Oh yes, the corner shops.

Our websites are just like the corner shops. They are small, well-run, highly efficient, have zero unnecessary expenses, and make a modest income (each) by offering genuine products and services, preferably to repeat customers.

Where the analogy most applies with corner shops is that by making each site unique we end up placing ourselves on lots of different virtual corners created by the vagaries of the search engines. If I have a laptop shop, do I optimize for laptop, notebook, netbook, or portable PC? It doesn't matter all that much because I can optimize for them all, placing myself on as many virtual corners as I like.

These days when people search for my products, I am confident that no matter what they call them one of my sites will appear in the organic search results. The money when they buy all goes into the same place.

Where the corner shop analogy stops working is when we have only a tiny financial investment per store, almost zero time commitment once it is up and running, and an ongoing residual income for the foreseeable future! So let's get duplicating.

Technical duplication tips

So we know that our stores must be different because we are not aiming for success through brand awareness, although you might surprise yourself and end up with one or more of your sites becoming well-known, but that is not our specific goal here.

Varying your payment provider

If you have a dozen thriving stores, you and your family are starting to live the life you deserve and all of a sudden, for apparently no reason, PayPal suspends your account. Hero to zero, and there is probably nothing you can do about it. Even if there is, it will almost certainly take time to get to the bottom of what got PayPal in a tizzy. And please believe me, they do get in a tizzy from time to time.

When you do your second PrestaShop, why not choose an alternative payment provider? There are others as well as the few options we looked at. Visit www.prestastore.com and www.presto-changeo.com to see the list of payment modules available for PrestaShop.

Once you have a few stores up and running with different payment methods, consider installing two or more options in each store. Then, if a payment provider becomes unusable for any reason, you can simply disable the unwanted one and enable another. You can also consider having more than one enabled at the same time to give your customers a choice.

Varying your web host

Problems can arise with web hosts. They can have downtime, get hacked, and so on. Keeping all of your websites on one host could be catastrophic. It is certainly okay to have a few per host, otherwise our web-hosting bill would quickly go through the roof but not too many with each.

The other good reason to vary your web host is that in a shared hosting environment the IP address that identifies your web server might be the same for all sites. This could potentially cause issues with the search engines, who might object to too many related sites on the same IP address.

Varying your content

This is crucial. You can save time by using your old content as a template and perhaps using some of the same images, but your category, product, and article pages must be unique or the site will not perform in search engine rankings, because it might be considered duplicate content.

Also, like the corner shops, vary your products. Once you are making a profit, which should be almost straight away, consider adding new products or even whole ranges. Vary the products and ranges that you put into different stores. After a year or two, it will start to become apparent which store is going to be your top performer and you can use this as your main store to try out new things and then move successful products into different stores.

Vary your cart software

PrestaShop is arguably the best. But there are loads and I mean loads of alternatives. The truth is that depending upon the criteria you use to judge the software, different products come out best. For example, if you are getting lots of visitors from your articles and there are lots more you could write, you definitely need to consider an open source solution where the focus is on the CMS but with a shop attached. Check out www.joomla.org and get a great book on the subject from www.packtpub.com.

If you want to stick with the traditional e-commerce model but want to help vary your structure and formatting (at the same time as getting your teeth into a new open source software title with different advantages and features), then go and have a look at www.zen-cart.com, www.oscommerce.net, www.magentocommerce.com, or www.cubecart.com. The latter of that list is not open source, but a fully functional free version is available. And get a great book on these subjects from www.packtpub.com.

Also consider some quick and simple regular HTML websites. Make yourself a really simple three- or four-page website using Nvu for free. Use template of your choice, for free, from `www.oswd.org`, and put on some simple "buy now" buttons, which you can create in your Google Checkout or PayPal account.

Try something totally new

I always wanted to have my own business but I never wanted one of the traditional forms of self-employment. I wanted to do something a bit different. The problem was I am risk averse. It never ceases to amaze me the courage shown by some entrepreneurs when financing their new venture: huge loans, re-mortgages, and so on.

The problem with this type of venture, of course, is that there are consequences if the business is not a success. I am for this reason a sort of do-it-yourself e-commerce kind of person. If a business fails, then I have lost some time, not my shirt, and if during that time I was earning money from other businesses, then it is not too much of a problem. As your experience of different software solutions grows, something happens inside your brain. Let me explain.

You begin to realize just how vast and varied the world of open source is. Just about anything can be achieved on the Web, for nothing or almost nothing, when you do it yourself, and you would be surprised how simple some of the things actually are, which you thought might be really hard.

As this world of possibilities dawns on you, if it hasn't already, you might find, all of a sudden that your ideas become much more varied and adventurous. For example, I found myself dabbling in the likes of education websites, product comparison, and business services as well as good old e-commerce.

Once you have a virtually passive income and just a little knowledge in a lot of fields, you will find that ideas for new websites come faster than you can possibly use them. Why not diversify totally? Think through these marvelous possibilities, plan how realistic they are, and dive in to your favorite. I have found, without exception, that there is always the opportunity for cross promotion with your existing businesses.

And if the fluffy teddy or guns business ever falls a bit flat for a year or two, your diversification will make your income more resilient. If you see yourself as an entrepreneur, I recommend investigating a few technologies. You do not need to master any of them, just understand the basics and how to use the hard work done by others to your advantage. If this is you, read about PHP, MySQL, AJAX, and jQuery writing for the Web and web development in general. You can get beginner's books on many of these topics from `www.packtpub.com`.

Have a go hero – John's 24-hour challenge

Yes, you guessed what all this is about. Think about this. You know everything there is to know about opening a PrestaShop. How long would it take you to install one now? Five minutes maximum. Okay, so the product descriptions might have taken a while, but you can use your existing images and sales copy as a template for the new ones and save time.

This is my challenge. Read the rest of this chapter, then sit down and plan your second PrestaShop. Write down in detail the precise list of steps you need to take. Plan it for a day when you will not be disturbed, get up early, and go for it. Install, open your store, and sell at least one product within 24 hours. I know it is a tough challenge, but it can be done. Here is a little tip to help a bit. You will probably have to rely on AdWords to get that first sale and be sure your domain is registered before the day you start proper work.

The future of e-commerce and PrestaShop

So you want to know what will be the next big thing. Well this is it. Are you ready? I don't know. Sorry.

We can only guess the changes that will occur in the world of e-commerce. New customer trends will surely come and go; new features we can only imagine will appear in shopping cart software. For example, in the short time while writing this book, PrestaShop went through two versions and had multiple upgrades.

As we have discussed at length, your first PrestaShop could be only the beginning. The possibilities are only restricted by our imaginations. All you need to decide is what part you are going to play. Keeping abreast of new developments in technology is the key to taking advantage of all the possibilities that future opportunities present. In the appendix, there is a list of online resources. Why not visit them all and join any forums that look interesting. Introduce yourself, watch the conversations that interest you, and join in the discussion when you can. Very quickly you will have your finger on the pulse of e-business.

Pop quiz – questions about Chapter 9

1. Why is creating brand awareness not necessarily the best policy for expanding our e-commerce business?

2. Can you find out by searching the Web what the top three open source shopping carts are?

3. With Google Analytics, which main options help us identify areas where improvement/optimization might help and which main option helps us prioritize those improvements?

Picture this

It's 6 o'clock on Monday morning. You are not really looking forward to another grueling week at work. Another five days of office politics. Another small chunk of your life dedicated to making somebody else rich—giving somebody else's family the finer things in life, while somebody else decides what you are worth by the hour!

And then you remember you don't do that anymore. You started your own online business about six months ago and gave your notice last Friday. You go downstairs and make a coffee. It smells good. You sit in your favorite chair and switch on your laptop. You check your e-mails.

You see you have made some more sales overnight. You log into your PrestaShop control panel and all of the payments have been confirmed. You process the orders. You check the news headlines as you sip your coffee. You shut down your laptop. You ponder your next big idea. The day is your own while PrestaShop works slavishly. What will you do and where will you go?

Summary

Well, that's just about it.

This chapter covered:

- The point of running our own e-business in the first place
- How to develop your business in an ongoing manner
- The big secret to multiply your business income whatever way you want
- The future of business on the Internet— it's hard to predict but with a bit of effort, simple to keep up with.

I wish you every success with your PrestaShop business and please let me know how you get on via www.prestashop-book.com. Much more than this, I hope you take advantage of the huge opportunity presented to us all through open source projects like PrestaShop.

In a world becoming more and more dominated by giant institutions, which can sometimes seek to control how much we earn and the type of lives that we lead, we can use the world of open source to take back what should be ours and find ourselves much better placed to provide for our families and serve our communities.

Control Panel Quick Reference

What follows is a really brief account of every tab and sub-tab. Where we have already covered the tab I will remind you in which chapter(s) this occurred.

Catalog

When you click on the catalog tab you can quickly create, edit, and delete categories and products. Here is what you will find on the sub-tabs.

Tracking

This is a summary of your shops categories including empty categories, disabled and out-of-stock products.

Manufacturers

This tab enables you to enter the names and details of the manufacturers of your products. Doing so is entirely optional but can have some benefits. See *Chapter 2* for details.

Suppliers

You can enter the names and extra information about your suppliers. There are a number of good reasons for doing this. If your supplier is a trade secret then this one is not for you. The details are in *Chapter 2*.

Attributes and groups

This is a very powerful feature that enables you define product attributes, group them and then assign them to products. This can be a big time saver as well as really useful to your catalog and your customers. See *Chapter 3* for full details.

Features

It is a great way to add a list of product features to a separate tab underneath the main product description. This is a good place to put all the information a customer might want to know without cluttering the main product description. See *Chapter 3*.

Image mapping

This is cool. Assign multiple clickable zones to an image so that different product pages can be opened by a single image. Go and have a look on the **Image mapping** sub-tab. A full guide is given there.

Tags

Create tags for any or all of your products and assign different tags for each language.

Attachments

This is potentially very useful. Here is an example. On the attachments tab add a new attachment. An attachment is a file. Perhaps an image or a PDF file. Then on your product creation page you can click on its attachment tab and add as many attachments as you like. Now on the product page that the customer sees there will be a downloads tab. This is great for technical documents, instructions, large images, or anything else you might want the customer to have access to but do not want to actually put in the product description.

Customers

Here you will find a list of customers. Click on one to view or edit the details. Here is a summary of the sub-tabs under the **Customers** tab.

Addresses

View and edit all of your customers names and addresses at a glance or a click.

Groups

View, add, and edit customer groups. Customer groups can be used to assign discounts to some customers. Full details are provided in *Chapter 8*.

Carts

Use this tab in conjunction with your statistics. See the carts that customers filled and if they made a purchase. There's more in *Chapter 8*.

Orders

Quickly see and sort all the orders you have received. Click on an order to process it. Order processing is covered in *Chapter 8*. Here is what you can do on the **Orders** sub-tabs.

Invoices

There are two main uses for invoices. First, our customers might want one, especially if they made a purchase for their business, and second, it is good practice to keep a copy for yourself for your accounting purposes. There's more in *Chapter 8*.

Delivery slips

Print off and configure delivery slips.

Merchandise return

Here you can enable merchandise return as well as specify the number of days after order that this is acceptable. There's more in *Chapter 8*.

Credit slips

View all your issued credit slips.

Customer messages

Review all of the messages sent and received.

Statuses

What is the status of an order. Statuses tell us and the PrestaShop software what is occurring with any order. Assign, change, or create your own statuses. Have a read of *Chapter 8*.

Order messages

Here you can add and amend customer messages. This is useful for sending messages that need to be sent many times. *Chapter 8* looks at how to create and send messages.

Payment

See at a glance and edit the payment modules you use as well as configure the currencies and countries you serve. The sub-tabs under **Payment** are as follows.

Currencies

Add, configure, update, and delete the currencies used in your PrestaShop. *Chapter 7* goes into lots of detail about this, including auto updating currency exchange rates.

Taxes

Select, add, and configure the different tax rates that you need. *Chapter 7* gives you the full low down on this.

Vouchers

Voucher management is important. There is much more to it than just giving a few vouchers. *Chapter 7* looks at creating and issuing vouchers. *Chapter 8* looks at using vouchers as part of a multi-pronged marketing campaign.

Shipping

Shipping has the potential to be the most complicated PrestaShop topic. But careful planning and implementation can keep things nice and simple. See *Chapter 7* for full details. Read the following pages for a summary of the **Shipping** sub-tabs.

Carriers

Add and configure the carrier options to be used by your customers. Read *Chapter 7* for all the ins and outs.

States

Add, remove, and configure the states that you ship to.

Countries

Add, remove, and configure the countries that you ship to.

Zones

Add, remove, and configure the zones that you ship to.

Price ranges

This is one of the key, fundamental methods of shipping price configuration. Read more in *Chapter 7*.

Weight ranges

The other key, fundamental methods of shipping price configuration. Read more in *Chapter 7*.

Stats

The subject of statistics is as wide as it is important. Set up PrestaShop to gather statistics in *Chapter 5*, learn to interpret statistics in *Chapter 9*, and make a plan for using statistics in *Chapter 9*.

Modules

Lists all of the different stats modules available. This is the same list you can see on the **Modules** tab but includes, as you might expect, only stats modules.

Settings

Choose your default graph and grid engine. These can also be changed on a per stat basis from each statistics page. Also decide how frequently your database is cleared of your statistics.

Search engines

A list of search engines and parameters that PrestaShop is already configured to gather referral statistics for.

Referrers

Options for indexing your site's referrers and cleaning the cache of referrer data.

Modules

Just about anything you want to add to your store is done from here. Modules are mentioned, installed, and configured in just about every chapter. There is just one sub-tab.

Positions

You can increase and decrease the priority of any module. If a module is at the highest priority (top of the list) it will be displayed first, within that position. Also you can list exceptions for pages where you do not want a module to appear.

Employees

This tab defines what users can do and who deals with each type of customer contact.

Profiles

Creating and assigning profiles for employees using your PrestaShop profile is both useful and makes good sense from a security perspective. Explore this idea more fully in *Chapter 6*.

Permissions

Assign permissions to your profiles and specify the amount of access, if any, that each profile has on each of the tabs. This is fully explained in *Chapter 6*.

Contacts

Define the options available to your customers in the drop-down list of contacts and who any messages should be forwarded to.

Preferences

Some explanations are repeated here for your convenience. Also see *Chapter 5* for detailed information about the options not covered anywhere else on the main part of the **Preferences** tab.

Contact

Fill out all of the contact details for your store. PrestaShop will automatically add relevant information to relevant places.

Appearance

Easily change themes, logos and icons. There's more discussion in *Chapter 2*.

Meta-Tags

Here you can define meta tags for your standard pages, site map, contact form, and so on. Simply click on the notepad icon next to the page you want to define and you know how to do the rest.

Products

This sub-tab has loads of options, all to do with products and how they are presented. There's more on this in *Chapter 5*.

Email

Configure or re-configure all of your e-mail options here. Have a look at *Chapter 5* before fiddling with these.

Image

Use these settings to customize the look and feel of your store. This is covered in *Chapter 2*.

Database

As suggested by the warning message, stay clear of this tab until you have read about backing up your store in *Chapter 6*.

PDF

PrestaShop creates PDF documents for us in several tabs. For example, invoices and delivery slips. Define your settings like font and encoding here.

Localization

Choose lbs, kg or any other unit of measurement that suits you.

Search

Configure the importance of different factors for PrestaShop search. More information is provided in *Chapter 4*.

Tools

Some explanations are repeated here for your convenience. Also see *Chapter 5* for detailed information about the options not covered anywhere else on the main part of the **Tools** tab.

Languages

Configure the languages available in your store. See *Chapter 4* for more information.

Translations

We cover translations in *Chapter 4*.

Tabs

Change, move, add, or delete tabs to get your admin control panel just how you want it. Learn more about tabs in *Chapter 5*.

Quick Accesses

Add and remove areas of your admin control panel that can be accessed via the quick access feature. There's more in *Chapter 5*.

Aliases

Create aliases to aid search in your store. *Chapter 4* has a tutorial about creating aliases.

Import

This handy tab allows you to import the settings and products from another PrestaShop.

Subdomains

Does your shop need to work on different subdomains? Shop.mysite.com and so on? If yes, specify the subdomain(s) here.

DB backup

Use this quick and simple database backup tool. Full backups are discussed in *Chapter 6*.

CMS

The PrestaShop Content Management System. Create and manage all of your articles here. The CMS is covered in *Chapter 4*, as well as how to write articles.

Generators

Generate `.htaccess` or `robots.txt` files. These are covered in *Chapter 4*.

B
Web Resources

Here are a few web resources to help you build your e-commerce business.

PrestaShop related

www.prestashop.com

The official home of the PrestaShop project including multi-lingual forum, wiki, and much more.

www.prestashop-book.com

The official website of the book. All the extra books and guides you might need, for free! There are also errors and updates for this book.

www.prestastore.com

Buy modules and themes for your PrestaShop.

www.prestabox.com

Turn-key hosting for PrestaShop.

www.ardianys.com

Loads of PrestaShop tips and tutorials.

www.presto-changeo.com

Loads of PrestaShop tips, tricks, and cool modules.

Sales and marketing

www.warriorforum.com

A bit hardcore but incredible information, advice, and feedback about all things marketing.

Technical

www.smarty.net

PrestaShop template engine.

www.php.net

Want to understand the code that makes PrestaShop run? This is the place to start.

www.w3schools.com

Easily the best resource for all things www coding. Just add /css to the URL for the best CSS resource bar none.

Resources

www.businessdreams.net/resources-making-money-online

All the best open source software, templates, and other resources in one place.

www.dreamstime.com

As many images at reasonable prices that you could ever want.

www.istockphoto.com

A bit dearer than dreamstime but some really high quality, arty stuff can be found here.

www.sourceforge.net

The largest free software site.

Other shopping carts and content management systems

www.zen-cart.com

www.joomla.org

www.oscommerce.net

www.magentocommerce.com

www.drupal.org

www.cubecart.com

Other

www.businessdreams.net

Loads of tutorials, resources, and a forum as well.

www.businesszone.co.uk

A general business forum and information site. Deals with all aspects of business but with a slant towards Internet enterprise.

http://smallbusinessonlinecommunity.bankofamerica.com/index.jspa

A great forum for all things business.

C
Pop Quiz Answers

Chapter 1

A few questions about Chapter 1

1	Simply create a sub-folder on your website. Call it 'shop2' or something similar. Then run the install process again using a new table prefix. Perhaps use 'ps2_'. To start the install process, just visit www.yourdomain.com/shop2.
2	**Stats**. Easy! Almost any function can be found on a very logical tab. The exceptions are **Preferences** and **Tools**, which will be covered later.
3	Use the quick access drop-down. Select **New product** and you will be there in a single page load.

Chapter 2

Themes and things

1	You probably guessed it. It's in the files you uploaded to the themes folder
2	There is a folder inside the theme folder that you uploaded called css. There are easily manipulated files within this folder to customize almost any element of your template. More next.
3	Look in the img folder of the theme folder you uploaded. You can change all the images. Make sure to replace them with images that are the same size and file name.

Chapter 3

A few product marketing questions

1	Try this. Sell a product at a killer price—even lower than the cost price. Make sure that the product you choose has plenty of high profit accessories and attribute upgrades. Always keep a close eye on this type of offer. Retailers do this all the time. Ever wondered how a shop can sell you such a great Plasma TV at such a low price? It's the profits in the £50 connecting cable and £10 per month insurance!
2	Feature: The new body toner uses
	Advantage: Your abs will be rock solid
	Benefit: The women will love you.

Chapter 4

PrestaShop search

1	Just change the category weighting to a significantly lower number than the short description and description weightings. Top of your search results would then be the category page with all the teddies.
2	It doesn't! It simply requests the nice search engines not to index certain parts of your website. We will take real security measures in *Chapter 6*.

Chapter 5

Tools and Preferences challenge

1	Simply click on **Email** in the **Preferences** tab, select **SMTP** and enter your e-mail settings from your ISP.
2	Yes. Just click on **Preferences**, scroll to the bottom, and select yes next to the label PrestaShop version 1.1 theme. It is worth mentioning that where possible you should stick to the themes that are designed for your version of PrestaShop. But if your dream template is made for 1.1 you can use it, but be prepared for some possible issues.
3	No. There are two elements to disaster recovery. The first is the database and the second is all the files from your web hosts server. We will cover this in full in the next chapter.

Chapter 6

Security

1	The reason for this is that as a company grows you will most likely have more than one person assigned to any given profile. Amendments to a profile can then be done quickly and easily by amending the profile and not everybody who is assigned to it individually. Having a profile name removes any ambiguity about the aims of the permissions assigned to a profile. What level of access should John have? It relies on memory, whereas 'IT illiterate' as a profile name is clear and unambiguous.
2	By giving users only the functions and access that they actually need you avoid some accidental errors. Also supposing a user's account is compromised, perhaps with a brute force attack, the minimal functions will mean an attacker can do less damage.
3	There is a way that PrestaShop can encrypt all user and customer logins as well as their entire session when in potentially sensitive areas. It is called SSL and is discussed next.

Chapter 7

A few product marketing questions

1	It encrypts (scrambles) the password between your web browser and your web host so somebody listening in, perhaps to your wireless Internet connection, cannot find out your password.
2	PayPal handles all the sensitive financial information on its website and just relays the basic, less sensitive details back to you. However, the information the customer enters on your website, like their contact details, can still be intercepted by someone listening in on the communication.

Chapter 8

Refresher questions

1	Google AdWords is a great way to instantly advertise your products. This is especially true if you have something new or unique. You can also use Twitter for instant product promotions. Don't make a habit of this type of promotion on Twitter or you might lose followers. Never do this type of promotion on Facebook unless you have a very specific group and you are confident the message will be well received; you might get reported for spam.
2	Shops with repeat purchase products that have lots of competition.
3	Each post has a link to your profile and your profile can usually be linked to your web site. Search engines give value to this type of link. It is possible that a forum uses a type of link called nofollow. This would mean a search engine would not then associate the link from your profile to your website. However there is still enormous potential benefit from direct visits from the forums users. It is also possible that forum users who have their own web site might decide to link to you.
4	Search for blogs related to your industry. Often blog owners allow comments and often within these comments they allow links to your site. Just remember the rules. No obviously blatant promotions and make your comments valid to the specific blog article. And you could always start your own blog; there are lots of free ones and you can link to your site as much as you like. Have a look at these sites that offer free blogs: 1. www.blogspot.com 2. www.wordpress.com 3. www.blog.com

Chapter 9

Questions about Chapter 9

1	This takes money. It's much simpler and cheaper to create a new presence and occupy more "virtual corners" on the Web by duplicating with variation.
2	Different sources vary and it depends how you grade them: fastest growing, most users, and so on. You would be just about correct if you named any of these: Magento, Zen Cart, OsCommerce, PrestaShop. Why not go and read up on their features and what makes them different to each other.
3	The **Visitors** and **Sources** options can identify things like where the visitors are coming from and the keywords they are using. The **Content** options show us clearly the volumes of traffic each page is getting. The pages getting significantly more page views should take priority when improving and optimizing.

Index

G

gift wrapping
  setting up 196, 197
GIMP 44
global.css 57
Google AdSense
  about 135
  advantages 135
  code, creating 136
  disadvantages 135
  installing 137
  setting up, in PrestaShop 136
Google AdWords
  about 215
  campaign, setting up 216-218
  optimizing 219
Google Analytics
  about 240
  content 243, 244
  installing 144, 145
  signing up 144
  summary 244
  traffic sources 242, 243
  using 146
  visitors 240, 241
Google Checkout
  installing 175
  using 175
Google Checkout account 175
Google Checkout payments
  setting up 176, 177
Google code
  creating 136
Google site maps tutorial 108, 109
graphics
  changing 60
  icons/buttons, changing 61
groups
  creating 226, 227
  using 226, 227
Guns4u.com, case studies
  Guns4u.com, case studiesabout 14

H

home page, PrestaShop
  content, adding 43, 44
  creating 41
  products 42
  USP 41
Home text editor 43

I

img/icons folder 61
img folder 60
improvement, PrestaShop
  about 244
  Adwords campaign, optimizing 244
  articles, optimizing 244
  category descriptions, optimizing 244
  Google Adwords, optimizing 245, 246
  new articles, adding 247
  product descriptions, optimizing 244
installation
  PrestaShop 20
invoices
  about 228
  disabling 228, 229
  enabling 228, 229

K

key modules
  arranging 33, 35

L

languages
  switching 111, 112
legal notice, must-have pages
  creating 45

M

MailChimp 133
manufacturers
  about 47
  defining 48, 49, 50
manufacturers block module 40
merchandise return
  enabling 230
merchant account 170
meta description 94
meta keywords 95

Thank you for buying
PrestaShop 1.3 Beginner's Guide

About Packt Publishing

Packt, pronounced 'packed', published its first book "*Mastering phpMyAdmin for Effective MySQL Management*" in April 2004 and subsequently continued to specialize in publishing highly focused books on specific technologies and solutions.

Our books and publications share the experiences of your fellow IT professionals in adapting and customizing today's systems, applications, and frameworks. Our solution based books give you the knowledge and power to customize the software and technologies you're using to get the job done. Packt books are more specific and less general than the IT books you have seen in the past. Our unique business model allows us to bring you more focused information, giving you more of what you need to know, and less of what you don't.

Packt is a modern, yet unique publishing company, which focuses on producing quality, cutting-edge books for communities of developers, administrators, and newbies alike. For more information, please visit our website: www.packtpub.com.

About Packt Open Source

In 2010, Packt launched two new brands, Packt Open Source and Packt Enterprise, in order to continue its focus on specialization. This book is part of the Packt Open Source brand, home to books published on software built around Open Source licences, and offering information to anybody from advanced developers to budding web designers. The Open Source brand also runs Packt's Open Source Royalty Scheme, by which Packt gives a royalty to each Open Source project about whose software a book is sold.

Writing for Packt

We welcome all inquiries from people who are interested in authoring. Book proposals should be sent to author@packtpub.com. If your book idea is still at an early stage and you would like to discuss it first before writing a formal book proposal, contact us; one of our commissioning editors will get in touch with you.

We're not just looking for published authors; if you have strong technical skills but no writing experience, our experienced editors can help you develop a writing career, or simply get some additional reward for your expertise.

Magento: Beginner's Guide

ISBN: 978-1-847195-94-4   Paperback: 300 pages

Create a dynamic, fully featured, online store with the most powerful open source e-commerce software

1. Step-by-step guide to building your own online store

2. Focuses on the key features of Magento that you must know to get your store up and running

3. Customize the store's appearance to make it uniquely yours

4. Clearly illustrated with screenshots and a working example

PHP 5 E-commerce Development

ISBN: 978-1-847199-64-5   Paperback: 356 pages

Create a flexible framework in PHP for a powerful ecommerce solution

1. Build a flexible e-commerce framework using PHP, which can be extended and modified for the purposes of any e-commerce site

2. Enable customer retention and more business by creating rich user experiences

3. Develop a suitable structure for your framework and create a registry to store core objects

4. Promote your e-commerce site using techniques with APIs such as Google Products or Amazon web services, SEO, marketing, and customer satisfaction

Please check **www.PacktPub.com** for information on our titles

Joomla! E-Commerce with VirtueMart

ISBN: 978-1-847196-74-3   Paperback: 476 pages

Build feature-rich online stores with Joomla! 1.0/1.5 and VirtueMart 1.1.x

1. Build your own e-commerce web site from scratch by adding features step-by-step to an example e-commerce web site

2. Configure the shop, build product catalogues, configure user registration settings for VirtueMart to take orders from around the world

3. Manage customers, orders, and a variety of currencies to provide the best customer service

4. Handle shipping in all situations and deal with sales tax rules

Selling Online with Drupal e-Commerce

ISBN: 978-1-847194-06-0   Paperback: 264 pages

Walk through the creation of an online store with Drupal's e-Commerce module

1. Set up a basic Drupal system and plan your shop

2. Set up your shop, and take payments

3. Optimize your site for selling and better reporting s

4. Manage and market your site

Please check **www.PacktPub.com** for information on our titles

1138781R0

Printed in Great Britain by
Amazon.co.uk, Ltd.,
Marston Gate.